PRAISE FOR *BLOOD BROTHERS*

"Stillman gives an account of the tragic murder of Sitting Bull that's as good as any in the literature."

—*Kirkus Reviews* (starred review)

"*Blood Brothers* is a story of sorrow and triumph—the sorrow of Sitting Bull's murder in 1890 and the triumph, barely understood at the time, of Buffalo Bill Cody's central role in preserving the robust culture of the Lakota and Cheyenne people, whom Sitting Bull had led in war."

—Thomas Powers, author of *The Killing of Crazy Horse*

"A well-researched, well-told story of two of America's bright icons, set against the background of the closing of the West."

—Robert M. Utley, author of *The Lance and the Shield: The Life and Times of Sitting Bull*

"The lives of two of the most iconic figures in American history intersect in a sad but fitting setting—a traveling Wild West show that gave both Buffalo Bill and Sitting Bull second lives after their frontier days had ended."

—Tom Clavin, coauthor of *The Heart of Everything That Is*

"Best of the West 2018. . . . Not to miss."

—Stuart Rosebrook, *True West*

"Two years ago I published an essay here called 'How the West Was Lost.' In it, a handful of gifted writers—Ivan Doig, Joan Didion, Edward Abbey, and Jim Harrison—offered their takes on how Americans have despoiled their frontier. . . . Now I would like to nominate Deanne Stillman for admission to this distinguished group."

—Bill Morris, *The Millions*

"Deanne Stillman's work is like one of Georgia O'Keeffe's landscapes, forcing a different perspective on the American West. Stillman re-catechizes our national mythology by putting symbols and personas that we already think we know into new light."

—Heather Scott Partington, *Los Angeles Review of Books*

"A compelling narrative that reads like a novel."

—Cynthia Romanowski, *Orange County Register*

"Splendid. . . . A strong sense of the spiritual power of place streams throughout."

—Bobby Bridger, *The Austin Chronicle*

"Deanne Stillman explores a historical anomaly with a researcher's skill and a storyteller's style."

—Tom McGowan, *Lincoln Journal Star*

"A thrilling and elegantly written saga. . . . By puncturing the mythology of the Wild West, Stillman proves once again that fact is always more surprising than fiction. A landmark achievement in American history!"

—Douglas Brinkley, Professor of History at Rice University, CNN Presidential Historian, and author of *The Wilderness Warrior: Theodore Roosevelt and the Crusade for America*

"Like a latter-day Joan Didion, Deanne Stillman has carved out an aspect of the American West. Not empty but populated by spirits, human and animal; the ghosts of lost tribes; and now a fascinating culture clash only she could have offered."

—Ron Rosenbaum, author of *Explaining Hitler* and *The Shakespeare Wars*

"Embedded near the heart of this surprising friendship lies an amazing portrait of the man who is arguably the greatest military/civilian leader in all American history—Tatanka Iyotake, Sitting Bull."

—Doug Peacock, author of *In the Shadow of the Sabertooth*

"Elucidating as well as entertaining."

—*Booklist*

"Riveting."

"One would think there would be little, if anything, left to be said about either Sitting Bull and Buffalo Bill. Leave it to Deanne Stillman to prove that notion wrong. *Blood Brothers: The Story of the Strange Friendship between Sitting Bull and Buffalo Bill* casts these two icons of American history in a refreshing new light. As with all Stillman's books, *Blood Brothers* is thoroughly researched and exquisitely written."

—W. K. Stratton, author of *Chasing the Rodeo* and Fellow of the Texas Institute of Letters

"Like a hybrid lovechild of Pete Dexter's great novel *Deadwood* and T. J. Stiles's nonfiction masterpiece *Jesse James: Last Rebel of the Civil War*, Deanne Stillman's *Blood Brothers* is both a celebration of the American West and a paean to its myths, similar to Evan S. Connell's bestseller about Custer and the Little Bighorn, *Son of the Morning Star*. Compelling and compassionate, *Blood Brothers* expands our understanding of two Western legends, Sitting Bull and Buffalo Bill Cody, and is a high-spirited, entertaining read to boot."

—William J. Cobb, author of *The Bird Saviors*

"Engaging. . . . Stillman uses her sources well and writes with a flourish worthy of two legends."

—*Wild West Magazine*

"A riveting ride that straps the reader into art and life, proving again absolutely that there really is no business like show business."

—Bill Ruehlmann, *The Virginian-Pilot*

"Read this book. . . . A rollicking adventure that proves Buffalo Bill still entertains."

—Robert Davis, *New York Journal of Books*

"Intriguing. . . . *Blood Brothers* brings Buffalo Bill wonderfully to life."

—Barbara Spindel, *The Christian Science Monitor*

ALSO BY DEANNE STILLMAN

*Desert Reckoning: A Town Sheriff, a Mojave Hermit, and
the Biggest Manhunt in Modern California History*

Mustang: The Saga of the Wild Horse in the American West

Joshua Tree: Desolation Tango

*Twentynine Palms: A True Story of
Murder, Marines, and the Mojave*

BLOOD BROTHERS

*The Story of the Strange Friendship
between Sitting Bull and Buffalo Bill*

DEANNE STILLMAN

Simon & Schuster Paperbacks

New York   London   Toronto   Sydney   New Delhi

To my dear, departed friend Michael Blake,
author and screenwriter, *Dances with Wolves*

To Bugz the wild horse, 1998–2009,
guide through the Dreamtime

Simon & Schuster Paperbacks
An Imprint of Simon & Schuster, Inc.
1230 Avenue of the Americas
New York, NY 10020

First Simon & Schuster trade paperback edition October 2018

SIMON & SCHUSTER PAPERBACKS and colophon are registered trademarks of Simon & Schuster, Inc.

For information about special discounts for bulk purchases, please contact Simon & Schuster Special Sales at 1-866-506-1949 or business@simonandschuster.com.

The Simon & Schuster Speakers Bureau can bring authors to your live event. For more information or to book an event contact the Simon & Schuster Speakers Bureau at 1-866-248-3049 or visit our website at www.simonspeakers.com.

Interior design by Carly Loman

Manufactured in the United States of America

10   9   8   7   6   5   4   3   2

The Library of Congress has cataloged the hardcover edition as follows:

Names: Stillman, Deanne, author.
Title: Blood brothers: the story of the strange friendship between Sitting Bull and Buffalo Bill / Deanne Stillman.
Description: First Simon & Schuster hardcover edition. | New York: Simon & Schuster, 2017. | Series: Simon & Schuster nonfiction original hardcover | Includes bibliographical references and index.
Identifiers: LCCN 2017006041 | ISBN 9781476773520 | ISBN 1476773521 | ISBN 9781476773544 (ebook)
Subjects: LCSH: Buffalo Bill, 1846–1917—Friends and associates. | Sitting Bull, 1831–1890—Friends and associates. | Entertainers—United States—Biography. | Dakota Indians—Kings and rulers—Biography. | Buffalo Bill's Wild West Company—Biography. | Wild west shows—History—19th century.
Classification: LCC F594.C68 S75 2017 | DDC 978/.020922 [B]—dc23 LC record available at https://lccn.loc.gov/2017006041

ISBN 978-1-4767-7352-0
ISBN 978-1-4767-7353-7 (pbk)
ISBN 978-1-4767-7354-4 (ebook)

They say there is to be a buffalo hunt over here!
They say there is to be a buffalo hunt over here.
Make the arrows! Make the arrows!
Says the father, says the father.

—Lakota Ghost Dance song

I want to ride to the ridge where the West commences
And gaze at the moon till I lose my senses
And I can't look at hobbles and I can't stand fences
Don't fence me in . . .

—Cole Porter, "Don't Fence Me In"

"Now that we've met, we've changed."

—from a Modoc Indian song

CONTENTS

Introduction   *xi*

CHAPTER 1
In Which Public Enemy Number One Comes Home
1

CHAPTER 2
In Which the Wild West Is Born—and Dies and Is
Resurrected from the Bottom of the Mississippi River
26

CHAPTER 3
In Which the Seventh Cavalry Is Defeated at the Battle
of the Little Bighorn, and Buffalo Bill Stars as Himself
in "The Red Right Hand, or the First Scalp for Custer"
59

CHAPTER 4
In Which Sitting Bull Is Hired and
Heads East for the Wild West
90

CHAPTER 5

In Which Sitting Bull and Buffalo Bill Join Up in the City
of Buffalo, and *Tatanka Iyotake* Reunites with Annie Oakley

117

CHAPTER 6

In Which an Indian and a *Wasichu* Certify
Their Alliance Across the Medicine Line

142

CHAPTER 7

In Which There Comes a Ghost Dance, or, a Horse from
Buffalo Bill Responds to the Assassination of Sitting Bull,
and Other Instances of the Last Days of the Wild West

185

Epilogue	*241*
Coda: Ghost Dance II	*245*
Acknowledgments	*251*
Notes on the Writing of This Book	*253*
Bibliography	*261*
Illustration Credits	*273*
Index	*275*

INTRODUCTION

For each of my books, there has been a precipitating incident that has caused me to venture into that particular story. The incidents are similar, for they involve acts of violence, the killing of people, wild animals, assaults on the land, and these acts have unfolded on a very big canvas, the American West. It is across this terrain that I see the incidents taking place, moments or months or years after they have happened; that is to say that I can literally picture them, in bas-relief, as the consequence of forces and matters that have long been in play, and when this picture begins to form, I know that the incident will become the prism through which I will tell my next story and there is no turning back.

Some time ago, while working on my book *Mustang: The Saga of the Wild Horse in the American West*, I learned about a strange and heartbreaking moment that had transpired outside Sitting Bull's cabin while he was being assassinated during an attempted arrest. A horse was tethered to a railing, and at the sound of gunfire he started to "dance," trained to do such a thing while he was in the Wild West, Buffalo Bill's famous spectacle of which Sitting Bull was a part for four months during 1885. I couldn't shake the image and as I began to look into it, I learned that the horse was a gift to Sitting Bull from Buffalo Bill, presented to Sitting Bull when he left the show to go home. The fact that Buffalo Bill had given Sitting Bull a horse upon his departure was significant. This was the animal that transformed the West—and was stripped from the tribes in order to vanquish them. It was a gift that Sitting Bull treasured, along with a hat that Cody had given him as well. After Sitting Bull was killed, Buffalo Bill bought the horse back from Sitting Bull's widows and according to some accounts rode it in a parade. And then the horse disappears from the record.

It was the legend of the dancing horse that led me into the story of Sitting Bull and Buffalo Bill, for it symbolized so much. As I thought about the steed outside Sitting Bull's dwelling as his killing was under way, a portal into something else opened up—exactly what, I was not sure of at the time, other than the fact that here was my next story, and it was calling and at some point I would head on down its trail.

Later, as I was well along this path, I came across another image. It's now on the cover of this book, and it too captured my attention. It was taken for publicity purposes while Sitting Bull and Buffalo Bill were on tour in Montreal, and its caption was "Foes in '76, Friends in '85." I began to imagine these two men on the road, Sitting Bull on that horse, crisscrossing the nation, visiting lands that once had belonged to the Lakota, appearing as "himself" on crowded thoroughfares that were built on top of ancient paths made by animals and the people who followed them, with William F. Cody, another mythical figure of the Great Plains, reenacting wartime scenarios that had one outcome—the end of the red man and the victory of the white—leading the whole parade in a celebration of the Wild West that became the national scripture. What were the forces that brought these two men together, I wondered, and what was the nature of their alliance? Were they each trapped in a persona, a veneer that was somewhat true? And behind the myths, the projected ideas in which they were preserved, who were they in day-to-day life? Theirs was certainly an unlikely partnership, but one thing was obvious on its face. Both had names that were forever linked with the buffalo ("Sitting Bull" refers to it, something that is not readily apparent from the name itself), and both led lives that were intertwined with it. One man was "credited" with wiping out the species (though that was hardly the case) and the other was sustained by its very life. They were, in effect, two sides of the same coin; foes and then friends, just as the photo caption said. So this image too entered my consciousness; here were two American superstars, icons not just of their era and country, but for all time and around the world. What story was this picture telling and how was it connected to the dancing horse outside Sitting Bull's cabin?

To take a close look at these matters and find out about other underpinnings of this story, I have spent much time on the plains. I have attended memorials of the anniversary of the Little Bighorn, the infamous battle from which this country has yet to recover, in which the Lakota and Cheyenne defeated Lieutenant Colonel George Armstrong Custer and his Seventh Cavalry in 1876, leading to the round-up of remaining "renegade" Indians; the flight of Sitting Bull and his people to Canada; his ultimate return as a pariah only to be blamed for the murder of Custer and then celebrated as a brave and defiant rebel. I have visited Mount Rushmore and the Crazy Horse Memorial nearby, traveled the Badlands where the remnants of the horse tribes sought refuge after the massacre at Wounded Knee, explored the terrain of William F. Cody in Cody, Wyoming, the town that he founded and which offers visitors a stay at the Irma Hotel, named after a daughter. I have visited the site of his defunct mine in Arizona, one of the ventures near the end of his life from which he could not recover. I have communed with wild horse herds that are said to be descendants of Buffalo Bill's horses on their home turf in Wyoming, where they flourished until recent round-ups obliterated them and their history, and I have spent time with mustang herds on a sanctuary in South Dakota where descendants of cavalry horses live out their lives, and where descendants of Sitting Bull's horses carry on in a national park nearby and where at night, under the northern lights, you can hear the thundering hooves of the ancient steeds if you get quiet and listen for the sounds behind the winds that are forever wailing.

What divided Indians and the white man is still in play. Out on the Great Plains, a staging ground for the original cataclysm, there is a face-off in North Dakota at a place called Standing Rock, where Sitting Bull was essentially a prisoner when the land became a reservation and before that lived in its environs as a free man. An oil company wants to force a pipeline through sacred lands on Indian territory and those who first dwelled there are saying no. They fear a spill that would contaminate the waters which flow nearby—the lifeblood of us all. They have been joined by thousands of Native Americans from across the country, who arrived on foot, by canoe, and on horseback. It has been the largest such gathering of the tribes in one place in America's recorded history, and many of these tribes are historic rivals. Regardless of the outcome at Standing Rock, one thing is certain: a shift is under way.

There was another momentous occurrence, and one that will reverberate for all time. In the frontier era, when the cavalry showed up on Indian lands, terrible things were afoot. Now, thousands of veterans had come to Standing Rock in support of Native Americans.

To celebrate this union and mark a victory against the pipeline, on December 6, 2016, at the Four Prairie Knights Casino and Resort on the reservation, descendants of soldiers who had fought in the campaigns against Native Americans knelt before Lakota elders. They were in formation by rank, with Wesley Clark, Jr., son of former army general Wesley Clark, Sr., at the forefront. "Many of us, me particularly, are from the units that have hurt you over the many years," Clark said. "We came. We fought you. We took your land. We signed treaties that we broke. We stole minerals from your sacred hills. We blasted the faces of our presidents onto your sacred mountain . . . we've hurt you in so many ways but we've come to say that we are sorry. We are at your service and we beg for your forgiveness." In return, Chief Leonard Crow Dog offered forgiveness and chanted "world peace" and others picked up the call. "We do not own the land," he said. "The land owns us."

The ceremony was marked by tears—and then whoops of joy. Outside, the winter snows began to overtake the plains and soon the veterans dispersed to the four directions.

Elsewhere, atonement and forgiveness between the white and red tribes has unfolded in a quieter manner. After a prolonged battle for course correction in the ongoing discussion of who determines American history and to what end, the U.S. Board of Geographic Names recently voted to change the name of Harney Peak in the Black Hills of South Dakota—"the heart of all there is" for the Lakota—to Black Elk Peak. This highest peak east of the Rockies was where Black Elk had his famous vision about a mythological figure known as White Buffalo Calf Woman, a dream that revealed the role of the buffalo and the horse and the four directions in the life of his people and showed how all these elements were woven together. The peak where it came to him was not the place where he had his vision (he was a young boy, at home), but the place to which his spirit traveled while experiencing it. As it happened, the site later became known to white people for something else—the Massacre at Blue Water, in which a number of Brule women and children had been killed in 1855, and it was named for General William S. Harney, who led the assault. Yet that incident didn't happen in South Dakota. It occurred in Nebraska.

The name change is significant. Black Elk was the second cousin of Crazy Horse, and he participated in the Battle of the Little Bighorn as a young boy. Later he fulfilled the vision that transported him to that mountain peak, and he became a medicine man. His teachings were passed on in *Black Elk Speaks*, regarded by leaders of many denominations as one of the great works of spiritual import. When the sacred hoop of his kind had been broken, when the Great Plains were no longer limitless and the circle that linked all elements and all living things was severed, he joined the Wild West and traveled the world with Buffalo Bill. "Pahaska had a strong heart," Black Elk said when Cody passed away, invoking the native name meaning "Long Hair" which many Lakota Indians used for both Buffalo Bill and Custer. It is a statement that many do not know or have forgotten.

In a recent ceremony to mark the transfiguration of the peak, two families gathered in a circle at a nearby trailhead. They were seventh-generation descendants of the general's family and the family of the chief whose people were wiped out. The rite was organized by Oglala Lakota Basil Brave Heart so that members of the general's family could apologize to members of the chief's, and to seek forgiveness and healing. In turn, members of the chief's family were there to publicly forgive and support the reconciliation offered by the renaming. The event had been several years in the making, involving many talks between the families, prayer walks, and facing down a range of anger and resentment in both communities. In fact, the renaming was something that few believed would happen.

When the ceremony at Black Elk Peak concluded, members of the families smoked the peace pipe and embraced, planning to continue acts of public healing between whites and Native Americans, culminating in a long-needed event at Wounded Knee. "Foes in '76, Friends in '85"—the slogan deployed for the partnership of Sitting Bull and Buffalo Bill—could have been the caption for a photograph of the ceremony at Black Elk Peak, with only a change of numbers. It would seem that America has embarked on the painful and necessary journey of healing our original sin—the betrayal of Native Americans. This is the fault line that runs through the national story, and perhaps the brief time that Sitting Bull and Buffalo Bill were together can serve as a foundation upon which this rift can be repaired.

And now, let us return to their final connection—the horse that Cody gave to Sitting Bull after his last performance in the Wild West. A while ago, I called Chief Arvol Looking Horse to seek his insight into this matter. He is the Nineteenth-Generation Keeper of the Sacred White Buffalo Pipe for the Lakota Indians, which was given to his people by the woman in Black Elk's vision. He has led ceremony regarding environmental and other sacred concerns at Standing Rock, the United Nations, and elsewhere. I had met him several years earlier at a wild horse preservation event in Las Vegas; at its conclusion, everyone in attendance joined him in a prayer circle in a ballroom at the South Point Hotel, hotels and their ballrooms with garish chandeliers being the location of many such events because they are among the central gathering places of our time. "What was the symbolism of the dancing horse outside Sitting Bull's cabin?" I asked him in our phone conversation. "Was he responding to the sound of the gunfire, as the story goes?" There was a long silence and I hesitated to break it. After a few moments, this is what he said: "It was the horse taking the bullets," he told me. "That's what they did."

Not everyone believes that the horse danced. But I do. And that's how I came to write this book, and perhaps after reading it, you'll have your own thoughts about what happened on a winter's dawn of 1890 and all of the matters and forces that preceded it.

CHAPTER ONE

*In Which Public Enemy
Number One Comes Home*

In 1839, artist George Catlin presented the first "Wild West" show in London, Brussels, and Paris. He had been painting Native Americans for years, investing all of his time and money into his obsession, traveling up and down the Missouri River and deep into the Great Plains, making portraits of various members of forty-eight different tribes. His gallery of Indians—he called it "Nature's dignitaries"—was admired by some and excoriated by others. Regardless of reception, he was determined to bring the plight of Native Americans to the world outside theirs, and to that end, he was now on the brink of ruin. His visits to the royal courts of England and Europe were an attempt to stave off the end—for him and the Indians he so revered. There was more sympathy for the aboriginals of America in these foreign lands than there was at home, and he felt that if he could bring his portraits alive, that would seal the argument for the preservation of the natives. At first, he hired local boys to don costumes and feathers from his own collection and adorn themselves in war paint and whoop it up in war dances before audiences of elite citizens and artists and monarchs. The performances were an instant success. He was soon joined by several groups of Indians—including twenty-one Ojibway and fourteen Iowa—who had been touring Europe with promoters. He hired them to reenact dances, hunts, and even scalpings, to the delight of many. But others wondered why the Indians would succumb to displays of this nature, and criticized the theatrical presentations as exploitive. The shows were becoming an entire scene unto themselves. In addition to reenacting their lives on the plains, the Indians posed for photographs and they were plied with gifts such as woolen blankets and various trinkets, all of which they would take home, and thus were the seeds of modern celebrity culture planted and scattered. Across Europe, women were taken with the "noble" savages, and later, it was said that in Paris, after Buffalo Bill's shows, some women were overcome, and would head directly to the cast encampments, wanting to touch the natives in backstage meet-and-greets, hoping that the Indians' sexual energy would be transferred.

Certainly a range of experiences was had by all, but the Indians had their reasons for participating in the spectacles, including the desire to meet with kings and queens and talk about encroachment on their lands. In some cases, they were able to have those conversations, to no avail. The wars against the Indian were hardly slowing back in America; in fact they were escalating, to ease for only a few years during internecine warfare between white men during the Civil War. And alas, poor George Catlin's situation did not improve at all. The cost of renting halls, traversing Europe with eight tons of paintings and artifacts, and taking care of his Indian entourage along with his own family (which included his wife, three daughters, and a son) only added to his financial distress. In 1845, his wife, Clara contracted pneumonia and died. The Ojibway got smallpox; two died and the others returned to the Great Plains. A year later, his three-year-old son died of typhoid fever. Catlin returned to America, bereft and broke. Yet his shows paved the way for Buffalo Bill and his spectacles of the Wild West, and it was through these shows that the American dreamtime was amplified, advanced, and came to live forever.

After the Battle of the Little Bighorn in 1876, Sitting Bull and his people were hounded and hunted for years. They found refuge in Canada, finally returning to the Great Plains five years later when the buffalo began to vanish in Canada as they already had in the United States. There was also another problem: Sitting Bull's renegade Hunkpapa band of Lakota Sioux had lost the protection of the Canadian government, which had succumbed to pressure from American officials, sending the Indians south, across what Indians called the Medicine Line, into their homeland, where they became prisoners of war.

"Sitting Bull Surrenders!" announced newspapers across the land, trumpeting the news that Public Enemy Number One had been captured and America should no longer fear the man who single-handedly killed Lieutenant Colonel George Armstrong Custer on the Little Bighorn battlefield. It was of no consequence that Sitting Bull did not participate in the final siege; Crazy Horse, the other leader of the assault on the Seventh Cavalry, had already been killed, and it mattered only that Sitting Bull, the remaining figurehead, had been rendered powerless.

Yet there was a weapon in his arsenal that his captors could never take: his fame. While in Canada as a fugitive, his fame only increased. He had many admirers there and few detractors. In the States, he had a lot of both, and the numbers would only increase exponentially over the years. Sitting Bull was well aware of how he was perceived, both inside and outside his tribe. At the time of his return he knew that the American government had dedicated much time and effort to his capture; he knew that he and his band of Hunkpapas were the last holdouts—or "hostiles"—on the plains, and that therefore his homecoming would be of significant note. Yet like anyone giving up his freedom, especially a wanted and presumed killer, his fear was that he would be locked up or assassinated—or at best, promised things that the government would never deliver, lied to as the *wasichu* (white man) had done to his people over and over again since the first treaties had been signed and broken. He was right on all three counts. But he could not have known that his stature would soon lead to a starring role in a traveling road show, of all things, making his name instantly recognizable around the world for many years to come, long after the Lakota and all other North American tribes had been subdued and confined to reservations.

Fort Buford was the most important military outpost on the northern plains during the Indian wars of the nineteenth century. Located at the confluence of the Missouri and Yellowstone Rivers, it was the major supply depot for military field operations. Much pomp and circumstance had been organized for all manner of visitors at this fort. Yet oddly, for a man who was so notorious among white people, and so revered within his own tribe, Sitting Bull's arrival there was not marked by fanfare or tribute, as would have befitted an officially arranged moment involving a high-ranking figure giving up his freedom. In fact, it was as if a beggar or some sort of wastrel had wandered in with his compadres, looking for food and shelter. If you hadn't heard that Sitting Bull and his people were coming in, the sight at Fort Buford on July 19, 1881, might have made you avert your eyes in shame or gaze in wonderment and horror at the wreckage. The weather seemed to match the dismal truth of the occasion. It was dull and windy, according to reports, and the sky was overcast. Six guards waited at a corner of the parade ground, and groups of soldiers and civilians gathered outside the post store. Major David H. Brotherton, the commanding officer of the Seventh Infantry, stood outside the entrance to his office. From the north, past the parade ground, columns of mounted Lakota and soldiers approached. The Lakota ponies were gaunt, reports said, and they contrasted with the well-fed cavalry horses next to them. The columns were followed by six wagons carrying women and children, and a number of carts carrying baggage from their camp. The carts, wrote Dennis C. Pope in *Sitting Bull: Prisoner of War*, "made a screeching noise that could be heard from afar, with the wheels running on ungreased axles that sounded like finger-nails being scratched across a pane of glass." The high-pitched and unnatural chord was a haunting accompaniment to the moment.

All together, there were 188 Lakota men, women, and children coming in that day. Their clothing was rotten and falling apart, and some were covered only in dirty blankets. As a pair of men at the head of the procession approached, the gathered watchers were transfixed. Next to the Indian trader Jean-Louis Légaré rode Sitting Bull, the formidable man who was said to have killed Custer, the cavalry star, now in tatters and starving; a man who drew power from his namesake, the buffalo, but also from wolf and horse and eagle, and rock and cave and wind, now beaten down and ill. He was wearing a threadbare calico shirt, plain black leggings, and wrapped around his waist was an old woolen blanket. A calico ban-danna was wrapped around his head, pulled low over his eyes to protect them from the light, as he was suffering from an eye infec-tion. Reports noted that his attire was among the shabbiest in the entire procession, and it added to the pity and disbelief that some onlookers felt as he passed by. But they did not know that for Sit-ting Bull, his dress that day was something of a choice; it would not have befitted a Lakota leader to look better than his people, and while he could have donned feathers or perhaps even a war bonnet, he did not, and the fact that his appearance was misunderstood by his captors was just the umpteenth item in a never-ending list of things that the *wasichu* did not know and would never know about the Indian. Still, Sitting Bull was clearly a man who needed food, clothing, and shelter, along with the others in his band, and that was why they were there.

It was a strange turnabout for the Hunkpapa chief. Beyond the fact that coming in marked the end of nomadic life for his people, Sitting Bull was bringing it to a halt at a place he had nearly dismantled. As a warrior he had often laid siege to Fort Buford, leading his men in a series of attacks during the 1860s, years before the battle at the Little Bighorn. The assaults often kept soldiers pinned inside, and during one particular siege, on December 23, 1866, the Hunkpapas almost took over the fort, commandeering the sawmill and the icehouse. On the following morning, Sitting Bull taunted the soldiers, singing to them while beating time on a large saw.

What he thought about having to give himself up at Fort Buford we do not know; most likely, he would have had the same thoughts about the turn of events no matter where it had transpired. Yet the closing of the circle would not have been lost on Sitting Bull, and perhaps it steeled his resolve against what was about to happen; later some of his surrendering remarks caused concern among authorities, who took them as statements of defiance rather than capitulation or simply a desire for his old life.

As his band entered the grounds of the fort, he rode in front of the column, along with other leaders such as Four Horns, White Dog, Spotted Eagle, High as the Clouds, Bone Tomahawk, and Red Thunder. They stopped in front of Major Brotherton, and Sitting Bull shook hands with the commanding officer. "Today I am home," he said. "The land under my feet is mine again. I never sold it; I never gave it to anyone." He explained that he had left the Black Hills in 1876 because he had wanted to raise his family in peace. He was returning, he said, because he knew that one of his daughters was being held at a nearby fort. "And now I want to make a bargain with the Grandfather," he continued, using the

Indian term for the president. "I want to have witnesses on both sides." So a council was arranged for the following morning—the act of official surrender with all of the ritual required.

For now, his men laid down their guns before the soldiers. Sitting Bull held on to his Winchester, planning to relinquish it during the ceremony on the next day. Then they gave up their horses. "My boy," he said, turning to his son Crow Foot, "if you live, you will never be a man in this world, because you can never have a gun or pony." And then he began to sing: *A warrior I have been. Now it is all over. A hard time I have.* The spontaneous keening may have startled the soldiers, and any reader of these pages who has heard such anguished chanting at Indian powwows or elsewhere has felt its power. It would have been clear that Sitting Bull was wracked with feeling, even though the *wasichu* did not understand the particular words. Of course the Lakota did, and the outpouring was not unusual. Such songs were traditional among the Lakota, utterances of the emotion that underscored significant events or acts. To the Indians, it might have been strange if Sitting Bull did not utter an elegy at this time. He was known for his ability in this regard, and this chant may explain why some would turn to him for help when composing their own fugues and celebrations.

Later that day, the Hunkpapas set up their camp. It was declared off limits to outsiders, as curious soldiers and their family members tried to have a moment with Sitting Bull, besieging him with requests for a handshake, an autograph, or just an acknowledgment. The admiration was a sign of things to come, and it grew over time, fraught with motives, and it would give him leverage in certain negotiations and it would also aggravate old rivalries. Now, as night fell, the Indians retreated to their tipis. Their years of flight were over, yet they probably did not rest easy, for there were no plans for their future—or at least any that had been made known to them. The next day broke gray again. Shortly before eleven in the morning, an army official entered the camp and told Sitting Bull that the time had come. Sitting Bull and Crow Foot led the way across the parade ground toward Major Brotherton's quarters. They were flanked by the other chiefs and headmen and they were all followed by thirty-two Lakota warriors. Sitting Bull was still wearing the attire in which he had returned, and the old kerchief was still wrapped around his head, nearly covering his eyes. The Indians were escorted into Major Brotherton's parlor, where they were greeted by a small group of soldiers and civilians, including the major, other army officials, a representative of the Northwest Mounted Police from Canada who had ridden in the night before, the trader Légaré, who had taken care of Sitting Bull north of the Medicine Line and then convinced him to return, an interpreter, and a reporter from the St. *Paul Pioneer Press*. Sitting Bull shook hands with all of them except Major Guido Ilges, a Prussian Civil War hero who had made a name for himself hunting down Apaches and who had also imprisoned Sitting Bull's father long ago.

The pivotal moment approached. Still carrying his rifle, Sitting Bull took a seat next to Major Brotherton. Then he lay down the Winchester, placing it on the floor between his feet. A few seconds of silence passed. The major broke it, as a translator relayed his remarks in Lakota. He explained existing policy toward those natives who had already surrendered and he told the new arrivals that they would soon be sent down the river to Fort Yates. This was a bit of good news; there they would be reunited with family members and friends, some of whom they had not seen since the days after the Battle of the Little Bighorn, when many surrendered shortly after, knowing that even though the Indians had been victorious, it was the beginning of the end, and others, sensing the same thing but thinking and hoping they could outrun it, became fugitives.

Major Brotherton continued to explain how things would work

now that Sitting Bull and his people were wards of the U.S. government. It was simple, generic, and stifling. They were advised to behave in such a manner that no harm would come their way, and if they did as they were told, they would be treated well. The Hunkpapas indicated their approval, except for Sitting Bull, who made no such acknowledging sound or gesture.

Major Brotherton now turned to the chief and asked him to speak. Sitting Bull remained characteristically silent for several minutes and then began. First he made a short speech to the Lakotas. It was not translated and there is no record of it. Did he give them a prelude of what he was about to say? Tell them not to worry—about tomorrow and the next day and the next? When the time seemed right, he turned to Crow Foot, telling him to pick up the gun and give it to the major. "I surrender this rifle to you through my young son," he said, addressing all of the officers, "whom I now desire to teach in this manner that he has become a friend of the Americans. I wish him to learn the habits of the whites and to be educated as their sons are educated. I wish it to be remembered that I was the last man of my tribe to surrender my rifle."

It was a statement that had to hang in the air, perhaps satisfying some of the soldiers, or giving pause to others. "The last man of my tribe to surrender my rifle"—what must they have thought when Sitting Bull said this? Did anyone hold back a sigh, a tear? Were some proud of their part in this play? And what of Sitting Bull himself? Which powers did he call on to get through this moment? Was it all of the animal tribes, all four directions, was it his ancestors, or was it buffalo only, the disappearing creature of endurance and strength? Somehow, on he declaimed, stripped of firepower and method of escape, asserting rights, asking for things, and trying to help certain friends. "This is my country," he said, "and I don't wish to be compelled to give it up. My heart is very sad at having to leave the Grandmother's country. She has been a friend to me, but I want our children to grow up in our native country." He then inquired about the possibility of continuing to trade with Légaré, and expressed his desire to visit two of his friends on the other side of the line—Major James Morrow Walsh and Captain Alexander MacDonnell—whenever he wished. He added that he hoped to have all of his people live together on one reservation on the Little Missouri River south of the line in their home territory. This meant that the people who were left behind during this final trek as well as those who were already confined on the Standing Rock Reservation—one of several government zones for the Lakota, each with its own army fort—would all be permitted to reconvene in one place. "You own this ground with me," he said, "and we must try and help each other."

In the end, regardless of the relinquishment of his weapon and ponies, and the simple fact that he was inside the gates of Fort Buford, it was as if Sitting Bull had not really surrendered, the reporter from the *Pioneer Press* wrote on the following day, and among many there was puzzlement, confusion, and fear. For the man who was thought to have killed Custer did not seem contrite, and some thought he might be indicted and tried for murder. In the newspapers, there was no discussion of the fact that Major Brotherton had denied most of Sitting Bull's requests, but he did agree to send scouts to escort the Hunkpapas who were still on the trail back to Fort Buford without incident.

After the meeting, the warriors stopped at the quartermaster's station and were each given a blanket. Later that day, there was another gesture of benevolence from the army: blankets were issued to the women and children and the men who had not attended the council. But the blankets were hardly enough for the destitute natives, as even officials at the fort recognized. The major sent a telegraph to headquarters, asking for three dollars per person to purchase clothing for the band. The request was sent up through channels to the Bureau of Indian Affairs, which declined it; due to the moneys already given to the hostiles who had surrendered months earlier, there were no funds left in the coffers. Clothing was then purchased for the Hunkpapas from the post traders on credit, and the War Department picked up the tab of $825.91. In their new garments, the Indians had some measure of protection against the elements, and the mood among the band seemed to lighten.

Over the next nine days, a parade of visitors made its way to the native encampment. Some simply wanted to be friends with the vanquished men and women. Others wanted souvenirs and to hobnob with Sitting Bull. A cottage industry in moccasins and saddles erupted and the Indians purchased more supplies from the trading post. It was good business for all concerned, another sign of the strange new path that natives and *wasichus* were now following, and further indication of Sitting Bull's budding star power.

On July 29, a week and a half after their arrival at Fort Buford, Sitting Bull and his band of Hunkpapas were transferred to Fort Yates, south of Buford, down the Missouri River, near the present-day border with South Dakota. Fort Yates presided over the Standing Rock Agency, and there the Indians would be reunited with their relatives. That morning after breakfast, the women packed up the encampment and took down the tipis. Then the men, women, and children boarded the *General Sherman*, a stern-wheeler that regularly plied the waterways of the frontier, carrying soldiers and civilians.

It's hard to imagine now, but steamboats—those stately and seemingly harmless vessels associated mainly with Mark Twain—were a common sight in the region, deepening the siege that horses had permitted the cavalry to make, allowing the *wasichu* to put the squeeze on Native Americans on land and water at the same time. Most likely, Sitting Bull and many of his followers had seen steamers like this before, but none had traveled on any, and once on board they would have trouble navigating such things as stairs. As the *Sherman* headed downriver, Major Brotherton dashed off a telegram to General Alfred Howe Terry, a revered Civil War general and military commander of the Dakota Territory. "Steamer Sherman left here for Standing Rock at six forty-five a.m.," it said, "with Sitting Bull and 187 of his people. Sent an escort of seventy under command of Captain Clifford, seventh Infantry. No trouble."

About 150 miles into the journey, the *Sherman* docked near Fort Stevenson for the evening. The women found wood and prepared dinner. Later, some of the Indians sang traditional songs until it was time to retire. As guards watched over them, the band slept under the stars, each covered in his or her army-issued blanket. The next morning, the women made breakfast, and then everyone reboarded the *Sherman*.

The next stop was Bismarck, the first white man's city that the Hunkpapas had seen. Here was the kind of fanfare that would soon greet Sitting Bull in many places, with citizens lining the shore for a close look at the famous captive. In this case, elaborate plans were afoot. Town dignitaries and officials of the Northern Pacific Railway had cooked up a gala event to welcome the Indians, and it seems that they must have been told to dress for the occasion. Now, contrary to how they looked upon surrender, many of the prominent Hunkpapas were wearing their most decorative clothing. But Sitting Bull continued to present himself with humility. He was wearing blue leggings, the reporter from the *Pioneer Press* later wrote, a dirty white shirt with three red stripes on each sleeve, and moccasins with little beadwork. His hair was in three braids, and his face and neck were streaked with red paint. His eyes were still painful, and to protect them he wore steel-rimmed goggles that were tinted green. On the little and second fingers of each hand he wore brass rings. He carried his pipe bag in one hand, and with the other he fanned himself with a large hawk's-wing fan.

When the Indians disembarked, they were each given two days of rations. Sitting Bull and some of the other headmen were separated from the band, and they were whisked away to a nearby train—the very thing that they had fought for years to keep out of their territory. There they were introduced to B. D. Vermilye, the personal secretary to the general manager of the Northern Pacific Railway, and Captain C. W. Batchelor, one of the principal owners of the Yellowstone Line. They explained to Sitting Bull that everyone would be attending a reception in his honor. He would meet the leading citizens of Bismarck and there would be a dinner. "We're traveling by rail to the Sheridan House," Vermilye explained, pointing to a plush railcar that would carry the party to downtown Bismarck. But it was the locomotive that seemed to interest Sitting Bull, wrote Bill Yenne in his book about the chief, and Vermilye told the engineer to steam it up and move it. To the secretary's puzzlement, Sitting Bull declined the offer for a ride, saying that he would rather walk to the hotel. Vermilye convinced him to head to the reception in an army ambulance drawn by a team of mules.

Sitting Bull sat in the front, along with Captain Batchelor and the driver. Behind them were the rest of the party, including Sitting Bull's sister Good Feather, his uncle Four Horns, White Dog, Scarlet Thunder, High-as-the-Clouds, and Bone Tomahawk, as well as the interpreter, Vermilye, and a guard. When the other Indians saw that their leaders had gotten into an ambulance, they panicked and began wailing, fearing that the chiefs were being taken to prison. Soldiers rushed in with their rifles, trying to control the crowd. Sitting Bull immediately stood up in the ambulance and addressed his people. His remarks were not recorded; he calmed them down, and the ambulance headed to the reception.

Outside of the Sheridan House, several hundred people had

gathered. Inside, Captain Batchelor escorted Sitting Bull and his group to a cushioned parlor upstairs. Chairs had been placed in a semicircle and everyone took a seat, with Sitting Bull in the center, and the armed guard behind him. He took out his pipe, lit it, and began to smoke. As he talked with some of the *wasichu*, he occasionally fanned himself. The other Hunkpapas talked with one another and occasionally laughed. As the event progressed, various people in the room approached Sitting Bull and asked for his autograph, including Captain Batchelor. During his exile in Canada, Sitting Bull had learned to write his name in English, reportedly to accommodate people who asked for souvenirs even then. He had become quite proficient at using a pencil. By all accounts, he warmed to this occasion in Bismarck.

It was just a prelude of festivities to come throughout the day. Soon the group headed downstairs, back into the ambulance, and over to the Merchants Hotel for a banquet. They were followed through the streets by large crowds, who pressed in outside the hotel windows once Sitting Bull and the other Indians were inside, hoping to get a good view of the event. The hotel owners had prepared a meal "as if for the Queen of England," said the *Bismarck Tribune*. To the surprise of their hosts, the Hunkpapas knew how to use knives and forks; they had learned such skills in Canada. Sitting Bull ate slowly, the newspaper would report the next day, stopping often to fan himself. The serving of ice cream for dessert was a great puzzlement for the Indians, who wondered how the *wasichu* could cook something so cold in such hot weather.

As the banquet concluded, Sitting Bull gave Captain Batchelor his pipe and Vermilye his goggles. The Indians then headed back to their encampment, and the guests at the hotel toasted the occasion with fine wine. The Hunkpapas who were not at the dinner had been having their own celebration as well. During the three hours that Sitting Bull was gone, they had eaten most of their two days' ration of food. After years of flight and deprivation, and now, un-certainty about where they were going, the seemingly large supply of sustenance must have been a relief, if only for a moment.

Back on board the *Sherman*, a group of prominent citizens was waiting to meet Sitting Bull. With the interpreter translating, the famous Indian was introduced to each one of them. One of the guests was Miss Emma Bentley, who presented Sitting Bull with a California pear, Yenne noted. He took it, retrieved his knife and cut off a piece, tasted it, and liked it. In return, he removed a ring from his finger and placed it on one of Miss Bentley's, folding her hand over it.

It was the kind of gesture that Sitting Bull would become known for, and for which he was already known within his band. The fact that he had so charmed Miss Bentley was not lost on the other women in attendance, or the men, and it only added to his appeal. For him, the soiree that night overturned his every expectation. It wasn't that he was surprised by what the white man was capable of; rather he began to learn the ways of the enemy. Beyond the fact that he did not trust them, he now realized that plenty of things were available once he was inside their world. Among his own people, he never wavered from his desire to get to Washington and sit down with the Grandfather. He would raise this subject from time to time with his captors, and in a few years he would discuss the idea with Buffalo Bill. For now, he was an imprisoned guest at the white man's party, asked to pay tribute to the Iron Horse, whose rails were now traversing and binding the frontier. While he may have liked the at-tention, he also understood its source. When the gala concluded, he and his headmen headed back to the *Sherman*, and boarded it along with the rest of the Hunkpapas for the next leg of the trip. At 6 p.m., a band on board struck up a festive tune. The celebration continued as the steamer traveled down the Missouri toward Fort Yates.

Debarking there the next day, August 1, Sitting Bull was greeted by his old associate Running Antelope. For the first time since his return, Sitting Bull broke down and cried. Later that day, he was reunited with his daughter, and they cried together. The Lakotas began to settle in at their new home, and almost immediately after his arrival Sitting Bull tried to get permission for a trip to Washington. When he surrendered in Canada and agreed to return to the Dakota Territory, he had been told by one of the officials that President James Garfield would indeed receive him in the White House. But by the time Sitting Bull arrived at Fort Yates, Garfield had been assassinated and Chester A. Arthur, the new president, "refused to allow the savage who was responsible for the slaughter of Custer to go to Washington," according to an army memo. In response, Sitting Bull sent a letter to President Arthur. It vacillated between defiance and capitulation and hope, and indicated that he was coming to a rapid understanding of his circumstances. "I wish that the Great Father would furnish me with farming implements," he concluded, "so that I can till the ground."

It was the plea of a man who was now concerned with the survival of his people, and very soon he would indeed become a farmer. But that would not happen at Fort Yates. A few weeks after the Lakotas had been living there, some cartridges were found in Sitting Bull's lodgings. There was to be no ammunition among the Indians and authorities at the fort began making arrangements to remove Sitting Bull and his band to Fort Randall, a more remote location where the isolation, it was believed, would help to control the Hunkpapas. Sitting Bull was not told of the plan until it was implemented, on the 10th of September. The white man had now broken another promise, for he had been told there would be no more removals. Once again, he and his band were ordered to board the *Sherman*, harried up the gangway at gunpoint. The lone Indian who refused, his nephew One Bull, was butted with a rifle between the shoulders, and sent sprawling. He got up and boarded the ship, and the Hunkpapas and soldiers headed downriver, this time for a week-long trip of four hundred miles to their new home near the present-day border of South Dakota and Nebraska.

There was no celebration on board and the riverbanks were not lined with admirers. Each night, the Indians left the steamer, set up camp, prepared dinner, slept, and returned in the morning to resume the journey. To the Hunkpapas' solace, no doubt, a different sort of tribute awaited them as the *Sherman* steamed past the Cheyenne River Agency. In anticipation of the passing, a large group of Lakotas had assembled on the riverbanks. "The most violent demonstrations of grief occurred," a newspaper reported. A few days earlier, 120 "ex-hostiles" from the Standing Rock Agency had been transferred to Cheyenne River. When they got word that Sitting Bull was in the vicinity, they had converged on the shores to demonstrate their high regard for the old leader. The display must have had an unsettling effect on the soldiers, and it was further indication that Sitting Bull must be closely watched and controlled. Meanwhile, amid the turmoil and sadness of the journey, one of Sitting Bull's wives, Four Robes, gave birth to a baby girl.

Life at Fort Randall was not as dire as Sitting Bull had expected, perhaps because it soon became clear that this was to be the final stop for the Hunkpapas, at least for a while. Sitting Bull had seemed finally to accept his fate. He asked to be supplied with wagons, plows, white-man clothing, horses, and cattle. The Hunkpapas were not quite ready for the implements of the new life that was planned for them, it was determined. All of these things would come in due time.

For now, the captives were to wait things out with little to do. They were guarded by the Twenty-fifth Infantry, one of four black regiments in the army, also known as "Buffalo Soldiers" because their curly hair resembled that of the buffalo. Although Sitting Bull had to live right next door to the fort, as opposed to farther away from it on the reservation grounds, he seemed to accept even that as the days and weeks and months unfolded. His statements appeared to be more conciliatory, though he continued to try to contact the White House, pressing for a visit.

Meanwhile, his celebrity status continued to increase, and he was besieged with visitors as well as mail from across the country and from foreign lands. There were requests for Sitting Bull's pipe, knife, tomahawk, and his autograph. He rarely replied unless the letters included a dollar. According to historian Stanley Vestal, he spent the income on paint and tobacco, "and other little luxuries at the post trader's." By now, his stardom was indelible. Offers from the many dime museums that were popping up across the country in the mid-1880s began to pour in. Circuses and road shows also wanted the popular chief. Major James McLaughlin, the agent in charge of Fort Randall, rejected all of the proposals. He was concerned that should Sitting Bull embark on any venture that made him even more famous, he would be impossible to control when he returned. In addition McLaughlin was rapidly becoming a nemesis of Sitting Bull's. Not only did he dictate the Hunkpapas' daily schedules—they followed army protocol, with reveille and so on throughout the day—but he also seemed to have it in for the leader, who represented everything that McLaughlin was not. Like many soldiers and settlers on the plains, McLaughlin was married to an Indian and was no stranger to their ways. Yet his interpretation of those ways was often inaccurate—or shaped by his own desires. And he firmly believed that if the Hunkpapas were to survive, they must succumb to the new order. Inside that order, he believed, it was necessary to relinquish any vestiges of the world from which they came.

But for the moment, he was fighting a losing battle. It was precisely Sitting Bull's stature as a man who would not give in, a rebel who had held his own against the U.S. army, that rendered him all the more popular, enabling him to remain an outsider and, in McLaughlin's view, cause trouble at Standing Rock. In the summer of 1883, the Northern Pacific Railway was planning to drive the last spike of its transcontinental route across the northern plains, in Gold Creek, Montana. It was decided that it would be advantageous to have an Indian chief at the ceremony in nearby Bismarck, adding to the glamour of the day. Of course, the choice was Sitting Bull, and perhaps because the event involved railroad officials, McLaughlin consented. On September 8, Sitting Bull arrived, accompanied by an army chaperone who spoke Lakota and worked with him to prepare a speech. They rode at the head of a parade, and according to some accounts, Sitting Bull carried the American flag. Then they took their places on the speakers' platform. Sitting Bull was introduced and began delivering his speech—in his native language. But he had changed the text. "I hate all the white people," he said. "You are thieves and liars. You have taken away our land and made us outcasts." The young officer was taken aback. And on Sitting Bull declaimed, "pausing occasionally for applause," as Dee Brown recounted in *Bury My Heart at Wounded Knee*, and then "he bowed, smiled, and uttered a few more insults." After he sat down, the interpreter stood up, and presented his translation, which was a short speech with a few friendly phrases. He added some "well-worn Indian metaphors," Brown wrote, and the audience gave Sitting Bull a standing ovation. Did he and his chaperone exchange a look at that moment? Or later, on the way back to Standing Rock, did they have some words or maybe even a laugh? All we can say for sure is that Sitting Bull had carried out a stealth campaign from inside what was essentially a jail. It belied the serious expression that is captured in the few photographs bearing his image. Clearly, here was a man who could smuggle in a joke and, at the same time, acquire new admirers at events of import.

Pressing his campaign to meet the president, Sitting Bull often asked McLaughlin if he could visit Eastern cities. He refused, until the day that he didn't, believing that if he could impress Sitting Bull with the advantages of city life, the chief would then be able to convince his people to accept American-style education and take up farming. In 1884, McLaughlin took Sitting Bull to St. Paul for ten days. He gave him a grand tour of factories, stores, churches, banks, theaters, a cigar plant, and the local firehouse. At the plant, Sitting Bull made "some very significant puffs," a reporter would write. At the *Pioneer Press* office, workers acquainted Sitting Bull with "the telephone eavesdropping racket." In admiration, he is said to have grunted "Waukon," which translated as "the devil." At the firehouse, Sitting Bull was taken by the sound of the clanging bell and asked if he could ring it. Everywhere he went, admirers turned out to greet him, offering gifts and ribbons and artificial flowers, and introducing him to their occupations and endeavors.

The tour of St. Paul continued throughout that week. Sitting Bull was taken to the Grand Opera House, for instance, for a performance of *Muldoon's Picnic*. On March 19, he went to the Olympic Theater to see the Arlington and Fields Combination— "combination" was a term for "repertory"—billed as "the greatest aggregation of talent" ever to appear in St. Paul. From a prominent seat in Box B, he watched the Wertz Brothers perform acrobatics, heard Allie Jackson sing a medley of songs, and saw Flynn and Sarsfield in a minstrel act.

But what impressed him the most—and would become a pivotal moment in his life—was Annie Oakley and her shooting routine. She began her performance by bounding onstage and snuffing out a candle with a bullet from her rifle. She continued to snuff burning candles with gunshots, and proceeded to blow corks off bottle tops and cigarettes from her husband Frank Butler's mouth. For the next few days, Sitting Bull dispatched messengers to Annie, asking if she would come see him. She was busy preparing for a shooting match and did not want to miss it, so she declined, lest she forfeit her entry fee. Money was important to the sharpshooter, and when Sitting Bull began offering it, she responded more positively. At first, he sent $65 to her room, asking for a photo. "This amused me," Annie later said, "so I sent him back his money and a photograph, with my love, and a message to say I would call the following morning. I did so, and the old man was so pleased with me, he insisted upon adopting me, and I was then and there christened 'Watanya Cicilla,' or 'Little Sure Shot.'"

It was a name that helped propel Annie's career (though its real meaning is "Little Person Who Does Good Things"). Two weeks later, on April 5, 1884, Annie's husband placed an ad in the *New York Clipper*. "The Premier Shots, Butler and Oakley, Captured by Sitting Bull," it said, referring to the chief's warrior status. The ad went on to note that Sitting Bull had given Annie a picture of himself, a feather from a Crow chief, and—as he had told her—the original pair of moccasins he had worn at the Battle of the Little Bighorn. Witnesses attested to the fact that Sitting Bull had actually done this, and if he had in fact said that the moccasins were worn at the battle, it would have been something of a grand gesture by which he acknowledged his presence at that event; outside Indian circles, it was still widely believed that Sitting Bull had indeed killed Custer. At the end of the week, Sitting Bull headed back to the reservation, and Annie headed east. They would soon meet again.

One month later, Buffalo Bill made his first attempt to hire Sitting Bull and a few members of his band for the Wild West show. McLaughlin declined to give permission, telling Cody that Sitting Bull "had already received so many propositions of the kind it has become considerable of a bore." While he thought that the show was a worthwhile form of entertainment and that Cody had made the request "in a very commendable manner," he explained that he couldn't consider "any such proposition at the present time when the late hostiles are so well disposed and are just beginning to take hold of an agricultural life." But he added that "if they would be permitted to join any traveling company, in conjunction with other attractions, I would prefer to have them in your troupe to any organized that I have knowledge of."

Launched in 1883, the Wild West—minus the word "show"— was a touring extravaganza that crystallized the frontier experience through a parade of moments and acts that had come to signify American history. It was cooked up by Cody, along with two part- ners. He was its figurehead and driving force. Already a major celebrity who was shuttling back and forth between the frontier (where he was known for his exploits) and Broadway (where he reenacted them), he provided employment for cowboys and Indians who were soon to be locked out of time itself. This almost instant theater—born of a history that did not even span a single century— was magic, a mesmerizing spectacle that was lie and truth, fable and news, a thing that inscribed the American story for the ages. But the magic behind the magic was horses, as Cody made a point of saying from the very beginning. Such deference was in the show's founding literature and programs; the presentation was essentially an equine drama, for without the flying manes and tails of the na- tional saga, the show would not go on. To that end, Cody hired the premier centaurs of the era—Native American warriors who embodied the spirit of freedom with their painted faces and feathers astride fast-stepping painted ponies. By 1884, the Wild West was on its way to becoming the premier frontier spectacle of its time—of all time—and it was only fitting that sooner or later, for many reasons, Sitting Bull would join Buffalo Bill on the mythology road.

But there were others who wanted Sitting Bull for their enterprises as well, all manner of impresarios and clerks of one religion or another seeking Sitting Bull's services. For instance, officials at the Bureau of Catholic Indian Missions in Washington wanted to take Sitting Bull on tour to raise money for the missions. McLaughlin didn't like the idea, and would have preferred Buffalo Bill's request, but it was too late in the touring season. Meanwhile, a group of McLaughlin's friends in St. Paul had been hoping to hire Sitting Bull for a tour of the East. Sitting Bull adopted a hard-line bargaining position, holding out for "big money" and letting McLaughlin know that he was "worth untold fortunes." Weeks later, the major agreed to Sitting Bull's demands, which also included bringing along more of his people.

The entourage was called the "Sitting Bull Combination," and in addition to the chief, there were eight Hunkpapas and two interpreters. On September 2, 1884, they left, embarking on a tour of twenty-five cities between Minneapolis and New York. It wrapped up on October 25, but the turnout everywhere was disappointing. McLaughlin was now convinced that only Buffalo Bill would make such a tour a grand success.

Possibly encouraged by the major, Cody wired the secretary of the interior the following spring. "Sitting Bull has expressed a desire to travel with me," he said, "and requests me to ask your permission for himself and seven of his tribe. I will treat him well and pay him a good salary. The agent at Fort Yates approves the idea." The request was refused. According to a response from the commissioner of Indian Affairs, the Indians should be busy planting crops and not "roving through the country exhibiting themselves and visiting places where they would naturally come in contact with evil associates and degrading immoralities." At the time, such a concern was not necessarily a disingenuous excuse to keep Indians on the reservation. Actors and performers are today's immortals, but in the nineteenth century "show folk" were disdained in many quarters, viewed as grifters and madmen and crooks, and this attitude launched a circuit of reformers and propelled political careers. The Indian Affairs authorities wanted to quash circuses and keep Native Americans on the straight and narrow; how else could they survive in a culture that had no place for their ways? Of course, such campaigns did not stop people from wanting to see novelty acts and death-defying performers, especially if cowboys and Indians and trick shooters and horses were involved, and later, many Native Americans wanted to join the Wild West and hit the road, earning a fair wage from the *wasichu* who honored his contracts while replicating a world which was vanishing. Buffalo Bill continued his campaign, getting letters of recommendation from General William Tecumseh Sherman and Colonel Eugene Asa Carr, former foes of Sitting Bull. Finally consent was given.

Two weeks later, on June 6, 1885, self-anointed "Major" John M. Burke, general manager of the Wild West show, arrived at Fort Yates. The show was already on the road, and he wanted to hasten the arrangements. After all, Sitting Bull was the man everyone wanted to see, and the sooner he could join the show, the more money to be made for all concerned. The contract was explained and signed in McLaughlin's office. Sitting Bull would be paid $50 per week, with a bonus of $125 and two weeks' salary in advance. Five other Indians would each receive $25 per month. And, agreeing to a request from Sitting Bull, Burke added a clause regarding additional fees for promotional material. "Sitting Bull is to have sole right to sell his own Photographs and Autographs," it said. By Monday, Burke and the Sitting Bull party headed to the train station in Mandan, Dakota Territory, and boarded the "vapor horse." They joined up with the show on the following Friday, greeted by throngs as Sitting Bull stepped off the train in a war bonnet with forty eagle feathers and an embroidered buckskin tunic. Coincidentally, this first stop on the chief's new path was a place whose name was resonant. It was Buffalo, New York, and within hours, Sitting Bull was part of a grand reenactment of a vanished era, hoping for a meeting with the Great Father, who was now Grover Cleveland.

CHAPTER TWO

*In Which the Wild West Is Born—and Dies
and Is Resurrected from the Bottom
of the Mississippi River*

In Europe, he was known as "Nature's Nobleman," a frontier self-sufficient with the sophistication of Western civilization; in America, he was "King of the Old West"—a title he deserved. He was a hunter, scout, shooter, rider, warrior, teller of tall tales, and man of adventure par excellence. His experiences in city and plain rendered him a kind of wise man, and presidents and generals sought his advice. His friends included Frederic Remington and Mark Twain and Pawnee chiefs; broncbusters who could drink him under the table and might have even been better riders; archdukes from foreign lands and ranch cooks who needed a job. He was open to all, he had no airs. What you saw was what you got, even if what you saw was sometimes a mirage. "He was the simplest of men," as Annie Oakley would say at the end of his life, "as comfortable with cowboys as with kings."

Everyone wants in on a success and superstar Buffalo Bill was surrounded by many who claimed to have helped him invent himself, said they had thought of the Wild West show, or suggested that he head the Wild West—or some combination of the fore-going. Like other superstars, and of course like all of us, he had plenty of help along the way. He could not have been Buffalo Bill without it. But it's not likely that anyone else could have been a repository of so many rivers, at a certain time and a certain place, and reflected those currents back to his comrades in a way that was affirming, uplifting, majestic even. Yet he was hardly a humble man; he was a fountain of charisma and charm with a personality that was much like the frontier that shaped him—big, exciting, dangerous, with a heart that was elusive and wild.

On a personal level, such a man is beyond reach. Many claimed a piece of him, yet few if any had one. Certainly, he had human yearnings, with a family and children and homes that he loved being in when he was there, having built and maintained two substantial ranches in Wyoming and Nebraska. Yet he was a man of huge appetites and the settled life did not fulfill them.

"My restless, roaming spirit," he later wrote, "would not allow me to remain at home very long." He was not a solitary traveler and he had a retinue of friends, partners, colleagues, cast members, and a number of women around him at any given time. Some of his female friends were close companions, and many came to his funeral, where his widow may have wondered or perhaps known who these figures were, having not just heard the rumors of his affairs but witnessed his behavior for a long time. A party in Omaha during the winter of 1877 is an illustration of the scrum of female adoration through which Cody's wife would have to navigate for access. A farewell celebration for a pre–Wild West theatrical troupe was under way, and "elegantly dressed, excited guests lined the hallway of a refined hotel," as Chris Enss wrote in *The Many Loves of Buffalo Bill*. "Waiters in tails and white gloves and carrying trays of champagne-filled glasses weaved around the congregation, as entertainers, businessmen and women, cattle barons, and politicians helped themselves to the abundance of wine and toasted one another's good fortune."

When the thirty-one-year-old Cody entered, guests turned their attention to the powerful force in their midst, applauding wildly as he made his way through the crowd. Everything about him was riveting. He was six feet one with dark, curly, shoulder-length hair. He had a mustache and goatee and wore a tuxedo-style waistcoat, vest, and perfectly pressed trousers. He liked the attention, although did not live for it, and that characteristic lent him an even more attractive air, confirming that he was a bad boy, after all, a rogue at heart, headed back to the wilderness as soon as the party was over. For now, everyone wanted to be near him, including "beautiful women in taffeta gowns and lace bonnets" who angled for proximity. When one of them slipped her arm into the crook of his, he did not mind. Soon, Enss continued, the crowd moved into the main suite and Cody regaled them with tales of his life, hitting the high points that had already been and would again be recounted in anecdotes and plays and biographies for as long as the republic endures. As he spoke, his female admirers paid rapt attention, and then his wife, Louisa, entered, not with fanfare and apparently he did not acknowledge her—or if he did, it was not noted by any who made a record of the event. She faded into the crowd as he continued telling his stories, then picked up a glass of wine and chatted here and there with a guest.

Like any longtime partner, she had heard the stories many times; possibly, upon occasion, they added to his allure. Soon, as Enss recounted, the party wound down and people began to leave, almost everyone except the actresses who had surrounded Cody. When it was time for them to go, they kissed him on the cheek, and then, with Louisa watching, he returned the kisses. For the first time that evening, she pushed through the remaining guests and approached her husband. She chastised him as partygoers grew silent and embarrassed under her heated words; after the exchange with Cody, she stormed out. Cody did not follow her, but watched and then said his goodbyes to the few remaining guests, wishing them well. After the party, man and wife headed home to North Platte and their Scout's Rest Ranch in silence.

They had fallen in love when they were young and much had happened since their wedding celebration on board the steamship *Morning Star* years earlier, when the handsome man in buckskin and fringe waltzed his bride, "a comely St. Louis girl of French descent" as he once described her, across the dining room floor. "My dear Lulu," he had written during their courtship, "I know you will forgive me for calling you this—because you will always be Lulu to me, just as I will be glad if I may always be Willie to you."

Years later, Cody the superstar, the most desirable man and foremost ruffian of the era, recalled the evening in Omaha, expressing puzzlement at his wife's reaction. "I do not think most wives would have felt a little angry to know and hear her husband in an adjoining room on Sunday morning, drinking beer and kissing theatrical girls of his company," he wrote. "I think they would have been rather proud of a husband who had six or seven months work with a party of people who were in his employ, to know and feel that they were on a kindly footing."

Of course, such was not Louisa's way, nor did she approve of other aspects of Cody's life, such as his gambling, one more thing that took Cody away, involving one more crowd of friends and hangers-on to get through in order to reach her husband. Whether on the road or at home, there was often something under way—card games, theater, public events, things and people who needed Cody and to which and to whom he felt an obligation. Over the years, it was all too much to keep up with, too much shuffling and reshuffling of the deck, and toward the end of his life, when things began to fall apart, he indulged his impulses to an even greater extent, trying to save things and keep up appearances, investing unwisely, in big ways—gambling well beyond the poker table, in

real estate, mines, and other enterprises. By 1913, the Wild West
had gone bankrupt and everything—horses, buffalo, cattle, stagecoaches, tipis—was turned over to creditors. Cody's powerful
friends—"the rulers of republics and mighty potentates of foreign
lands," as one newspaper put it—did not come to his aid. In the
end, like everyone, he was down to a few good friends, red man
and white man alike. A thing that most anguished them was the
fact that Cody's horses would be sold off. They all knew that without the horse, on foot and looking inglorious, they were diminished. Along with the country's newspapers, they rallied around
the sale of Cody's beloved Isham, a horse he had ridden since it was
given to him years earlier. "BUFFALO BILL MUST SACRIFICE
FAMOUS HORSE ON AUCTION BLOCK," screamed the headlines in August of that year. "Isham belongs to the company," Cody
said, holding back tears, as he talked to reporters who had gathered.
"We were together for a long time, and we know each other better
than brothers. . . . I would not want to even estimate the number
of shots that I have fired from Isham's back. I do know that he has
taken as much interest in my exhibitions as I have. And at any time
I scored more misses than I was entitled to make, Isham showed his
sympathy by his looks and actions. And when I made full scores, he
would prance off the grounds like a conquering hero."

A few days later, an auctioneer took the podium at the Over-
land Park arena in Denver. As he offered Isham, many in the
packed house choked up. He then explained that Cody could not
save him due to insufficient means and announced that a man from
Nebraska had come "to buy this faithful animal for the purpose of
presenting him to his owner." Carlo Miles, an Indian aide to Buffalo Bill, rode into the arena leading Isham. The crowd fell silent.
"Ten dollars," the Nebraska man called, opening the bidding.

"Twenty dollars," called the Indian. Unbeknownst to Cody,
each bidder was planning to give Isham back to him, but none

knew that each was bidding for the same reason. Other bids came quickly, almost simultaneously—twenty-five dollars, thirty-five, fifty. Carlo Miles called out, "Seventy-five dollars." "Eighty dollars," called someone else, then a hundred dollars from the man from Nebraska—Colonel C. J. Bills as it turned out, an old friend who had fought with Cody in the Indian wars. "I would sooner lose my life than see Buffalo Bill lose that white horse," he had told a reporter before the sale. "It doesn't make any difference who bids, or how many want the horse. I am going to buy it and the next minute turn it over to my old friend. I know how he loves the animal, and I know how I love Colonel Cody. It would hurt me even worse than it would him to see the horse fall into the hands of others."

Miles upped the bid to $110. And so the bidding continued, and finally Miles started to cry, not having received word as to what Colonel Bills was planning and concerned because he couldn't go much higher than the current bid of $150. "If the man who buys that horse don't give him back to Colonel Cody, I'll steal the horse tonight and take it to him," he said, and he swore an oath. Isham went to Bills, and then Bills turned him over to Cy Compton, a Wild West cowboy who had cared for the horse for years. Compton sat down and wept. The show had folded but its lifeblood—horse and rider—had been preserved. As for Buffalo Bill, there is no mention of him in coverage of the auction. Most likely he had decided not to attend.

What he made of this matter, or many other matters involving his inner workings, we do not know. The fact that he teared up while talking to reporters about the possible loss of Isham tells us much. When another of his favorite horses, Charlie Joe, fell ill at sea upon return from the Wild West's triumphant presentation to Queen Victoria and her court, Cody was bereft. He did everything he could to try to save the ailing steed, spending hours with him belowdecks as Charlie continued to falter. When the horse died, the crew took him to the main deck, wrapped him in a canvas shroud, and covered him with an American flag. He lay in state for a day, and everyone recounted their stories of the horse. When it was time, Cody stood alone near Charlie and uttered a prayer. "Old fellow, your journeys are over . . . obedient to my call, gladly you bore your burden on. . . . Willing speed, tireless courage . . . you have never failed me. Ah Charlie, old fellow, I have had many friends, but few of whom I could say that. . . . I loved you as you loved me. Men tell me you have no soul; but if there is a heaven and scouts can enter there, I'll wait at the gate for you, old friend."

At eight o'clock that evening, candles were lit and with all hands and members of the Wild West assembled, the band played "Auld Lang Syne." Charlie was lowered into the depths.

There is nothing sadder than the cowboy who fights off tears, the frontiersman who is overcome by the thing he cannot bear. But when it came to people, Cody's reminscences or writings or statements are not as fraught. After all, he was often billed as the King of the Old West, and his best friend was his trusty and beloved steed—of which he had many over the years. While he was certainly more talkative than the stereotypical cowboy who said only what was needed, going way beyond "Yes, ma'am" and "No, ma'am" and "Wait for me," behind his urge to tell tales and engage an audience, he was true to the form. There was not much second-guessing or self-doubt or hints of pain or regret—except within letters to women he was courting or loved or with whom he was infatuated, such as Annie Oakley, who starred in his show for many years. Some of his comments to reporters about Sitting Bull and Native Americans also laid bare pangs of remorse and occasionally something bordering on outrage, but he could also make disparaging remarks about them that were indicative of the era.

The writings of others in his circle, much of which was designed to promote him and some of which was borne of resentment or other unreliable seeds, betray little underlying feeling. But we do know that he was a man of action, and that tells us much, especially when the record is examined closely. He was also a man of his time, and in that regard he had a not uncommon rough-and-tumble childhood involving violence and bloodshed. He took it all in stride, and later he quelled his demons with lots of liquor—a fact of life during an era when self-reflection was hardly a social convention. Who can say how much the fog of whiskey shrouded his secret longings and wounds and fears? One way or another, in Cody's later years, it was apparent that his demons were mighty, try as he would to right some very large wrongs.

Before the term was forever linked to his name, William F. Cody grew up in the Wild West. Once, he was a boy, not a superstar, not named for the animal that he would kill by the thousands (others, for the record, killed more), but just a boy who played with Indians on the Great Plains, perhaps even members of Sitting Bull's extended tribe who would pass through territory near his home in Kansas as they followed the buffalo. So too, by his own account, did he kill an Indian in his youth (and others later), while he was employed as a wagon train hand. But of course he was not aware that the curtain would soon fall on their way of life—and that he would participate in that last act as well as try to preserve what came before. Once he was just a boy, who helped his struggling family eke out a living on the frontier, as many children of the era did, engaging in tasks and acts that would now violate every child labor law on the books. En route, he learned a keen sense of justice from his father, who became embroiled in the great abolitionist struggle of the day, ultimately speaking out against slavery—an act that would have consequences.

William Frederick "Buffalo Bill" Cody was born near Le Claire,

Iowa, on February 26, 1846. Although associated via name with the iconic animal which would later represent the West as the Department of the Interior symbol and on the nickel, Cody was first and foremost a horseman, one of the best of his era. Galloping steeds and the men who rode thunder were the driving force behind the Wild West show, which included few scenes of men on foot. Quite simply, horses were the defining part of Cody's life, as they were for many in his time. Beyond that, although he and his future employee and friend Sitting Bull both carried the buffalo in their names, it would be through the horse—specifically a dramatic act initiated by Buffalo Bill—that their time together in the theater of the West would be finalized in the most haunting of ways.

Young William F. Cody learned and absorbed all aspects of horse culture in Le Claire, where his father, Isaac, managed large farms for absentee owners, including the six-hundred-acre farm known as Breckenridge Place, after a state senator. Isaac was contracted to survey it and build a large stone house in which he and his family could live. "Young Billy followed his father everywhere," wrote his sister Julia Cody Goodman years later in one of several biographies of her brother. "To break the land, 25 separate plows were used, each drawn by a yoke of oxen, one driver to each team. Other men followed, dropping seed corn into the fresh furrows. Behind both crews rode Mr. Cody, with Billy perched on the saddle horn, watching the long line of ox teams creep slowly across the field—turning 25 ribbons of green earth downward. As the boy and his father rode back and forth, up and down, they could hear other men, all strong, sturdy, dependable German laborers, working in the quarry, getting stone for the new house." Beyond the farm, another world called. There were thick forests, full of bears, wild hogs, deer, and wildcats, and young Will was enraptured, gazing wide-eyed "as wild deer raced down from the bluffs and skipped effortlessly over the fences" their father had built around the farm.

Life was a kind of wilderness school, and Will was a natural student, studying the woods and animals and how they moved on the land. But it was to horses that he seemed most drawn. In addition to managing farms, his father ran a stagecoach business between Davenport and Chicago. With his six siblings, Cody would stand on the riverbank and watch his father's horse-drawn coach pass by—perhaps an early seed for a scene he would later re-create in his show in a much more dramatic fashion involving a famous stagecoach from Deadwood. Recalling his first experience as an equestrian, Cody later wrote that "Somehow or other I had managed to corner a horse near a fence, and had climbed on his back. The next moment the horse got his back up and hoisted me into the air. I fell violently to the ground, striking upon my side in such a way as to severely wrench and strain my arm, from the effects of which I did not recover for some time. I abandoned the art of horsemanship for a while." A year later his father let William ride one of his horses.

In 1853, his oldest brother, Sam, who was twelve, was killed by a bucking mare. The family was devastated. According to some accounts, Will himself was involved in a violent incident of his own around this time, brawling with the class bully in the schoolyard in order to impress a girl, and finally slashing him in the leg with his Bowie knife. "I've been killed," the fellow called out, but Cody the young hunter could tell that he wasn't, and their schoolmates staunched the bleeding with rags. A teacher punished Cody with a hazel switch, and then he fled the scene, returning later with friends to confront the teacher and the bully. The frightened teacher dismissed the class and fled as well. Meanwhile, the girl for whom Cody had fought was said to be duly impressed, gazing longingly at him as she left with the class.

A year later, the Codys moved from the scene of their family tragedy to the Kansas Territory, declared open for settlement by Congress, with settlers permitted to vote up or down on the question of slavery. "Northern abolitionists hurried from Illinois to fight the pro-slavery Missourians rushing in from the South. They fought with gun and Bowie knife," wrote Henry Blackman Sell and Victor Weybright in *Buffalo Bill and the Wild West*. Taken by their six horses—four pulling a wagon filled with the family's goods and two pulling the stage that carried the family—they were among the earliest white settlers. A relative named Horace Billings continued Cody's education in things equestrian, teaching him to ride a small, fast horse named Little Gray that the family had purchased along the way. "I made rapid advances in the art of horsemanship," Cody later wrote. It was a skill the young man soon put to good use.

When the Codys arrived in Kansas, the territory was roiling with the question of slavery. "A brutal and quarrelsome breed of men had followed the Codys into the Salt Creek Valley, where they settled," wrote Sell and Weybright. "'If I had my way, I'd hang every Abolitionist!' screamed an editor named Stringfellow from the Missouri side of the river. 'And everyone born north of the Mason-Dixon line is an Abolitionist!' At his behest a mob of horsemen rode into the valley and declared that slavery was 'thereby instituted in the Territory of Kansas.'" Some locals announced that the state was ungovernable, like hell, and others vowed to wipe out abolitionist strongholds such as Lawrence. In 1856, the question of slavery exploded once again when "a pro-slavery mob swarmed into town, wrecking and burning the hotel and newspaper office" in Lawrence, Robert A. Carter noted in his book *Buffalo Bill Cody*. Three days later, John Brown led his infamous antislavery raid in which a band of abolitionists besieged pro-slavery settlers, dragging five of them from their homes and hacking them to death. This was a signpost on the way to the Civil War. Three weeks after that, a ripped-from-the-headlines drama called *Osawatomie Brown* (referring to John Brown) opened on

Broadway. It was one of various presentations blazing the trail for Cody, the future stage attraction.

The heated scenes that played out over slavery in the Kansas Territory soon involved Cody's father. Like many new settlers, Isaac Cody was against slavery, though he did not seem to make a point of it. But he had a reputation as a good public speaker, and one day, shortly after the family arrived, when he was riding past Rively's Trading Post, the site of many a debate, he was dragooned into giving a speech against a resolution that sanctioned slaveholding and outlawed abolitionists. "I believe in letting slavery remain as it now exists," he said from atop a box amid the noisy crowd. He meant that it had no place in the Kansas Territory. "And I shall oppose its further extension. These are my sentiments, gentlemen, and let me tell you—"

"You black Abolitionist!" someone shouted. "Get off that box!" came another cry, and he was hauled down as someone pulled a Bowie knife and then he was stabbed twice in the chest.

In his first autobiography (there were several), published in 1879, Cody wrote that "his father shed the first blood in the cause of freedom in Kansas." After the attack, a neighbor came to Isaac's rescue, according to some accounts, and took him to a nearby cabin. In another account, written years later by Cody's sister Helen Cody Wetmore, Will sprang to his father as he fell, "and turning to the murderous assailant, cried out in boyhood's fury: 'You have killed my father. When I'm a man, I'll kill you.'" Then, supported by Will, "father dragged his way homeward, marking his tortured progress with a trail of blood." Although this is one of various stories about Buffalo Bill that has been disputed, or recounted in several ways, its essence would seem to be accurate, which is to say that Cody's father was indeed attacked as he proclaimed an anti-slavery position amid a pro-slavery crowd, given a newspaper article published in the apparently pro-slavery *Democratic Platform* of Liberty, Missouri, on September 28, 1854: "A Mr. Cody, a noisy abolitionist, living near Salt Creek, in Kansas Territory, was severely stabbed while in a dispute about a claim with a Mr. Dunn, on Monday week last. Cody is severely hurt, but not enough it is feared to cause his death. The settlers on Salt Creek regret that his wound is not more dangerous, and all sustain Mr. Dunn in the course he took. Abolitionists will yet find 'Jordan a hard road to travel!'"

From then on, Isaac Cody's house was a site of Free Kansas rallies, and the family was harassed by pro-slavery neighbors in nearby Missouri. But Isaac was determined to stake his claim in Kansas Territory, and in 1857 traveled east to recruit settlers for a colony he was building in Grasshopper Falls. "As a result," Cody's sister Helen later wrote, "our house overflowed, while the land about us was white with tents; but these melted away as one by one the families selected claims and put up cabins." Perhaps this was a blueprint or inspiration for an aspect of Cody's Wild West spectacle, serving as instruction for how to organize large numbers of people in the makings of a sprawling tent city. In any case, Isaac's activities continued to agitate his enemies. "One night," Will recalled later, "a body of armed men, mounted on horses, rode up to our house and surrounded it." His father escaped by dressing in his wife's clothes and making his way through a pack of mounted vigilantes, then hiding in a cornfield. Later, gangs from Missouri torched the Codys' hay field and stole their horses, including Prince, a favored sorrel.

"The loss of my faithful pony nearly broke my heart," Cody said later. Death threats against Isaac continued, and there were ongoing raids on the property. One night as ten-year-old Will lay in bed with the flu, his mother roused him and told him of a plot to kill his father. "The boy arose and clambered onto a horse," Louis Warren reports in *Buffalo Bill's America*. Cody carried a letter about the plot to his father, who was several hours away in Grasshopper Falls. After riding eight miles, young Cody realized he was being followed. "The boy put his heels to his horse, and for nine more miles the men chased the sick and terrified child," Warren recounts. "He finally reined up at the home of a family friend . . . the would-be assassins turned and fled. . . . The animal was covered in lather, and flecked with the boy's vomit."

Shortly after this episode, Isaac returned home. A wave of scarlet fever and measles had broken out in the tent settlement on his property, due to overcrowding. While working with the new arrivals in the rain, Isaac Cody contracted pneumonia. Weak since the stabbing at the trading post, he soon died. It was 1857 and William Cody was ten years old. He had watched his father stand up to bullies and take an unpopular, even life-threatening, stand. Beyond that, he had tried to save him, riding hard across miles of rough terrain to head off his father's assassins. Like many a frontier child, he was a crack shot and a good rider. "I thought these qualities might earn me a living," Cody wrote in *True Tales of the Plains* many years later. "They did." He became the principal breadwinner for a family of six—not so unusual for the offspring of hardscrabble frontier families. He would later provide employment for many who experienced a similar rugged upbringing.

After Cody's father died, young Bill went to work herding cattle with a mule as a small mount. His next job was serving as an "extra" on a wagon train headed by a friend of Cody's father, based out of Leavenworth. He earned good money and graduated from playing with Indians to killing one—or so he wrote. "The pay was $40 a month," Cody recounted, "a fortune it seemed to me then. The work was the sort usually entrusted to a grown man, and it meant not only perpetual hustling, but a lot of danger as well. For the plains in those days were anything but free from Indians. This latter thought frightened even my brave mother. Boy-like, I was delighted at the idea."

This job was essentially a tryout; if Cody did well, he would be hired on a permanent basis. As it turned out, Cody demonstrated that he was both a worthy hired hand and someone who would not shy away from life-or-death battle. The wagon train to which he was attached generally served the army and was usually a large one, with twenty-five wagons each carrying seven thousand pounds, each drawn by six yoke of oxen and guided by a bull-whacker, with loose cattle in tow. On Cody's audition, the train was smaller, consisting of three wagons, and the men were driving a large herd to Fort Kearny for the use of Colonel Albert Sidney Johnston and his command, who were on their way to Salt Lake City to fight the Mormons. His experiences as a young boy helping his father drive the teams of oxen at Breckenridge Place would serve him well. As one of several extras, Cody's duties "were to assist in driving and herding the cattle," he reported in one of his autobiographies, "and to make myself generally useful when we pitched camp. It was a busy trip till we came to Plum Creek, thirty-five miles west of Fort Kearny. Though we always set guard, no Indians had appeared."

But stopped for dinner one noon, Cody and his crew were "loafing on the grass, waiting for the pot to boil." They heard a volley of shots and some bullets and arrows whistled by. At the first shot, everyone jumped, but three of the men immediately fell. Two bands of Indians were racing for Cody and the other hands. One band ran off the cattle and the other rushed the men. Briefly repelled, the Indians were joined by others, soon outnumbering the wagon hands eight or ten to one. "We bolted for the South Platte River with the savages at our heels," Cody wrote, and then the men sheltered behind the banks, firing at the Indians. "I blazed away with the best of them," Cody said, "but in the confusion no one could tell whether he or someone else dropped the man he fired at."

To get to safety at Fort Kearny the men followed the Platte, staying hidden under the riverbanks. Knee-deep in water and quicksand, they began a thirty-five-mile march, keeping it up for half a day. "By nightfall," Cody wrote, "my short legs wouldn't keep up with the procession. I dropped back, little by little, still plodding on as fast as my aching feet could move. We thought we had given the Indians the slip, but I still lugged my rifle, a muzzle-loading 'Mississippi Jaeger,' and carried a slug and two buckshot to each charge."

The moon had risen and Cody was trying to catch up with the rest of the men. Suddenly, against the moon and high above him on a riverbank, Cody spotted the head and war bonnet of a chief. His gun was leveled at Cody's compadres, and they did not see him. Cody halted, aimed, locked on to a spot just below the feathers on the bonnet, and pulled the trigger. The report echoed from bank to bank, and the chief tumbled down over the edge, "rolling over like a shot rabbit," Cody wrote, landing in the water. The Indians swarmed the bank, but the men drove them back. The following dawn, Cody and the others limped into Fort Kearny. Some soldiers set out for the Indians, but the search was fruitless. Next to the wrecked and looted wagons, the men found the slashed and scalped bodies of their dead brothers.

It was a turning point; now Cody the boy was a warrior, and it was announced to all. "The proudest minute I'd ever known," he wrote, "came when Frank McCarthy swung me up on his shoulder and announced to everyone in the barracks: 'Boys, Billy's downed his first Injun! And the kid couldn't have made a prettier job of it if he'd been a thirty-year scout!'" It was an unofficial ritual, though not unlike the more formal one in which Sitting Bull's prowess as a warrior was proclaimed by an uncle after a skirmish in which the young boy felled a member of a rival tribe.

Soon Cody would in fact become an army scout, but for now, one of his next jobs was riding for the Pony Express. He signed on at the age of fourteen. Certainly, his midnight ride to warn his father had prepared him for this part of his career. Later, it would become one of the key elements of the showman's official biography, as well as of the Wild West show itself, although various investigators of Cody's life have suggested that the Pony Express part of his story is exaggerated if not an outright lie. But his accounts have the ring of truth, unlike some of the more florid tales, and being a Pony Express rider ("Orphans Preferred") was a likely vocation for someone with Cody's background. After his stint as a pony-bound messenger, he later claimed that he made a 322-mile ride—the third longest in the history of the mail service. (The longest ride was 384 miles and was made by Bob Haslam, whom Buffalo Bill would later hire for his Wild West show, in the persona of "Pony Bob.")

Of course horses were important to the Pony Express, and Cody often spoke of his mounts. Years later, he recounted an episode that sums up the glory of his life's path:

> One day, when I had nothing else to do, I saddled up an extra Pony Express horse, and arming myself with a good rifle and a pair of revolvers, struck out for the foothills of Laramie Peak for a bear hunt. Riding carelessly along, and breathing the cool and bracing autumn air which came down from the mountains, I felt as only a man can feel who is roaming over the prairies of the far West, well armed and mounted on a fleet and gallant steed. The perfect freedom he enjoys is in itself a refreshing stimulant to the mind as well as the body. Such indeed were my feelings on this beautiful day, as I rode up the valley of the Horseshoe.

There's always a point, or several, at which a person passes from merely human to legend. Certainly, for William Cody, acquiring the name Buffalo Bill was elemental. But first he had to earn the name. After his career with the Pony Express, Cody was chief of army scouts for the Fifth Cavalry, "mastering the accomplishment of riding bareback and leaping off and on his horse while the animal was galloping at full speed," reports Agnes Wright Spring in *Buffalo Bill and His Horses*. In 1866, he met the woman he would marry, Louisa Frederici, through a runaway horse. "More than once," wrote his sister Helen Cody Wetmore, "while out for a morning canter, Will had remarked a young woman of attractive face and figure, who sat her horse with the grace of Diana Vernon." Vernon was a character in the popular book *Rob Roy* by Walter Scott, and an accomplished rider. "Will desired to establish an acquaintance with the young lady, but as none of his friends knew her, he found it impossible. At length, a chance came. Her bridle-rein broke one morning; there was a runaway, a rescue, and then acquaintance was easy."

A year later, there came a new form of employment—the railroad was coming through, and he began hunting buffalo to feed construction crews who were building the Kansas Pacific. One of many whom the writer Mari Sandoz referred to as "the portentous men of '67," he followed on the heels of prolific hunters such as Wild Bill Hickok and Charley Reynolds. "Cody had killed buffaloes for the railroad the summer before," Sandoz wrote, "and he knew how it should be done. He hired [a fellow named] Tennis, an experienced plainsman who had hunted the Republican and Smoky Hill region for several years. There were five more men, and each man furnished his own blankets, grub enough for two months, and his arms, as well as two horses, one for packing. Old timers like Tennis would not be hampered. 'Indians ain't never slowed down by wheels,' he said, gnawing off a chew of tobacco, 'an if you ain't got no army to stand 'em off you better keep to legs—horses' or yours.'" Cody's crew would outfit at Fort Hays, heading west with their pack horses and camping on streams. "They didn't use Cody's fine showy method of shooting buffaloes from a running horse as he did for visiting celebrities and sportsmen," Sandoz wrote. "That called for years of practice and would require a large relay of fast horses, day in and out—enough to tempt the best Sioux and Cheyenne raiders. Tennis taught the men how to ride close in to a herd, hobble the horses and creep up against the wind, usually without stampeding the buffaloes until they had several fat young cows down. . . . The buffaloes were not skinned but they were bled like beeves and gutted of all but the heart and liver, ready for the haulers who followed close."

As the owner of the hunting outfit, Cody presided over the business from a saloon at Hays. Ever mindful of presentation, "he had a special table," Sandoz wrote, "conspicuously placed to set off his fringed buckskin, the fine belly-tan hat and his flowing yellow hair for the easterners: speculators, railroad promoters, hide buyers, and the sportsmen seeking new experiences and new trophies, as well as the gamblers, gunmen, road agents and the ladies at Drum's." On the not-so-frequent occasion that he joined the hunt, he rode a horse named Brigham, after the Mormon leader Brigham Young, purchased from a Ute Indian. Cody often said Brigham was the best horse he ever had for chasing buffalo, referring to him as "King Buffalo Killer." Riding Brigham, he wiped out buffalo by the hundreds.

Eighteen months after Cody began working for the railroad, he boasted that he had killed 4,280 buffalo. Around this time, people started calling him Buffalo Bill—a shadow version of the names accorded Native Americans for whom the buffalo was an ally, pathway to the Creator, font of rebirth if bearing a coat that was white, source of sustenance and shelter and clothing and warmth, symbol of strength and endurance. On January 11, 1868, the *Leavenworth Daily Conservative* reported that "Bill Cody and Brigham started on a hunt Saturday afternoon, and came in Tuesday. The result was nineteen buffalo. Bill brought in over four thousand pounds of meat, which he sold for seven cents per pound, making about $100 per day for his time out."

While Cody's reputation as an effective hunter was flourishing, a man named William Comstock also became known as Buffalo Bill due to his voracious hunting. To determine "the owner" of the name, they had a contest to see who could kill more buffalo. Here is how Buffalo Bill himself described the grim dance of death and the role of Brigham:

> Comstock and I dashed into the herd, followed by the referees. The buffaloes separated; Comstock took the left bunch and I the right. My great forte in killing buffaloes from horseback was to get them circling by riding my horse at the head of the herd, shooting the leaders, thus crowding their followers to the left, till they would finally circle round and round. On this morning the buffaloes were very accommodating, and I soon had them running in a beautiful circle, when I dropped them, thick and fast, until I had killed thirty eight; which finished my run. Comstock began shooting at the rear of the herd, which he was chasing, and they kept straight on. He succeeded, however, in killing twenty-three, while mine lay close together. I had "nursed" my buffaloes, as a billiard player does the balls when he makes a big run.

After eight hours of shooting, Cody won—69 to 46. Then he removed Brigham's saddle and bridle and rode bareback into the herd. As a parting flourish, he began firing again, now using his breech-loading .50-caliber Springfield, which he called "Lucretia Borgia," after the famous, beautiful, and deadly woman of the Renaissance. Cody went on to kill an additional thirteen animals with the rifle that has become one of the most well-known firearms in American history.

To understand the blood purge that was unfolding on the Great Plains, we must look past numbers and ammunition categories and nicknames for people and guns. Throughout American history, greed and lust has led to wildlife extermination, including birds whose feathers looked good in hats; beaver and bear for their pelts; wolves and bobcats because they were in the way; and all manner of other creatures disappeared from their lands because we're bored, we're hungry, we need to make way for roads and rails and stores, and in our free country we can do what we want. Alas, for the buffalo, it offered not just a beautiful hide, but its end was the Indians' end, as stated in government policy and as Native Americans such as the Cheyenne chief Yellow Wolf predicted after observing the *wasichu* as far back as 1846. He had even tried to hire an army herder to teach the Cheyenne to grow the white man's cattle, according to Mari Sandoz, so the Indians need not die when the buffalo vanished. "His prediction received only laughter," she noted, "and now he was dead, killed in the Sand Creek fight in 1864"—a most brutal massacre in which a chief named Black Kettle and his tribe were mowed down and mutilated after the chief raised an American flag in a gesture of peace.

And so the assaults unfolded. "The hide boom only lasted a dozen years before the buffalo ran out," wrote Steven Rinella in *American Buffalo*. There were probably about fifty million buffalo on the range when the pursuits began, consisting of four great herds—the Republican, the Arkansas, the Texas, and the Yellowstone, but the exact number is not known; the buffalo seemed endless and the idea that an animal could be completely "hunted out" was not known or considered, except to some of those who had lived with the buffalo for generations. "The first big hunting push was in the vicinity of Dodge City," wrote Rinella.

In 1871, the hide hunters killed so many animals so close to town that residents complained about the stench of rotting carcasses. That winter, a half-million buffalo hides were shipped out of Dodge. The hunters spread out from there, organizing their hunts along the east-flowing rivers of the Great Plains. They hunted out the Republican River, near the Nebraska-Kansas line. Along the south fork of the Platte River, hundreds of buffalo hunters lined fifty miles of riverbank and used fires to keep the buffalo from getting to the water at night. In four daytime periods, they gunned down fifty thousand of the thirst-crazed animals. . . . By 1878, there weren't enough buffalo on the southern plains to warrant the chase.

Generally the animal parts were left where the bodies were felled, and when stripped down by wind and weather and hungry creatures, all that remained was a pile of bones on the Great Plains, adding to the mountains that were stacking up across the land, later transformed into porcelain as fine bone china or fertilizer for farms, a complete rendering of the far-flung and mighty animal from sovereign creature to cash within a span of two decades. "Many Indians and even some breeds and white men who had lived close to the great herds a long time refused to believe that these multitudes had been all killed off by hunters," Sandoz wrote. As an old Hudson's Bay Company employee said at the time, "Man never could have exterminated them; they went back into the earth from whence they came."

When it was over, "the portentous men of '67" whose livelihood depended on the lord of the plains were out of a job. Buffalo Bill himself had not spent much time acquiring the name which would make him a superstar. By 1868, the Kansas Pacific suspended work, and his most valuable possession had to go: he raffled off Brigham, who spent the rest of his life on the speed-and-endurance-contest circuit. Soon Bill resumed his scouting duties for the army and it wasn't long before he met the writer Ned Buntline, who was trolling the West for material. By then, Buffalo Bill had invented himself as a man who had ridden fast and fought Indians and bears and had a way with guns, and even helped the army during the Civil War, but it was Ned Buntline, another adventurer with a flair for promotion, who immortalized Cody.

Buntline was born in 1823 in upstate New York. His original name was Edward Zane Carroll Judson, and somewhere along the way he adopted a Mark Twain–style moniker, which invoked a steamship reference in his surname, and became a writer, like Twain. But he was more like Cody than Twain, and to a degree more like Cody than Cody—minus the looks, charisma, and frontier gravitas—participating in much of the historic turmoil of the era, and surviving an array of cataclysmic events including a hanging and jail time.

Buntline ran away from home as a young teenager and fought in the Seminole wars; then he returned to the East Coast, where he picked up the pen and began spinning tales. In 1845, he launched *Ned Buntline's Own*, a magazine that published his sensational stories about pirates, outlaws, and frontier romance. In 1846, he was lynched—and lived to tell that story. It seems that the wandering scribe had fallen in love with the teenage wife of an acquaintance in Nashville. Their affair angered her husband. A duel ensued and Buntline killed the man. As a consequence he was tried for murder. During the trial, his girlfriend's brother shot and wounded Buntline, who ran into the streets, where an angry mob roped and hoisted him to a tree. But he was cut down by rescuers while still alive and he left town with a new tale—just the kind of thing that would delight patrons of New York bars and gossip salons.

In Manhattan, the notorious fellow soon became embroiled in politics, joining the Know Nothing Party, which among other things advocated for nationwide abstinence; oddly (in that regard), he would later hitch his wagon to Buffalo Bill—a man who was no stranger to firewater and saloons. Buntline also became a key figure in a now bizarre moment that was emblematic of its era, the Shakespeare riots of 1849, which pitted the acting styles of two famous actors, Edwin Forrest (American) against William Charles Macready (British), in violent class warfare involving a serious question of the day: how should the classic playwright Shakespeare be performed in the start-up land of America?

Behind that question was another one, which went to the heart of the national identity via New York: "Shall Americans or English rule this city?" This query was posed on flyers that were nailed to barroom walls all over town, and interested parties were told to attend Macready's upcoming performance of *Hamlet* and unleash havoc. Ten thousand people converged, lining the streets and bombarding the theater with rocks and stones, while at the same time engaging in running battles with the police. Inside the theater, the show went on, with Macready finishing his scenes as beatings unfolded just beyond the entrance. Among those taking part in the assault was Ned Buntline, later arrested, tried, and convicted of riot-related crimes, including attempted murder. After his release from jail, he saw the dispute as a way to further increase his notoriety, and also have a hearty answer to the question posed by the theater riots. It was America first and out with the Brits—a statement Cody himself later made more elegantly in a triumphant performance of his Wild West show before Queen Victoria and her court in London, during which he led his mounted procession to Her Majesty's feet, carrying the American flag, and bowing with his horse.

Amid all of the tumult of the era, Buntline continued writing, penning hundreds of short novels, earning the nickname "Father of the Dime Novel," and blazing the trail for many others from Owen Wister to Zane Grey to Louis L'Amour. Yet in terms of sheer word count and impact, Buntline's literary output perhaps remains unmatched considering that such tales influenced many young boys to hit the trail and reinvent themselves where the buffalo roamed. When he himself finally headed westward and met Buffalo Bill, the pair of self-promoters formed a natural partnership. Buntline clearly recognized that there was much to be gained. While the men had a lot in common, Cody possessed certain attributes that Buntline lacked. Both figures may have been larger than life, but Cody was actually large in stature. And his feats were associated with the West, which was different from hanging out with Seminole Indians, or even surviving a lynch mob. Cody had battled those who were portrayed as the demons of the era, recognizable figures of menace in war paint and animal skins and streaming rivers of feathers, facing them down in man-to-man combat, and, like many a great warrior, absorbing some of their characteristics along the way. His life itself was a kind of frontier victory dance, or as Buntline put it, he was "a compendium of clichés." And thus was a literary alliance born.

After his westward journey, Buntline returned to New York and penned the serial *Buffalo Bill, the King of the Border Men* for *New York Weekly*. The serial included epic tales of buffalo massacres and battles with Indians, and Buntline kept churning out the episodes, capturing the fancy of both high- and lowbrow readers across the land. Capitalizing on the popularity of Cody's dramatized adventures, Buntline went on to write *The Scouts of the Prairie*, a play that opened on Broadway in 1872. It starred Buntline and famous scout Texas Jack Omohundro as themselves. It also featured Buffalo Bill, who periodically dropped in to play himself as well, literally "just in from the Indian wars." The critics loved him, and he appeared in the play for eleven seasons.

In 1876, as Sitting Bull was heading for the arms of the Grandmother after the victory at the Little Bighorn, the nation's centennial was unfolding in Philadelphia—a grand event that signified the American march. In a moment of great fanfare, President U. S. Grant flipped the switch on the Corliss steam engine, and it has rolled ever since. Across the fairway, another feat of technology was unveiled: the telephone. Giving it a whirl, none other than the emperor of Brazil put his ear to the speaker, and Alexander Graham Bell delivered a message. Of all the things he could have uttered, of all the written texts and narratives that had been passed down through the ages, it was Hamlet's soliloquy, which he read in its entirety—quite possibly as Sitting Bull was crossing the Medicine Line.

"To be, or not to be," Bell intoned, *"that is the question . . .*
Whether 'tis Nobler in the mind to suffer
the Slings and Arrows of outrageous Fortune,
Or to take Arms against a Sea of troubles,
And by opposing end them: to die . . ."

"I am looking to the North for my life," Sitting Bull told the Canadians in his own echo of the speech, and inventor Bell concluded the moment on the strange new contraption. "My God, it talks," said the emperor from Brazil.

Meanwhile, another American was hatching a plan that would soon make him a key player in the Wild West saga as headlined by Buffalo Bill. This was Nate Salsbury, actor, entrepreneur, impresario. The world was awash with traveling show folk, and while he was trekking through Australia with his theater company, Salsbury's Troubadours, he became engaged in a heated argument with a circus agent from Iowa over whether the jockeys of Australia were better than those in other nations. The agent disagreed, and this propelled Salsbury into a patriotic challenge. They argued until the dinner gong sounded, but Salsbury couldn't shake the question. "Before I went to sleep," he later wrote, "I had mapped out a show that would be constituted of elements that had never been employed in the history of the show business." He realized that various circus managers had tried to reproduce the equestrian culture of the Great Plains with professional riders, "but they never had the real thing." Pondering the idea over the years, Salsbury became convinced that such a presentation needed a famous head-liner. The answer: William F. Cody. His reasoning was that Ned Buntline had written Cody into the history of the Great Plains, dripping from the writer's pen as a hero. Consequently, Cody was known "in the uttermost parts of the earth as a showman." Yet ac-cording to Salsbury, but for the humility of another man, it might have been otherwise. Buntline had first tried to boost Major Frank North (later, a member of Cody's show), but "being a real hero," North rejected the idea and, in a fateful act, pointed him toward Cody during a visit to an encampment in the Great Plains. He was asleep under a wagon. "Between story and the stage," Salsbury wrote, "Cody became a very popular man with a certain class of the public and was notorious enough for my purpose."

In 1882, Salsbury and his Troubadours appeared for a week at Haverly's Theatre in Brooklyn. Cody was appearing in New York at the same time, and Salsbury arranged a meeting at a restaurant next to the theater. "Have you ever thought of going big?" Salsbury may have said, knowing that Cody had played out his real-life ad-ventures in theater revues. "I mean very big—as in circus?"

"Yes, indeed, the thought has crossed my mind," Cody may have replied.

"Well, my friend," Salsbury went on, "you have packed the house in Delaware, Columbus, and even on Broadway. You have entertained archdukes on the prairie and won the admiration of generals and Presidents. You are a betting man. Don't you think it's time for a parlay here? Say, London town? With Queen Victoria and her court in the orchestra section?" Cody liked it, for he knew that the dime novel and his exploits were quite the thing in the Mother Country, and the following summer Salsbury traveled abroad for a look-see, and then returned with his assessment. The plan was most feasible, although it would require much thinking and organizing, and the men talked of the mechanics of such an extravaganza—all the cowboys and Indians they would hire (possibly Sitting Bull was mentioned, a most valuable asset; he had just been transferred to Standing Rock, and therefore might be available), the staff, acquiring the horses and other animals for the "Wild West" (in the original configuration, the term "show" was not attached). There would be much more than two of everything, dozens and dozens more, a Noah's Ark of the West, and in the grand scheme it would bear the essence of the American myth, not because the men thought of it that way, but because that was the thing that came through.

Meanwhile, a few blocks away or perhaps around the corner, some other citizens were having their own Indian dreams. They too were meeting, perhaps over drinks and a meal, and they were wondering how to prevent the atrocities on the Plains, the assaults on natives, what they could do to save the tribes. "Well, we have Red Cloud and Gall," someone may have added, for it was true; the well-known leaders had added their names to the new campaign for Indian rights. "It's made a difference. Congressmen are listening. We have gotten some sympathetic coverage." Everyone agreed and then someone may have pointed out how necessary it was to have a really big name and the conversation may have turned to Sitting Bull, because they were not unlike other *wasichus* in certain ways, and ever since he had surrendered, everyone wanted him for their openings, their ceremonies, their cause. And as these various parties conferred about their hopes and dreams for America and their own endeavors, into the harbor chugged a steamer from France, carrying the arm of the Statue of Liberty, soon to be fully erected in New York harbor at Bedloe's Island. The arm was tall and heavy and it carried the flaming torch of freedom—the thing that was being extinguished for the aboriginals on the Great Plains even as it was coming into full flower for all of the arrivistes.

On May 19, 1883, Buffalo Bill launched his equine extravaganza in Omaha, Nebraska. Nate Salsbury was not involved—although that would soon change. The progenitor of the spectacle that Cody would take into history, it was called *The Wild West, WF Cody and WF Carver's Rocky Mountain and Prairie Exhibition*. (Carver was a dentist and sharpshooter who briefly partnered with Cody until he left amid ongoing rancor due to a business dispute, and subsequently launched his own competitive dramas.) Interestingly, the title of the Wild West did not include the word *show*—it was not presented as something removed from the frontier, but rather as the Wild West itself. Anticipation of the event was keen, as this newspaper account of a dress rehearsal at Buffalo Bill's Nebraska ranch chronicles:

> In the afternoon in company with Mr. [James] McNulty and Hon. W. F. Cody we visited the germ of the great show which is to spring into existence the latter part of this month at Omaha and which will sweep all before it when once fairly started. . . . On a piece of level meadow land was pitched the tents for the men while the buffalo and a large number of horses were grazing in an adjoining pasture. A number of elk were expected in a day or two and men were engaged purchasing the most famous bucking horses that Nebraska afforded. "Buck" Taylor, who is to be one of the star riders of the combination, gave an exhibition on a

wall-eyed calico horse that would astonish the effeminate easterners, and if he lives long enough the performance will be repeated for their benefit during the summer. Another wing of the show is getting under way at Omaha, where the Indians will join it, and about the 17th of the present month the western Nebraska wonder will give its opening exhibition at the state's metropolis.

The actual production was a huge hit, although mules deranged the premiere, panicking while dignitaries in the Deadwood stage came under mock attack from a party of Pawnees. Once the kinks were worked out, Cody and his partner took the show on the road, staging it around the country. Attendance was spotty, and Cody was concerned; at heart he was a businessman and he wondered if he would be able to recoup the large investment he had made in his new endeavor. He was looking forward to a special presentation at the World's Industrial and Cotton Centennial Exposition in New Orleans, in December of 1884. It would be easy for crowds to attend, he reasoned, as the city had a streetcar. He even planned a finale just for the event, a re-creation of the Battle of New Orleans in which he would play Andrew Jackson. "At least he had the hair," Ned Sublette wrote in *The Year Before the Flood*, his book about Hurricane Katrina.

But as it happened, Cody's plans were thwarted by a shipwreck and another historic flood. He had hired his old pal and cast member Pony Bob Haslam to make travel arrangements. In Cincinnati, Pony Bob secured a steamboat to carry the show down to Louisiana. But the job was above Pony Bob's pay grade; at stops en route, the Wild West did not fare well, and the tour was losing money every day. "Near Rodney Landing, Mississippi, the showboat collided with another steamer and sank within an hour," wrote Don Russell in *The Lives and Legends of Buffalo Bill*. Wagons, equipment, guns, and ammunition were lost, along with much of the ark's precious cargo, including buffalo, donkeys, and an elk.

Over the years, as the show gained stature and a bigger cast of people and animals, there would be other, more catastrophic accidents and collisions. This time around, all of the horses were saved, and none of the show's employees was injured or perished. But Cody was broke and had lost his way—and his production. The Wild West would miss its opening date at the Cotton Expo, and quite possibly the rest of the tour. He telegraphed his former co-conspirator Nate Salsbury, who was appearing with the Troubadors in Denver. "Outfit at bottom of river," he said, "what do you advise?" As legend has it, Salsbury was about to take the stage and sing when Cody's message arrived, and asked the orchestra leader to play the overture again so he could think about Cody's question. "Go to New Orleans," Salsbury replied, "reorganize, and open on your date." He himself continued with his show, and so did Cody, rounding up herds of buffalo and elk, and wagons and other equipment within eight days, just in time for the opening.

But there came an Old Testament–style storm and it rained for forty-four days, never once stopping at showtime. The fairgrounds were a quagmire of mud, and one day only nine people bought tickets. A ticket seller wanted to cancel the show, but Cody rejected the idea. "If nine people came out here in all this rain to see us, we'll go ahead," he said. Yet in spite of the foul weather, the *Daily Picayune* praised the show, weighing in with a booster's report: "The performers include Indians, Mexicans, cowboys and special marksmen and riders. Among the animals are a hundred horses, including all grades from the roughers to the bucking mustang. The entertainment . . . is a dime novel pictured by the heroes themselves. It is much to see Buffalo Bill riding and shooting with a grace and unerring air that belongs to no other." All in all, the show was "exciting, interesting and of the highest order."

That winter, the Wild West lost $60,000—no small sum at the time. The cast dispersed for the season, with some of the Indians heading home for spring plowing, and Cody himself planning to head off on a drunk. "Just to change my luck," he wrote to Salsbury, "I will paint a few towns red hot—but til then I am staunch and true—with my shoulder to the wheel." Fortunately for Cody, all was not lost in New Orleans. One day an important figure materialized out of the floodwaters. This was Annie Oakley. She and her husband were in town with the Sells Brothers Circus, and they heard that the Wild West might have a job opening. After she demonstrated her skills, Cody hired her immediately. Together, she and Buffalo Bill would take the frontier spectacle to new heights of glamour and excitement. But that was just the beginning. Cody had been trying to recruit Sitting Bull for nearly two years, ever since his transfer to Standing Rock after his imprisonment at Fort Randall, thereby becoming "available." Sitting Bull was the one man who could make the show into a guaranteed blockbuster—and the one Indian whose fame was as great as Buffalo Bill's. Sitting Bull was not interested—until he saw Annie's picture on postcards for the Wild West. He had never forgotten meeting her in St. Paul, Minnesota. Once he learned that Annie was part of Cody's show, he was ready to entertain an offer from the *wasichu* who was also named for the buffalo.

In 1873, a circuit-riding physician and homesteader named Brewster Higley wrote a poem called "My Western Home." It was published in a Kansas newspaper called *The Pioneer*. A year later a friend convinced Higley to turn it into a song. A fiddler was rounded up, a tune conceived, and as cowboys came through Kansas, they picked it up and carried it into history. Somewhere along the trail, it became known as "Home on the Range," and today stands as an unofficial national anthem, with its sonorous refrain about the range as the place where the deer and antelope play, a discouraging word is rarely heard, and the skies are not cloudy all day. But it carried a darker truth, and it went like this:

> The red man was pressed from this part of the West,
> He's likely no more to return
> To the banks of Red River where seldom if ever
> Their flickering campfires burn.

At some point, that verse disappeared. But it would be reenacted in the Wild West, where cowboys and Indians were running away together, accompanied by the traveling thunder of the American dreamtime.

CHAPTER THREE

*In Which the Seventh Cavalry Is Defeated at the Battle of the
Little Bighorn, and Buffalo Bill Stars as Himself in "The Red
Right Hand, or the First Scalp for Custer"*

On April 20, 1876, two months before the Battle of the Little Bighorn would claim George Armstrong Custer and transform Sitting
Bull into America's Most Wanted Man, William Cody was about to
go onstage in Springfield, Massachusetts. He was touring in a play
called *Life on the Border*, along with his compadre J. B. Omohundro,
whose cowboy role was "Texas Jack." The theater company—"Cody's
Combination"—also included assorted ruffian and Native American
characters. It would be several years before the officially designated
Wild West show emerged, but this play, and others like it, had the
hallmarks of the great spectacle to come, with Cody playing himself
in an early re-creation of American life. In these touring productions, Cody and the cast were portraying events that had just happened, including shootouts, buffalo hunts with foreign dignitaries
and prominent Americans, and battles with Indians. Although the
players were usually critically panned—they weren't acting, after
all; they were just being themselves—this play and others like it
were hugely popular. Audiences loved the rawness, the authenticity,
and Cody himself had serious charisma—the kind that always fills a
house, wherever it is and whatever is being presented.

As the curtain opened on the first scene on that night in Springfield, Cody was presented with a telegram from his wife, Louisa. His beloved son, Kit, Kit Carson Cody, named after the famous scout and friend of Buffalo Bill's, had been diagnosed with scarlet fever. He did not have long to live. Cody finished the first act, and then rushed to catch the overnight train for his home, which was now in Rochester, New York.

"I found my little boy unable to speak," Cody wrote of his six-year-old in his *Autobiography*, "but he seemed to recognize me and putting his little arms round my neck he tried to kiss me. We did everything in our power to save him." But Kit died in his father's arms and was soon buried in Mount Hope cemetery. A bereaved Cody missed the next performance in Worcester, where the local paper said that "Without Buffalo Bill, the play, which is not a high order in itself, is a poor affair." He soon rejoined the tour for a final performance and bow in Wilmington, Delaware, still subdued and grieving.

Another drama—the Indian wars on the plains—was heating up and Cody was summoned by the Fifth Cavalry to reprise his long-time role as scout. It was something he generally did in the summers anyway, after his acting career began to take off, reserving theater performances for the colder months of the year when the plains were covered in ice and snow and it was preferable to be inside. But he was also happy to leave his domestic life. Being a husband and father were kind of adjunct roles for him, not that they didn't take up significant time, and not that he didn't love his children, and perhaps his wife in a certain way. Quite simply, he was not essentially sustained by that part of his life. Still, after his son died, he was so distraught that he did not feel up to performing. Comfort would be found in the wilderness, in action in it and on it, and there he went, retreating to the place he knew best, the terrain he himself played in as a boy and where later he found some of his best friends.

When looking at history, we tend to forget or are not aware of the fact that a particular luminary lives and thrives among a circuit of people—not just a list of names—and that these people are friends and acquaintances much as you or I would have today. For Cody, this circuit consisted of the well-known and the ordinary, white men and natives, artists and writers, kings and queens, generals, foot soldiers, trappers, hunters, miners, settlers, and all manner of frontier entrepreneurs and drifters. A particularly celebrated member of Cody's circuit was Lieutenant Colonel George Armstrong Custer, the Civil War hero known for his numerous charges on the battlefield, and now, at the height of the Indian wars, a figure both revered and reviled in his capacity as leader of the Seventh Cavalry under General Philip Sheridan, another celebrated Civil War figure.

Cody himself had served in the Civil War as a scout for the Union, first in campaigns against the Kiowa and Comanche who were "in the way" as the army advanced into Texas and New Mexico, and then later in the Seventh Kansas Cavalry, where he guided troops through swaths of Missouri and Tennessee. When the war was over, he continued his work as an army scout, based out of Fort Ellsworth, Kansas. It was during his years in that role that he met Custer, and the two men, along with General Sheridan, went on to host the most famous buffalo hunt of the era—and perhaps the most celebrated hunt in American history. It was because of the bonds formed during this hunt, especially between Cody and Custer, that Cody would go on to avenge Custer's death at the Battle of the Little Bighorn. Later, he incorporated the scene of vengeance into his Wild West program.

Thanks to newspapers, the burgeoning cult of celebrity worship, and an abiding American urge to leave civilization and go wild, organized buffalo hunts on the frontier were becoming *de rigueur*, especially if the pursuit was led by a wilderness icon such as Buffalo Bill. In 1871, Cody and Sheridan had hosted a much talked about hunt that was kind of the warm-up for a coming extravaganza. This first one, for East Coast bigwigs, came to be known as "The Millionaires' Hunt." It included prominent financiers, lawyers, reporters, and newspaper publishers. "One of the most glamorous hunting parties in the history of the Plains," Louis Warren observed in his book *Buffalo Bill's America*, "it expressed the confluence between the urban power elite of the East and Midwest, the U.S. army, and sport hunting on the Great Plains." For the occasion, Buffalo Bill selected his clothing carefully. As Cody himself said in a kind of Twainesque way, it was "a nobby and high-toned outfit which I was to accompany." With members of the party awaiting his arrival, he made a grand entrance from the Fort McPherson staging grounds in Nebraska, sending at least one man into a linguistic reverie that today one might read in *Vanity Fair* runway coverage.

On the first morning, recounted Henry Davies, a district attorney from New York, Cody rode down on a white horse, dressed in a light buckskin suit, "trimmed along the seams with fringes of the same leather, his costume lighted by the crimson shirt worn under his open coat, a broad sombrero on his head, and carrying his rifle lightly in one hand, as his horse came toward us on an easy gallop." Davies' elaborate description of Cody's attire was included in full accounts of the hunt, which were published around the country, adding to the flamboyant plainsman's allure. It was almost a century after the thirteen colonies had thrust off the shackles of royalty, but America was developing its own. The cast included frontier icons, and Buffalo Bill would soon be the king. The hunting extravaganza that sent Cody into the stratosphere was the Royal Buffalo Hunt, so named for its star member, Grand Duke Alexis Alexandrovich, the fourth son of Russian Czar Alexander II. Wanting to leverage a business arrangement between America and Russia, and harboring a serious desire to meet Buffalo Bill and accompany him into the wild, the duke and his entourage had set sail for America in August of 1872; in September, he arrived at Falmouth, England, and from there was escorted by a Russian battle fleet to New York harbor. There he debarked in November with much fanfare. On the 21st of that month, he began a quintessential tour of America, attending a Thanksgiving service at the Russian chapel in downtown Manhattan, and in the following days went on a shopping spree with a stop at Tiffany's. He then traveled to a host of other cities, including Springfield, Massachusetts, home of the Smith & Wesson factory, where he was presented with a pistol; Cleveland, Ohio, where he visited the iron mills of outlying Newburgh Heights; Buffalo, New York, to see Niagara Falls; and Washington, D.C., for a state dinner with President U. S. Grant. From there, he hopscotched around the continent, arriving by train in North Platte, Nebraska, in January of 1872, where he would live his dream, joining Buffalo Bill and other iconic Western figures on a buffalo hunt, including the famous military men Sheridan and Custer, now leading the war against the Indians of the Great Plains.

At the time, there was turmoil in the Dakota Territory—although nothing like what would be coming in the next few years. The second Treaty of Fort Laramie, in place since April 29, 1868, and named for the famous army fort in Wyoming where a so-called peace council was held, stated in its essence that the sacred Black Hills would remain in the possession of the Sioux Nation forever. In exchange, the tribes of this nation—the Brule, Oglala, Minneconjou, Yanktonai, Hunkpapa, Blackfeet, Cut Head, Two Kettle, Sans Arcs, Santee, and Arapaho—would agree to move onto reservations. Some natives in attendance at the council refused to sign the treaty, including Sitting Bull, who had spent the spring of that year raiding forts on the upper Missouri. Having his approval was critical to ending the Indian wars. Shortly after the council, General Alfred Sully sent a delegation of Indians who had signed the pact to Sitting Bull's camp on the Yellowstone River. The group also included a prominent Catholic priest, Father Pierre Jean de Smet, known to the Indians as "Black Robe." He carried a personal invitation from Sully. At the camp, the men met with Hunkpapa leaders, including Black Moon, Four Horns, Red Horn, No Neck, Crawler, Gall, and Sitting Bull. In response to de Smet's request for peace, Sitting Bull—a warrior at the age of forty-one—said this:

> I hardly sustain myself beneath the weight of white men's blood that I have shed. The whites provoked the war; their injustices, their indignities to our families, the cruel, un-heard of, and unprovoked massacre at Fort Lyon [Sand Creek] of hundreds of Cheyenne women, children, and old men, shook all the veins which bind and support me. I rose, tomahawk in hand, and I have done all the hurt to the whites that I could.
>
> Today you are among us, and in your presence my arms stretch to the ground as if dead. I will listen to your good words. And as bad as I have been to the whites, just so good am I ready to become toward them. . . .
>
> Listen my friend. I have a message for the Grandfather. I do not want anyone to bother my people. I want them to leave in peace. I myself have plans for my people, and if they follow my plans, they will never want. They will never hunger. I wish for traders only, and no soldiers on my reser-vation. *Wakan Tanka* gave us this land, and we are at home here. I will not have my people robbed. We can live if we can keep our Black Hills. We do not want to eat from the hand of the Grandfather. We can feed ourselves.

Later that day, lest his views were somehow unclear, Sitting Bull added some details. He told the visitors that he did not want white men to cut down his tribe's timber, "especially the oak. I am particularly fond of the little groves of oak trees . . . they endure the wintry storm and the summer's heat and, not unlike ourselves, seem to thrive and flourish by them." Each statement was followed by one more emphatic statement, and Sitting Bull's final remark could not have been more final. Yet there was one more thing he had to say in response to General Sully. "Those forts filled with white soldiers must be abandoned; there is no greater source of trouble and grievance to my people." And then he suggested to Gall that he go to the council and find out what the white men had to say. "Take no presents," he added. "We don't want them. Tell them to move the soldiers out and stop the steamboats; then we can have peace."

But to Sitting Bull's disappointment, Gall signed the treaty, and the steamboats were not stopped. Nor was anything else, including of course the soldiers. Sitting Bull continued his raids, incurring the wrath of one more Civil War veteran, Colonel Regis de Trobriand, now the commander of Fort Stevenson in Dakota Territory, perhaps the first to officially put a price on Sitting Bull's head, calling him "one of the most dangerous and evil Indians in [the region]." As the frontier wars became more heated in the next few years, this was the sort of language that would be used by various army leaders in their characterization of Sitting Bull, and it was picked up by reporters who restated it in newspapers from the *New York Times* to lesser known periodicals across the land. To amplify his description and heighten the belief that Sitting Bull was a savage figure who needed to be eliminated, the colonel said that the "Dakota [Territory] has become the theater of his depredations and killings. [Sitting Bull] is bent on vengeance, he has always done us every harm in his power and is the spirit or arm of all the coups attempted or accomplished against us." To some degree, this was true. Sitting Bull—and Crazy Horse and others—were indeed the spirit of all that the invaders wanted to squelch. They were not backing down, if that can even serve as language that explains the nature of a spirit or path.

It was into this atmosphere that Grand Duke Alexis and his party were traveling by special train, accompanied by various railroad executives, an official Western Pacific telegrapher, reporters, and Russian and American military luminaries, including General Sheridan. The engine of the train was draped with Russian and American flags, pulling five Pullman cars of the duke's imperial suite, and two private cars for Sheridan. The procession traveled at about twenty-five miles per hour, not fast, but a good clip for the time. On the evening of January 12, 1872, Alexis invited Sheridan and his party, as well as other prominent travelers aboard, to dine in his car. Sheridan was seated at the duke's table and according to the Beatrice, Nebraska, *Express*, a fine Pullman feast was served.

On the following day, the train arrived at North Platte station at about 7 a.m. After breakfast in the cars, members of the hunting party disembarked. The weather was cool, about 46 degrees, certainly not as brutal as it often was at that time of year—perfect for a winter hunt. They were met by Buffalo Bill. He was the picture of frontier adventure, in his fur-trimmed buckskin suit, accompanied by twenty saddle horses, a cavalry company, and horse-drawn ambulances or carriages. "Your Highness," General Sheridan said, "this is Mr. Cody, otherwise and universally known as Buffalo Bill. Bill, this is the Grand Duke."

"I am glad to know you," Cody said.

Alexis and Sheridan took their seats in a four-horse open carriage, and the moment was recorded with much fanfare in newspapers such as the *Lincoln Daily State Journal*, which announced the morning arrival of the Grand Duke and his party. Later that and other episodes of the adventure were written about by Cody himself. "The whole party [dashed] away towards the south," he said, "across the South Platte and towards the Medicine, upon reaching which point we halted for a change of horses and a lunch." Lunch consisted of sandwiches and champagne, after which the celebrated posse resumed its ride, reaching Camp Alexis just before sunset.

"As we ascended some rising ground," wrote the *New York Herald* reporter, "we came in full view of a splendid military camp. The Stars and Stripes were seen flying from a towering flagstaff on a broad plateau. A cheer arose from every member of our party as this scene burst upon our sight. A few moments more and the band of the Second Cavalry was playing the Russian hymn." The party gathered around a large campfire, and it soon became apparent that not everyone was there. Some important army officials were missing. Had they been waylaid in a skirmish with Indians? That was something that crossed the minds of a few of the hunters. In particular, where was George Armstrong Custer, that other American icon whom Alexis was expecting? Such hunts were really not official without him; he had a long history of not only sport hunting but of hosting hunts with visiting royals. With the possibility of commerce with Russia around the bend, Custer's presence was critical.

Just as Sheridan was about to send out a search party, there came the gallant horseman—on foot, carrying his buffalo rifle on his shoulder, striding down the hill, followed by the others. Five miles away, their ambulance had broken down and the men had had to walk to get to camp. It was probably not the way that Alexis had imagined Custer making an entrance—and nor do we think of him on foot today—but no matter; the camp was now ready.

Camp Alexis itself, for all its splendor, was hastily concocted for the duke's arrival. According to the trio of authors Douglas D.

Scott, Peter Bleed, and Stephen Damm in their book *Custer, Cody, and Grand Duke Alexis*, it was situated on about four acres of a low grassy plateau at the junction of Red Willow Creek and one of its small, frozen tributaries. The snow had been removed by a special crew after Cody had scouted the area in advance, selecting the site for a nearby buffalo herd and the ample space provided. The encampment included two hospital tents (used for dining), ten wall tents, and tents for servants and soldiers. Three of the wall tents had flooring, and the duke's had a carpet. There were box and Sibley stoves inside the hospital and wall tents, along with what a reporter called "an extensive culinary outfit." The dining area was festooned with flags. Under the dazzling constellations of a clear Great Plains night, the men toasted each other and their enterprise with fine wines, and dined on several courses of local game, including a prairie chicken that had been shot in the head by Custer, to satisfy a request from the Grand Duke to taste the indigenous fowl.

By today's standards, Custer would be considered bloodthirsty—and even by yesterday's. He was known for his hunting prowess, but also for the extensive menagerie of stuffed animals that he had felled—elk, bear, buffalo of course, and numerous other creatures; his voracious hunting appetite was something that some of his colleagues noted, and visitors were sometimes taken aback when they viewed the numerous specimens of caged wildlife at his Kansas headquarters. He was also hard on his horses. While lowering his gun at a buffalo during his first hunt, his horse shied and the bullet hit his horse in the head, killing it instantly and sending Custer into the path of the bull. This became an anecdote for the dinner party circuit—along with numerous other stories of horses that had died in Civil War charges with Custer in the saddle. The hunt with Alexis would provide one more such story for the frontier joke arsenal, involving another ill-fated horse. By contrast, fellow equestrian Buffalo Bill—though known for the vast number of buffalo that he had killed—viewed horses as true partners, much as the Indians did—and in fact the horse, one in particular, would become a critical part of his friendship with Sitting Bull.

Day one of the hunt, January 14, was the twenty-second birthday of Duke Alexis. Custer, Cody, and Sheridan wanted to provide him with a fitting experience. After all, he had chosen to spend this birthday in America, with the elders of a celebrated hunting and military tribe, and his hosts would make sure that it was one for the Russian history books. Early in the morning, Cody left to scout for buffalo, returning just before ten to report that a herd was about fifteen miles away on the divide between Red Willow and Medicine Creeks. Sheridan wasn't feeling well and did not hunt that day. Cody, assigned as tutor, gave Alexis a quick lesson in buffalo pursuit, and he was given Buffalo Bill's famous buffalo horse, Charlie Almost Human, as his mount. When asked about his weapon of preference, Cody explained that the Grand Duke could use either a gun or pistol. For the occasion, Alexis had brought the revolver that he had received at the Smith & Wesson factory, a special gift, crafted with him in mind. It was a Russian model with an engraved and carved pearl grip, sought after to this day on gun forums.

En route, Custer further instructed Alexis in the way of hunting the buffalo. When the trio reached the herd, Custer charged through, singling out a bull for the Grand Duke, having promised him the first kill. At the right moment, he signaled Alexis, who then rode in and fired his gun—perhaps the Smith & Wesson. But he was firing wildly, Cody later said, so he rode up to Alexis and gave him his "old, reliable Lucretia"—his favorite weapon.

"I advised him not to fire until he could ride directly upon the flank of a buffalo," Cody later wrote, "as the sport was most in the chase. We dashed off together and ran our horses on either flank of a large bull, against the side of which the Duke thrust his gun and fired a fatal shot. He was very much elated at his success, taking off his cap and waving it vehemently, at the same time shouting to those who were fully a mile in the rear. When his retinue came up there were congratulations and every one drank to his good health with over-flowing glasses of champagne. The hide of the dead buffalo was carefully removed and dressed, and the royal traveler in his journeying over the world has no doubt often rested himself upon this trophy of his skill on the plains of America."

On day two of the hunt, to the delight of the Grand Duke, Spotted Tail and eight Brule warriors joined the hunting party as they had promised Cody before Alexis had arrived. They ranged across fifteen miles of rough terrain to find their quarry, and then killed a total of fifty-six buffalo, including eight by Spotted Tail and his band, who put on their own Wild West show for Alexis. Displaying their hunting methods, they surrounded a herd and—in an act that dazzled onlookers—a warrior named Two Lance shot an arrow straight through a buffalo. Then another Brule, bearing a lance with a one-foot-long steel head, singled out a gigantic bison while racing full speed alongside it, and thrust his lance right through the animal's heart. "Considerable skill was necessary to apply the momentum of the horse in just the right way to send the stoke home," Cody later wrote, "it being necessary for the hunter instantly to let go of the lance or be pulled from his steed."

As the party returned that evening, they fired their guns in celebration and the camp threw up a cheer. It had been a grand day of hunting, though not without casualties beyond the buffalo. One soldier's horse had foundered and was led back to camp. And not widely reported was the fact that Custer had ridden his horse so hard that it collapsed and died upon reaching Red Willow.

Yet the show must go on. There was a sumptuous feast and the men, especially Alexis and Custer, flirted heavily with "red-skinned maidens" as newspaper accounts of the time recorded. Then Spotted Tail and his band of several hundred, bedecked in war paint and feathers, enacted a war dance, with "outlandish contortions and grimaces, leaps and crouchings, their fiendish yells and whoops making up a barbaric jangle of picture and sound not soon to be forgotten," in the words of Helen Cody Wetmore years later.

As the evening concluded, Alexis gave the warriors $50 in silver half-dollars, twenty blankets, and a cache of hunting knives with ivory handles. In return, Two Lance presented Alexis with the arrow he had used to fell the buffalo earlier that day.

The grand finale of the hunt came on the following day. General Sheridan wanted the Grand Duke to have a stagecoach ride. "Shake 'em up a little, Bill," Sheridan said as the party headed back to the train depot, "give us some old-time driving." Buffalo Bill cracked the whip, and the horses broke into a run. With a light load to pull, they increased their speed over the divide that led down into the valley of the Medicine. There was no brake and Cody couldn't stop them. "All I could do," he said, "was to keep them straight in the track and let them go down the hill, for three miles." They made it in six minutes, the rear wheels periodically striking a rut and then not touching the ground again for fifteen or twenty feet. "The Duke and the General were kept rather busy in holding their positions on the seats," Cody said, "and when they saw that I was keeping the horses straight in the road, they seemed to enjoy the dash which we were making. I was unable to stop the team until they ran into the camp where we were to obtain a fresh relay, and there I succeeded in checking them." The Grand Duke asked Cody to take it easy on the rest of the drive.

Back at the North Platte station, Alexis invited Buffalo Bill into his private car and showered him with gifts, including a diamond and gold stickpin, a Russian fur coat, and jeweled cuff links and studs. The fanfare at the farewell departure of the Grand Duke was well deserved, for Cody, along with Custer and the U.S. Army, had put on a grand show. But the superstar in the constellation was Cody, as everyone knew, and as the extensive press coverage inscribed. From then on, the stagecoach ride back to the station was an official moment, known as "Shake 'Em Up, Bill." And it was destined to be enshrined in the Wild West show—a carefully managed event that would be reenacted many times, one of various episodes that when replayed, turned American history into scrip-ture and transformed it into a hall of mirrors.

With the hunt concluded and the Grand Duke winding up his birthday celebration, the curtain fell on this band of brothers. The men dispersed to points west and east, with Custer accompa-nying Alexis to Colorado for more hunting outside Denver, and Cody heading back east for a possible military commission and the welcoming arms of the nation's capital. Could the American enterprise have been any more golden? Custer and Cody, standing in for citizens everywhere, dominated a savage terrain and helped advance an alliance with an important new ally, Russia. Their parts had been played well. And behind it all, there was the thing that bonds warriors: secrets had been passed on by way of animal sacrifice and although the killing was wanton, for the buffalo were not eaten or partaken of in a way that honored them, the ritual most certainly drew the men close as they faced off danger and watched the blood flow. Elsewhere, warriors in different garb and skin of another color were waging their own hunts, including Sit-ting Bull himself, possibly coming upon evidence of the festivities at Camp Alexis and noting that once again after these invaders had moved on, there was so much waste and pointlessness, you see, all these buffalo parts had been left behind, the carcasses had been picked over for souvenirs like hooves and tails and of course their hides, but that was it, not like the way his people engaged with the animal, their life source and spiritual font, and quite possibly he thought yet one more time about what he could do to stop the advancing *wasichu*.

In 1874, gold was discovered in the Black Hills. Thirst for the yellow flakes that peeked through the gulches and valleys of the region intensified with a landmark Custer expedition of that year. Geologists and topographers accompanied the venture, to give it a veneer of respectability and to suggest that it was not driven by lust for riches. One of the soldiers had even brought along an "odometer cart," charting the way into the hills and measuring the miles with a strange contraption that he rode. As the men advanced, the region became more beautiful. "An Eden in the clouds," a reporter from the *New York Tribune* proclaimed along the steep banks of the Red Water. "How shall I describe it!" Taking in the expanse below, Custer named it Floral Valley, and the soldiers were overtaken by a certain spirit. "Teamsters picked blossoms to decorate the harness of their mules," Donald Jackson wrote in *Custer's Gold*. "Infantrymen plumed their hats; young officers slipped petals into their notebooks to take to their wives. On either side the limestone hills were thick with pine, and the woods rang with the cry of the sandhill crane." As the men descended into the valley, the band played "How So Fair" and "The Mocking Bird," and then Custer spotted a crane. He raised his arm to halt the column, and then went ahead and shot it. Soon his Arikara scouts spotted five Sioux lodges, and Custer dispatched interpreters to assure the Indians that he meant no harm. The expedition continued its foray into the hills. Somewhere in this region dwelled Sitting Bull. At the moment he could have been anywhere—in the mineral caves below, possibly a cool respite in the summer heat, or perhaps he was away hunting. Custer hoped that he might encounter him during his explorations, but for now, the most desired quarry was gold.

As tales of gleaming veins over yonder began to circulate, reporters filed heated dispatches. On August 12, the *Bismarck Tribune* proclaimed Custer's Valley as "The El Dorado of America." "STRUCK IT AT LAST!" announced the *Yankton Press and Dakotian* on August 13. "Rich Mines of Gold and Silver Reported Found by Custer. PREPARE FOR LIVELY TIMES! Gold Expected to Fall 10 per Cent.—Spades and Picks Rising.—The National Debt to Be Paid When Custer Returns." Two weeks later, the reporter from the *New York Tribune* cast doubt on such announcements. "Those who seek the Hills only for gold must be prepared to take their chances," he wrote. "Let the over-confident study the history of Pike's Peak. The Black Hills, too, are not without ready-made monuments for the martyrs who may perish in their parks."

But gold fever was sweeping the nation, and many a prospector was now buying supplies and heading to the heart of Lakota territory, advancing the course of empire with a pick and a mule. Across the country, financial markets were heating up. Native lands were seized by the government, and Indians who had not agreed to live on reservations continued their raids on settlers. Angered that the Treaty of Fort Laramie had been violated, Sitting Bull allied with the holdouts.

"Give them whiskey," said General William Tecumseh Sherman, Civil War hero whose name invoked a legendary Shawnee chief. "Kills them like flies." General Phil Sheridan, also with valiant service in the Civil War, had another idea. "Obliterate the red man." Indians who refused to surrender—"hostiles"—would be quelled with a massive, three-pronged attack. The plan was this: At Fort Abraham Lincoln, Custer would be met by General Alfred Howe Terry's column, leading the Seventh Cavalry west and then north toward Montana Territory. There, they would hook up with General George Crook's column from the south and General John Gibbon's column from the west—and wipe out the enemy encampments of Sioux and Cheyenne led by Sitting Bull and Crazy Horse.

On May 17, the Seventh Cavalry marched off to war. As the column departed, guidons of each regiment snapped in the breeze. Custer was riding one of his favorite horses, and he was dressed in his signature buckskin pants and jacket. He also wore his trademark red silk cravat, which many men in his outfit sported in imitation. Custer's wife, Libbie, joined her husband on horseback at the head of the column. When they passed the Indian quarters, where their allies from the Crow tribe were living, the squaws, old men, and children sang death songs, and when the column passed Laundress Row, wives and children of soldiers lined the road, and mothers held their babies aloft for a last look at their departing fathers.

After fourteen miles, the column separated from camp followers and Custer leaned down from his horse to embrace his wife. "Watch for our return," he said, but for now she stopped and watched the departure, "a scene of wonder and beauty," she later wrote. A little while later on that fine spring morning, five weeks before the most famous cavalry and Indian battle in American history, Libbie Custer had an omen. The wife of the warrior with the long golden locks saw something that disturbed her as she watched the line of pack mules, ponies, cavalry, artillery, infantry, soldiers, orderlies, cooks, Indian scouts, veterinarians, and surgeons that stretched for two miles march off into the morning mist. As it vanished, there appeared a mirror image of the procession in midair, halfway between heaven and earth—a ghost train of horse and riders, swallowed by the sky.

Unbeknownst to Custer, scores of Indians had been assembling in the Valley of the Little Bighorn, coming together as they often did just before summer began, in May, the Month When the Ponies Shed, for the annual Sun Dance. In previous years, they would meet elsewhere, but in 1876, things were different. Sitting Bull wanted the tribes to gather in a remote place while they discussed how to respond to the latest developments. They had camped at nearby Ash Creek, but their horses—perhaps as many as fifteen thousand—had grazed the grasses down, and a few days before the troops arrived, they moved into the valley, where the forage was lush and as high as a horse's belly. It was the biggest encampment the tribes had known, with ten thousand Indians stretching for two miles along the western side of the Little Big-horn River.

Two weeks before the battle, there was a Sun Dance ceremony at Deer Medicine Rocks. It was the ritual from which *Tatanka Iyotake*—Sitting Bull—and his people derived their power and demonstrated their union with the Great Mystery. This Sun Dance would be one for the annals. At the center of the Sun Dance lodge was a sacred tree. It had two hide cutouts of a man and a buffalo attached to the top. "Buffalo robes had been spread out around the tree," Nathaniel Philbrick wrote in *The Last Stand*, "and Sitting Bull sat down with his back resting against the pole, his legs sticking out and his arms hanging down."

He was planning to give *Wakan Tanka*—the Great Mystery—a "scarlet letter," fifty pieces of flesh from each arm. His adopted brother Jumping Bull began cutting Sitting Bull's left arm with an awl, "starting just above the wrist and working his way up toward the shoulder," Philbrick recounted, describing the painful process. "Fifty times, he inserted the awl, pulled up the skin, and cut off a piece of flesh. Soon Sitting Bull's arm flowed with blood and he cried out that he wanted to be at peace with all, wanted plenty of food, wanted to live undisturbed in their own country. Jumping Bull repeated the cutting on Sitting Bull's right arm, and soon, his limbs and fingers were covered in blood. He rose to his feet, and beneath a bright and punishing sun, his head encircled by a wreath of sage, he began to dance." He danced for a day and a night, all the while with an eagle-bone whistle in his mouth, slowly breathing in and then slowly breathing out, and on the exhale, the whistle made a frantic sound that urged the celebrants on. "Around noon on the second day," Philbrick wrote, "after more than 24 hours without food or water, he began to stagger." Several warriors rushed to his side and laid him down, reviving him with drops of water. He whispered to Black Moon and then Black Moon made an announcement. *Tatanka Iyotake* had seen a vision—an echo of Libbie Custer's, suggesting that when our senses are on high alert, especially when the winds of war are stirring, we are all dreaming a version of the same dream. Many soldiers and horses, along with some Indians, were falling upside down into a village, like grass-hoppers. The soldiers did not have ears, which meant that they did not listen. But there was also a warning. The voice in Sitting Bull's vision said that although victory was at hand, his people were not to remove objects from the battlefield, lest a terrible fate subsume them.

During the summer of 1876, the campaign against the horse tribes of the Great Plains met with unexpected resistance. General George Crook was leading his troops toward the encampment at Ash Creek shortly before the Bighorn conflagration. When Crazy Horse got word from his scouts, he took off from the encampment with Cheyenne and Lakota warriors to confront the troops. After a long fight on June 17, the Indians routed the cavalry, shoot-ing Crook's horse from under him, killing a number of soldiers, seizing their weapons and horses, and sending survivors away on foot. The encounter became known as Battle of the Rosebud, an important victory for Native Americans. With plans for July 4th and the American centennial unfolding across the land, newspapers responded in kind. "This war is not bringing much honor to the national flag," said the *St. Louis Times*. "The savages must be stopped." The moment now fell to Custer, the Civil War hero.

As Custer surveyed "the hostiles," he split the Seventh into three battalions, one led by Major Marcus Reno, another by Captain Frederick Benteen, and the third by himself. Each battalion headed off into a different direction. Indian scouts quickly spotted signs of their advance, and word was passed up and down the riverbanks, from the Hunkpapas and the Oglalas to the Minneconjous, the Sans Arcs, the Blackfeet, the Cheyenne and the Yanktonais and the Santee. Crazy Horse readied for battle, riding either his prized bay or sorrel, and then stopped at a wall of sandstone near Ash Creek and carved a petroglyph. It depicted a horse—undecorated and on the move—with a snake hovering above. It is said that somewhere en route, he followed the information he had received in a vision, anointing himself and his animal with gopher dust and paint, and placing a stone pendant over his heart.

Other warriors prepared in a similar fashion, grabbing their horses and applying war paint and items of power. The Oglala Standing Bear had killed a red bird shortly before the battle; now he placed it atop his head as an offering, and joined his fellows. But they were already under siege. Bullets were flying and women and children were running for safety. The men galloped past the timber and down into the valley. A young Hunkpapa named Iron Hawk hesitated for moment. "The earth is all that lasts," Little Bear told him, and then he headed into the fray with his tribe. "Hoka hey!" people called out amid the dirt clouds kicked up by the ponies, and they made the wartime tremolo and the scream of eagle bone whistles was everywhere. Dust and smoke enveloped the land and shadows lurked and there was shouting and gunfire and the thunder of hooves.

Down in the valley, the Seventh Cavalry began to collapse quickly. The horses had grown thirsty in the summer heat and they faltered; amid the battle, some stopped at a ford for a drink. Later, hungry mounts halted in their tracks and ripped snatches of prairie grass from the ground, no match for the fast-running and well-fed Indian ponies that swarmed them. Reno's battalion was quickly surrounded. He ordered the soldiers to dismount and fight, with every fourth man taking the horses and heading for ravines as the others skirmished on foot. The men were overwhelmed. Some of the horses were spooked and ran back toward the water, where soldiers grabbed their tails and used them as life rafts. Others were run off by Indian women who waved buffalo hides. A bullet ripped through the Crow scout Bloody Knife's skull and his brains splattered across Reno's face. Reno issued a flurry of commands, some not even heard, and then quickly ordered another retreat. The battalion headed for the bluffs and was soon joined by Benteen and his men. There they would spend the night, their wounded in a hollow, tended by the only surviving doctor and surrounded by horses and mules for protection.

At about 3:30 p.m., Custer passed through the Medicine Tail Coulee on the east side of the river, approaching what would soon be called Last Stand Hill. A figure was heading in from the southeast, alone and moving fast. "Crazy Horse is coming! Crazy Horse is coming!" someone cried out. When exactly he arrived at the fight is a mystery; perhaps, as per his vision, the gopher dust made him disappear until he galloped onto the battlefield.

Custer was now leading his column north, followed by Captain Myles Keogh's. Another battalion, heading east, was met by thirty Indians, who were soon joined by Sioux chief Gall and the warriors who had just finished off Reno's brigade. "Our young men rained lead across the river," Sitting Bull later recounted, "and drove the white braves back." With Gall's band in pursuit, Keogh led his men up a ridge, riding the battle-scarred steed Comanche, named for courage displayed while facing off with Comanche Indians years before. He gave orders to dismount and form a skirmish line; the battalion kept the Indians at bay for half an hour, then withdrew and headed up another ridge. Keogh again told his men to dismount and form a line. The Indians ran off a number of horses; with soldiers now on foot and without ammunition, they began fighting with pistols and retreated.

Cheyenne warrior Lame White Man mounted a lightning raid, hitting Custer's flank and forcing the soldiers back to Keogh's position atop a hill. Within minutes, Custer and his men were surrounded, and the Indians launched arrows and blasted them with rifles, carbines, muskets, and pistols, felling dozens of troopers and horses. Then the Cheyenne attacked Keogh's battalion head-on; from either side of the ridge, the Lakota raced in at the same time. The shooting was quick, and throughout the attack one man was galloping back and forth in front of the skirmish line, drawing fire until he was blasted from the saddle. This was Captain Keogh, who died on the field.

By 4:30 in the afternoon, Custer was waging his final fight, on a ridge where he had planted his banner. He was joined by survivors of the other battalions as Crazy Horse and his men and warriors from the various tribes closed in. A large group of soldiers broke away, running down a gulley toward the river. They were finished off in a ravine, and so too were Custer and the remaining troops, fighting from behind a bulwark of horses that they had shot for protection.

Exactly how Custer died is a question for the ages. Some say that he was done in by Crazy Horse, while others contend that he was killed by Rain-in-the-Face. According to various Native American accounts, he never really had a last stand. He was killed in the river before his battalion made it to the hill, then was later dragged there by the army to readjust the scene. Yet others believe that he killed himself.

When the battle was over, Cheyenne participant Wooden Leg said that a crowd of old men and young boys rushed their ponies onto the field and began to move among the bodies. A wounded captain, dazed, raised himself on an elbow and glared wildly at the Indians. They thought he had returned from the spirit world. A Lakota warrior wrested the revolver from his weakened hand and shot him in the head. And so passed the last soldier to have fought with Custer, his identity unknown—although he's believed by many to be Myles Keogh, the dashing, stouthearted warrior from Garryowen, Ireland, who had raced in front of the skirmish line to protect his men earlier in the day.

Many of the soldiers were stripped of possessions and their bodies were mutilated. Out of respect for his bravery, Keogh's was not. Custer's body was left intact as well, save for a stick in the ear. According to Native American accounts, he was spared because one of the women on the field was a Cheyenne who had a child conceived by Custer in the aftermath of his attack on Black Kettle's tribe ten years earlier on the banks of the Washita River. On the night after the battle, there was a celebration at Ash Creek, with big fires and kill songs and dances all night long. Years later, the Lakota Black Elk sang one of the songs for his biographer:

> *Long Hair has never returned,*
> *So his woman is crying, crying.*
> *Looking over here, she cries.*
> *Long Hair, guns I had none.*
> *You brought me many. I thank you!*
> *You make me laugh!*
> *Long Hair, horses I had none.*

You brought me many. I thank you!
You make me laugh!
Long Hair, where he lies nobody knows.
Crying, they seek him.
He lies over here.
Let go your holy irons.
You are not men enough to do any harm.
Let go your holy irons!

After the victory celebration, Black Elk was so tired that he lay down on the spot where he was dancing and went to sleep. He was about ten years old.

Soon after that, the Indians of the Great Plains dispersed, dressed in cavalry gear and adorned with pocket watches and other items, carrying saddles and weapons seized in victory—contrary to Sitting Bull's warning about taking things of desire from the battlefield. They struck their vast impromptu village that had covered miles of prairie and faded into the wilderness, followed by thousands of ponies whose ranks now swelled with army horses. "Henceforth," Sitting Bull said when he saw what had happened, "you shall always covet white people's belongings."

When General Terry and his battalion arrived two days later, the field was baking in the summer furnace and strewn with bodies—the dead, mutilated, and scalped bodies of men and the bodies of dead and dying horses. The soldiers traversed the grounds and carried off their dead. The service of the men in this battle has been recounted in many places, from every point of view, exploring at length who may have died on what ridge, how long they may have fought after suffering the first wounds, the possibility that Custer's last recorded message—"come quick—need help"—may have been improperly written down by the Italian bugler, who did not speak good English, what impetuous or self-destructive or inevitable plan of Custer's the men of the Seventh may have been following. Scraps of their clothing, their riding gear, mementos they carried into battle were long ago gathered and held on to forever by the legions of people who have swarmed across these grounds looking for answers—soldiers, widows, sons, great-granddaughters, politicians, archaeologists, students of forensics, historians, citizens who partake of the Little Bighorn like the blood of Christ on a wafer. What secrets are here? they—I—want to know, for I too have traversed this field. If I stay here long enough, will I touch America's heart?

These are riddles without answer, yet of this we are certain:

The Lakota had delivered a shattering message, and it could not have arrived at a more significant moment. A week after the battle, the country was about to celebrate its centennial. The brash and young country, which had broken free of the Old World in a bloody and prolonged revolt, had just seen its most adored military figure destroyed on the battlefield. It was an unexpected event, especially on the eve of the nation's 100th anniversary. As it happened, there was one survivor of Custer's unit—the war horse Comanche. This time, he had been found bleeding from seven or eight bullet wounds, lying in the greasy grass amid the carnage. He was roused with some bourbon from a soldier's hat, helped off the field, taken to a nearby steamer and then up the Yellowstone River to Fort Randall, where he was retired with full honors. Over time, he was nursed back to health, though he had developed a taste for booze. He was billed as "the lone survivor of the Battle of the Little Bighorn" (although others had made it through, including many Native Americans), just in time for centennial celebrations; as such, he joined the parade of frontier superstars on the national stage. Years later, he was an eyewitness to Wounded Knee, serving in the army pack train in spite of retirement.

While Comanche's survival conveyed hope as news of the Custer massacre reverberated, the national mood had darkened. The campaign against the Lakota had failed and the cavalry was humiliated. Recall that Buffalo Bill was scouting for the Fifth Cavalry in Wyoming, trying to escape the grief caused by his son's death. He did not get word of the Little Bighorn and Custer's demise until July 6, while staging from Sage Creek with the army as they pursued Indians who were dispersing after their victory. Early the next morning, he rushed into camp with the shocking news. Four days later, the Fifth was told to head for Fort Laramie, but early on the morning of July 14, they learned that a thousand Cheyenne were planning to flee the Red Cloud Agency in Nebraska so they could join Sitting Bull, who was en route to Canada. The Fifth headed in that direction, with Cody and two other scouts leading the way. At daybreak on July 17, at Hat Creek, they engaged the Indians. It would be Cody's fourteenth fight against the enemy since he had become the official scout for the Fifth in 1868. And it would be his most glorious, involving a duel that sent his reputation into the stratosphere.

According to war correspondents from various newspapers on the scene (including the *New York Herald* and *Chicago Times*), as well as eyewitnesses to the skirmish, and Buffalo Bill himself, Cody and Colonel Wesley Merritt were lying on an outpost behind a hill. They sighted Cheyenne war parties on a ridge above. Three miles to the south, a wagon train carrying infantry was on its way, led by two couriers who did not see the Indians. A small party of Cheyenne galloped up the ravine to attack the two riders. Cody rushed back to camp, rounded up fifteen men, returned and started a running fight. The soldiers were quickly swarmed by many Indians.

"I know you, Pahaska," said a young chief known as Yellow Hand or Yellow Hair, breaking out of his line and riding up and down before his men. "If you want to fight, come ahead and fight me!"

It wasn't unusual that this Indian had singled out Buffalo Bill. His luxuriant hair had given him the nickname invoked by Yellow Hand, which many natives used. Plus he was all dressed up that day, in a stage costume no less—a black velvet vaquero outfit, bedecked with lace, silver buttons, and scarlet ribbon. Ever the showman, he had been wearing it for the past eighty miles, en route to either his death or one more near-miss. But he was not dressed this way just to impress reporters or to display his version of war paint for the Indians. His choice of regalia that day had all to do with a little-known mania for truth; he later said that he wore it so that in future reenactments of this battle he could wear the suit and honestly say that it was what he was wearing at Hat Creek.

Cody accepted Yellow Hand's challenge. "I galloped towards him for fifty yards," he later wrote,

and he advanced towards me about the same distance, both of us riding at full speed, and then, when we were only thirty yards apart, I raised my rifle and fired; his horse fell to the ground, having been killed by my bullet. Almost at the same instant my horse went down, he having stepped into a gopher hole. I instantly sprang to my feet. The Indian had also recovered and we were now both on foot, not more than twenty paces apart. We fired at each other simultaneously. My usual luck did not desert me on this occasion, for his bullet missed me, while mine struck him in the breast. He reeled and fell but before he had fairly touched the ground, I was upon him, knife in hand, and had driven the keen-edged weapon to its hilt in his heart. Jerking his war bonnet off, I scientifically scalped him in about five seconds.

Cody was immediately swarmed by Indians, while Company K hurried to his rescue. As the soldiers converged, Cody held the "top-knot and bonnet" aloft, shouting, "The first scalp for Custer." Blood splattered across his face as he waved the scalp, and the beautiful war bonnet to which it was attached. Within hours, telegraph wires were ablaze with the story and the moment was trumpeted in newspapers across the country. Custer had been avenged.

For a while, Cody carried Yellow Hand's arms, shield, and scalp on scouting expeditions. It was war loot. Those who rode with him begged him to discard the scalp, for it had a stench which was unbearable. On the day after the taking, a cavalry scout is said to have observed Cody with the scalp over his belt as he played pool at the Red Cloud Agency, where members of Yellow Hand's Cheyenne tribe lived. It was at Red Cloud that Cody learned the name of the man he had killed and that his father was a leading chief named Cut Nose. Some time later, Cut Nose sent a white interpreter to Cody at his camp in the Bighorn Mountains, offering to trade four mules for his son's scalp, war bonnet, ornaments, gun, pistols, and knife, all of which Cody had taken. No deal was struck and from then on, whenever he could, he brandished the very scalp and war bonnet, arms, and decorative items he had seized at Hat Creek. While touring with his theater troupe, he arranged for the display of the items in a prominent window. He had joined a long line of ancient warriors, from the Scythians in 700 BC to his contemporaries, the Apache and Comanche and Mohawk and other tribes for whom the taking of a decorated whorl of hair woven with feathers and beads was not just war booty but the capture of a soul. By the time he got to New England, his victory war dance would come to a halt. He was met by reporters and clergymen who railed against "the blood-stained trophies of his murderous and cowardly deeds." He did not exhibit them anymore, finally putting the scalp in a box and mailing it to his wife in Rochester. But first he sent a telegraph that said to expect a surprise. The scalp arrived before his message and according to some accounts, when she opened the package, she fainted. "Will Cody," she said upon his return, "don't you ever send me another Indian scalp as long as you live." After Cody died, Yellow Hair's scalp passed down through the generations to his grandchildren. It is said that the scalp was intact, still tied with two leather strips, just as Yellow Hand wore his hair. In 1957, the family sold it to the Buffalo Bill Historical Center, where it is maintained in a "sacred vault" to which only certain Native Americans and museum staff members have access.

Soon after the duel at Hat Creek, the *New York Weekly* published "The Crimson Trail, or, Custer's Last Warpath, A Romance Founded Upon the Present Border Warfare, as Witnessed by Hon. W. F. Cody." By then, Sitting Bull had escaped to Canada and Crazy Horse was hiding in the Black Hills. "The Indians are tired," Cody declared. "There is little prospect of any more fighting. I determined to go east as soon as possible to organize a new dramatic combination, and have a new drama written for me based on the Sioux War. This I knew would be a paying investment as the Sioux campaign had excited considerable interest."

There were still some skirmishes on the frontier, even in the height of winter when the thermometer had frozen at more than fifty degrees below zero. A year later, General Sheridan reported that the war against the Sioux was over; the Indians had ceded all titles to the Black Hills. Meanwhile, Cody was appearing on stage in a playlet about the duel with Yellow Hand. It was billed as follows:

FIRST APPEARANCE SINCE HIS RETURN
FROM THE INDIAN WARS
BUFFALO BILL COMBINATION
(HON. W. F. CODY)
SUPPORTED BY CAPT. JACK,
THE POET SCOUT OF THE BLACK HILLS
IN THE NEW DRAMA FOUNDED ON INCI-
DENTS IN THE LATE INDIAN WAR
ENTITLED
THE RED RIGHT HAND
OR
BUFFALO BILL'S FIRST SCALP FOR CUSTER.

He did not scalp another Indian. In a few years, he would be
hiring them. They would play themselves in the reenactment of
the duel with Yellow Hand and other incidents, including the Battle of the Little Bighorn. But it was not until Cody hired Sitting
Bull that the Wild West would have its most successful year. When
Sitting Bull entered the circus ring on tour, he was often, though
not always, booed, for Americans believed that it was he who had
killed the golden boy, George Armstrong Custer. What really happened was this: *Tatanka Iyotake*, according to his own account, had
engaged briefly with one of the units which was not Custer's and
not near it, and then departed to protect his village, watching the
battle with noncombatants from a vantage point nearby. Among
those who watched with Sitting Bull was One Bull; according
to him, Sitting Bull was dressed in a characteristic unassuming
manner—not at all like the warrior who would ride into the arena
as part of the Wild West. He wore buckskin clothes, said One Bull,
and not a war bonnet, but a feather. Human hair hung from his

sleeves and his face was not painted. On the day before the battle, the two men had visited the field. As they smoked a ceremonial pipe, they laid down a bison robe and placed small bundles of tobacco tethered to sticks of cherrywood nearby.

"Pity me," Sitting Bull had called out to the Great Mystery, in one of his famous lamentations. "Wherever the sun, the moon, the earth, the four points of the wind, there you are always. Father, save the tribe, I beg you . . . Guard us against all misfortunes or calamities. Pity me." The men were praying on the spot that became known as Last Stand Hill. Someone else had killed Custer, but *Tatanka Iyotake*'s medicine was all over the place.

CHAPTER FOUR

*In Which Sitting Bull Is Hired and
Heads East for the Wild West*

Everyone wanted a piece of the Plains Indians, especially the Lakota and Cheyenne, the holdouts, the rebels, the "last ones to
come in." Even as they were being purged from the lands, the white
man was preserving their clothing, their dwellings, their art, their
spoons, their hair; their very heads were shipped to far-flung repos-
itories where they were studied and calipered and gazed at in wonderment, scientists gathering in a torqued-out version of Hamlet
contemplating his own mortality, but in this case, it was someone
else's because the *wasichu* could not grasp that he too would meet
the end some day, and that the other was in fact himself.

Buffalo Bill well knew the desire for communion with Native
Americans; he had led dukes and financiers on treks to meet them
and he had led soldiers on missions to find and kill them and he
had learned their ways. Later, when the frontier began shutting
down and he took Indians across America and around the world,
the spectacles were transformative, a magic act, and to further
partake, people would visit the villages where the traveling Indians lived in order to touch them. It was a scenario that hinted
at the power of ritual and dance and music to set people free, and
a hundred years later, girls would faint at the sight of handsome

crooners who hit certain notes and gyrating dancers who moved just so and there would be attempts to shut the whole thing down because sometimes it involved other races and could lead to a general breakdown in the scheme of things.

It was only fitting that John M. Burke was dispatched by Buffalo Bill to make an offer to Sitting Bull to join his show, the last and most famous of the "last holdouts." Larger than life and a man whose actions mostly matched his words, Burke had been part of Cody's circle since the early theater days in the Midwest and on the East Coast. A character actor himself, he appeared in many repertory productions around the country, and was well known in the acting community. Experiencing the eternal fate of performers, he took on other jobs in theater when he couldn't find work as an actor. When he couldn't find jobs in theater, he worked on newspapers, where he met the important reporters of the day and acquired skills that would make him a publicity man par excellence. In 1873, while Cody was appearing in *The Scouts of the Prairie*, Burke developed a serious crush on one Mademoiselle Morlacchi, a beautiful Italian actress who was playing Dove Eye, the Indian Maiden of this play. According to the *Chicago Tribune*, she had "an Italian accent and a weakness for scouts." To Burke's dismay, she was in love with Texas Jack Omohundro, a long-haired frontier scout who was handsome, six feet tall, and carried Indian scalps on his belt. The pair soon married, and the portly and not especially suave "Arizona John," as Burke was known (though he had no connection with Arizona), threw himself back into his own career, which included managing celebrities as well as a troupe of acrobats. He also committed himself to Buffalo Bill. When Cody starred in *The Red Right Hand, or the First Scalp for Custer* after the Battle of the Little Bighorn, Burke helped publicize the sensational show, which featured Yellow Hand's scalp, and from then on he was an indispensable part of Cody's enterprises, soon to include the Wild West.

Over the years, Burke came to idolize Buffalo Bill, and in some ways resembled him. In stature, he too was large. He had a bushy mustache, and he was flashy, often wearing a big Stetson and a diamond in his lapel. Like Cody, he had shoulder-length hair. He also told a lot of stories about himself (in his case, often untrue), and in addition to invoking the Southwest with the name "Arizona John," he allied with the army, calling himself "Major Burke" (sonorous it was, but he had never served; it was one more element of the glittering vapors around Cody and his show).

By 1884, he had become the primary advance man for the Wild West. "Was there a notice to be published in the *Podunk Gazette?*" wrote Shirl Kasper in *Annie Oakley.* "Was there an entertainer or a government endorsement to be had? Burke secured it." His stock-in-trade was "wind and brass," according to friends, and not surprisingly he was beloved by reporters around the country. Like Burke, they were enamored of Cody, and Burke took pride in the fact that he was a major port of entry to the international idol. But the alliance between Burke and Cody went beyond acolyte and adored. They were making history, mainly because they were simpatico on the mechanics of show business. While certainly the Wild West could not exist without Buffalo Bill, Cody knew that he could not be the only figure to carry the show over time. Plus, there was clearly a fortune to be had, if certain arrangements were in place and all of the right elements converged. The frontier was not just a jackpot of gold and animals with thick coats and birds with pretty feathers, but it was yielding great characters who had been formed by their lives on it—and they themselves were now proffering their stories and experiences in the endless wilderness bonanza.

For instance, Wild Bill Hickok—a friend of Bill's—had experimented with a Wild West show long before Cody's, and it was probably on Cody's mind when he cooked up his own. "Securing co-operative Indians was not too difficult," Sell and Weybright wrote in their book about Cody, "but capturing wild buffalo was a much more perplexing problem." In 1870, the notorious gambler and gunfighter Hickok rounded up a herd and shipped them to Niagara Falls. But it was not possible to get the animals into the arena in Buffalo, and mayhem erupted. The buffalo escaped, and the Indians chased them through the streets while dogs and children followed. A grizzly bear that had been caged in a railcar also broke loose, rushing for a vendor's hotdogs. Soon, the buffalo were herded into a dead-end street, and Hickok sold them to raise train fare for the return to the plains. The audience had seen an accidental buffalo hunt for free—and loved it. As for the buffalo, one can only hope that their travails came to an end quickly. Knowing of the strange event, Cody and his associates planned their show accordingly, with logistics that would head off a buffalo stampede outside any arena—and make sure to have one that they could control. Of course, the main idea was to turn a profit.

To that end, on June 6, 1885, John Burke boarded a train in Chicago where the Wild West was playing and headed for Mandan, Dakota Territory, site of the Standing Rock Agency, where Sitting Bull had been transferred after being a prisoner of war at Fort Randall. Signing Sitting Bull was almost a done deal. Prior entreaties from Cody had been turned down by Major James McLaughlin, the army official in charge of Standing Rock, but now he had changed his mind. McLaughlin is a controversial figure in frontier history, often viewed as a villain whose mission was to obstruct Sitting Bull in every way, and occasionally presented as a complicated man who believed that the only way to save Indians was to help them acquiesce to the ways of the white man. Weighing the many accounts, it seems clear that McLaughlin, a company man who was no doubt tormented, had a problem with Sitting Bull. He generally scorned his most well-known resident, often condescending to him, a façade that barely covered his fear of Sitting Bull's power among his own people. But with a Native American wife, McLaughlin had his own allies among the Indians at the agency.

When McLaughlin finally relented to Cody's request to meet with Sitting Bull and extend an offer of employment, he was still concerned with how best to handle him. Sitting Bull had been learning to farm, as required of all the Indians at the agency, but it was simply his presence that continued to vex McLaughlin, a thing that needed to be controlled and contained. Yet, in a very palpable way, McLaughlin's behavior toward Sitting Bull is a lesson in human contradiction, for in spite of his fear of Sitting Bull's fame, he himself had tried to use it. In 1884, he helped Alvaren Allen organize the "Sitting Bull Combination," which took him to St. Paul where he had the fateful meeting with Annie Oakley. McLaughlin was hoping that the tour would educate Sitting Bull in the ways of the white man—simply put, aren't lamps better than fire?—and demonstrate the value of giving up his old life. While it did introduce Sitting Bull to the various wonders of the conquerors' world, it also became an embarrassment for McLaughlin. When the train carrying the actors returned to the plains, it stopped in Bismarck, where a reporter came aboard and interviewed Sitting Bull. When asked what he liked about the tour, Sitting Bull replied that he liked the dancing girls in the East, and then reportedly gestured in imitation of what he had seen. That response was unexpected and, moreover, the tour had been sanctioned by a group of Catholic missions, according to assurances from McLaughlin to the federal government. Now it sounded as though the production was a party. The commissioner of Indian Affairs rebuked McLaughlin, who then replaced Sitting Bull with Gall, another prominent Lakota and Little Bighorn veteran, in the upcoming Dakota exhibits at the New Orleans Cotton Expo. It was shortly after that incident that he approved Buffalo Bill's request for a meeting, again hoping, perhaps even more fervently, to get Sitting Bull off his hands—and trying to make things right with Interior Department secretary Henry M. Teller. More importantly, no less a figure than General Sherman had endorsed the idea. "Sitting Bull is a humbug but has a popular fame on which he has a natural right to 'bank,'" Sherman said.

As Burke neared Standing Rock, it was almost time to make his pitch. This one would be different—after all, he would be talking with Sitting Bull—yet much like the others. If it worked, Cody and Burke were ready to deal with whatever else may have followed. In the two years that the show had been in existence, the men had managed many a flamboyant character or temperamental personality. With years of theater experience, they knew what to do and what not to do when it came to quieting and reassuring nervous actors, many of whom in this case were warriors and cowboys who were prideful and did not step away from a fight. For instance, years earlier, Cody had hired Wild Bill Hickok for a production of *Scouts of the Prairie*. Living up to his name, Wild Bill would sometimes shoot at the feet of extras to make them jump. Another time, feeling disrespected by an audience member, he fired his gun at a spotlight, blasting it to smithereens. Now, dozens of Native Americans, primarily Pawnee, were in the employ of the Wild West. Burke and the show's staff were well versed in the ways and needs of Indians. These were not solo operators who would stage unnecessary dramas like Hickok or some of the touring cowboys who liked to go into town and drink, but they often came with their own rivalries and ongoing feuds, which erupted offstage in their tent community or while they were making their cross-country trips by rail or steamboat.

As an advance man whose success with Buffalo Bill's shows spoke for itself, Burke, we can assume, had done his homework when it came to Sitting Bull, probably "scouting" him as a prospective member of the troupe. Having read about Sitting Bull's travels in various theatrical enterprises, he would have learned that the medicine man was eager to acquaint himself with modern machinery, and also that he wanted to understand how the white man was living and how his culture was being passed on to his children. If he had read of Sitting Bull's journey to New York City in 1884 to appear at the Eden Musee, a Madame Tussaud–like enclave on West 23rd Street that presented "the Wonders of the World in wax," he might have learned that the performance—consisting of "a tipi on the stage and the Indians in full dress smoking and cooking"—drew six thousand people during the matinee and evening productions on the first day. This was a huge audience and would have further convinced Cody and Burke to add Sitting Bull to their lineup. Yet the Eden Musee did not treat Sitting Bull in a fitting manner; he did not ride a horse at the Eden Musee nor was he presented with any sort of stature or grandeur other than his name. With that in mind, Burke would want to make sure that the Lakota war hero understood that he'd be an honored cast member of the Wild West.

Still, Burke must have wondered about a few things. Would Sitting Bull be difficult to work with? Having already forged alliances with various Lakota while scouting on the Plains, no one knew better than Cody that Sitting Bull was a powerful figure with strong medicine—not a man to be trifled with. Would there be a problem if a dispute arose and things didn't go his way? On a more mundane front, how many people were in his entourage and would they all be on the payroll? If Sitting Bull declined the offer, should Burke offer a Plan B—and what was it? These were probably some of the questions he pondered and discussed with Cody as they formulated a presentation.

As for Sitting Bull, what had gone through his mind before Burke's arrival? We can say he had a very good idea of his own value by that time, having already appeared at various events around the country, publicized as a warrior who had survived bloody battles and the man who killed the beloved Custer. Now "Major Burke," the emissary of a famous *wasichu* hunter and showman, was coming to meet him. This might have underscored Sitting Bull's understanding of his stature to himself, his tribe, and the soldiers who watched and said yes or no to his comings and goings. But humility, not self-aggrandizement or adulation, was a virtue in Lakota society, and Sitting Bull's standing among whites would serve only to help him negotiate a good deal—nothing more and nothing less. There was another, more important question that he likely would have considered: could he trust one more white man with a piece of paper requiring his signature? So far, not a single *wasichu* had risen to this level. And what if he didn't trust Burke? Would he send him back to Cody after a courteous farewell, even though McLaughlin had sanctioned the meeting? In his heart, before Burke outlined his proposal, Sitting Bull knew the answer. Behind his curiosity about the pending offer was a desire to go to Washington and meet the Grandfather. He had been promised such a thing on previous tours. He still wanted to talk face-to-face with the headman of this new American empire. What was what? he wanted to know. What goes on in this man's heart? Buffalo Bill was the way to such knowledge, and Sitting Bull was ready to sign.

To the Lakota, summer was known as *bloketu*, the Time of the Warm Moons, and there were three of them, one for each month of the season. It was during the Moon of the June Berries that Burke arrived, stepping off the train and heading to Fort Yates. There, he and Major McLaughlin exchanged pleasantries and then climbed into a wagon with two interpreters, William Halsey and Joseph Primeau. They were heading southwest away from the Missouri River and across the grasses of the Plains—as tall as a horse's belly—with displays of color responding to the heat and sunlight everywhere, sunflowers, primrose, and goldenrod betraying not a hint that those who lived on this land were confined to it.

The men camped en route and there may have been a steady

wind blowing, for at any given time on the Great Plains, the air, unchecked from the Mississippi to the Rockies, is stirring and swirling and it might have carried the scent of sage or rain if the clouds were swelling, and overhead a falcon may have ridden the current, for that was one of Sitting Bull's protectors, and surely the winged and the four-leggeds would have been on guard in some way, alerted by a derangement in their surroundings and the silent news that an important member of the circle would be leaving it for a while.

On the second day, the men arrived at Sitting Bull's cluster of lodges along the Grand River. Here he lived with his two wives and ten children and some of their extended families. It was late. The visitors settled in for the evening, and on the third day Major Burke had a meeting with Sitting Bull. We do not know if, when the men were introduced, they shook hands, and if they did, in what manner it occurred. It was said that when Sitting Bull met a white man and shook hands with the fellow, he generally did it with two fingers rather than his entire hand, simply because that was his custom with the *wasichu* as they generally did not warrant a full handshake—even from someone for whom that was not his method of greeting. "[The chief] was fifty-one years old," wrote Walter Havighurst in *Annie Oakley of the Wild West*. "He stood five feet eight inches, with a massive head and bull-broad shoulders, a tapering waist and neat, small feet. His stern face was pitted with smallpox scars from an epidemic in his youth. They were two big men, Burke and Bull, and both were fond of ceremony. Arizona John spoke of his great gratification at meeting a chief whose fame was known afar. While the interpreter put that into Sioux, the chief stood impassive." After all, although the Indian wars were over, there was no arguing with his gravitas: he was still the leader of the Hunkpapa, the most powerful tribe of the Lakota Nation.

Finally, Sitting Bull spoke, welcoming Burke and asking him to explain his proposal. Burke said that he "wanted Sitting Bull and a party of Sioux warriors and their women to travel with the Wild West show," wrote Havighurst. "They would be well paid, well fed, well treated. They would see the cities and towns of the white men, they would have fresh beef in their tepees and fine horses to ride. At the end of the summer they would be brought back on the railroad to their camps in Dakota."

Sitting Bull invited the men into his tipi, and they sat on a buffalo robe. "Through the open flap came the smell of cooking where the women bent over the scattered feast," Havighurst recounted. "The sun sank in a rosy haze over the buttes and the long summer twilight softened the plain. They ate their supper and lighted their pipes, and still *Tatanka Iyotake* did not give his answer."

On the following day, Sitting Bull was ready to hear the details of Burke's offer. Along with eight of his men, he climbed into the wagon and joined the visitors as they all headed back to Fort Yates. In the agency house, Burke sat at a pine table and wrote out a contract. It made Sitting Bull the highest paid performer in the show, and in addition to including a paid entourage, it provided for an interpreter whom Sitting Bull chose.

This was a critical component of the contract. Many a frontier disaster or just plain absurd or deadly misunderstanding had occurred because of inaccurate translations, both purposely or by accident. For instance, there was the infamous Grattan massacre in 1854, an early confrontation between the army and the Lakota, which was initially a dispute over the killing of a cow that belonged to a party of Mormons and then quickly escalated into the killing of Conquering Bear and twenty-nine soldiers, including Lt. John Lawrence Grattan. There was the time that Sitting Bull's own remarks in Philadelphia were said to be the opposite of what he had stated, although no one was the wiser until much later when it didn't matter. And perhaps one of the greatest tragedies in the Indian wars, the killing of Crazy Horse, was partly the result of a bad translation. On May 7, 1877, almost a year after the victory at the Little Bighorn, he and a remaining band of followers surrendered to army authorities. Several months later, possibly as a ruse, he had reportedly agreed to help the cavalry fight Chief Joseph and the Nez Perce, who had been holding out for months along the Canadian border. But his remarks were translated as planning to kill white men. Then he defied an order, and was literally stabbed in the back with a bayonet to the kidney as he resisted an unexpected imprisonment. Sitting Bull had trusted William Halsey as an interpreter since he had been transferred to Standing Rock, and such a relationship on the Great Plains was a thing to be honored. Much could have gone wrong during the time that Sitting Bull traveled with Buffalo Bill; what if an interpreter said incorrectly to a reporter, for instance, that Sitting Bull hated Boston and it became front-page news? There are no reports of misunderstandings due to poor translations of anything that Sitting Bull stated when Halsey was interpreting, and the negotiations with Burke proceeded accordingly.

Other elements of the contract included $125 as a gift, a kind of "signing bonus," and two weeks' salary in advance. Burke also promised to pay all of the expenses for Sitting Bull's party to and from Standing Rock. As an indication of the ad hoc nature of the contract, Burke then added an interesting postscript, a result of something Sitting Bull asked for as the negotiation was under way. He became quite proficient at using a pencil. "PS," the notation at the end of the contract said. "Sitting Bull is to have sole right to sell his own Photographs and Autographs."

That was the final request from *Tatanka Iyotake*, and all agreed and then Burke and Sitting Bull signed the contract, McLaughlin and Primeau as witnesses. As a result of the late-breaking request,

Sitting Bull would go on to earn a substantial amount of money during the four months that he was in the Wild West, much of which he gave away to family and friends, and also to strangers in need, especially the many poor orphan boys he encountered in cities while on tour. This was a thing that caused him great sadness and dismay, and made him ask a question that lingers to this day: in a land where the people have made such great advances, why can't they feed all their children?

For now, Sitting Bull was ready to leave his camp at Grand River on the Standing Rock reservation, and see more of the world. On June 8, cavalry aide William Zahn, a former member of Custer's regiment, helped him and his entourage load their belongings onto the wagon that would carry them to the Northern Pacific railhead at Bismarck, along with Major John M. Burke and interpreter Halsey. Traveling with Sitting Bull were Crow Eagle, Fool Thunder, Fishing Elk, Iron Thunder, Crow's Ghost, and Slow White Bull—all "warriors of distinction," said a telegraph sent to newspapers around the country. There were also various women among the party, including Great Black Moose's daughter, Mrs. Crow's Ghost, Mrs. Slow White Bull and her daughters as well. On the plains, weather can be counted on for a grand gesture, and the party encountered heavy storms and violent winds en route. They crossed swollen rivers and slippery trails and for a while the sun disappeared. It was the most treacherous weather some had seen in years, nature's response to the departure of a thunder dreamer—Sitting Bull, who years later would perform a ceremony that ended a drought. At the station, a small crowd had gathered, and the soldiers and Indians watched the travelers board. Then they waved goodbye as the vapor horse galloped away on the Iron Road, the parallel lines that had split the vast buffalo herds in half, carving right through the heart of the Great Plains. Three days later, the group arrived in Chicago and transferred to the

Atlantic Express. Sitting Bull and his interpreter were ushered into a stateroom in the Pullman car, and they headed east for the Wild West.

Imagine being born into a world where your tribe was the most powerful in all the land and within that being born at the climax of its power. Imagine that in your lifetime, you witnessed a thing that consumed nearly everything you loved and were nourished by and that nearly everyone you cherished or parlayed with was destroyed, altered, killed, or locked up. Imagine being a person who lived through such a thing, sought to head it off directly and softly, was both celebrated and hated for doing so, and yet, because of an alliance with the natural world and it with you, saw the whole thing coming—even your own end. And then, finally, imagine embracing life with all of your might and force, your generosity and joy, trying to contain the wellspring of sorrow and blood that was flooding your world and drowning it, knowing that a river cannot be stopped but that there are many different ways to ride it. This was Sitting Bull's fate and condition, and this is how it unfolded.

Translating Lakota winter counts to the American manner of marking time, Sitting Bull was born in 1831, either on the Grand River near Many Caches in what is now South Dakota, according to the major historians of that era, or in Montana, on the banks of the Elk or Yellowstone River, as it is now called, according to his great-grandson Ernie LaPointe in his book *Sitting Bull: His Life and Legacy*, which was published this century. The book casts certain oft-stated elements of Sitting Bull's life with different details. To some, this would seem inconsequential, but the differences derive from long-standing rivalries between factions and relatives around Sitting Bull—basically, those whose ancestors betrayed Sitting Bull in the end, and those who stood by him. There is even some question as to exactly who is a direct descendant, but after a five-year investigation, the Repatriation Office at the Smithsonian's National Museum of Natural History determined that LaPointe and his three sisters are Sitting Bull's only living relatives. Told by his mother about her grandfather when he was a young boy on the reservation, LaPointe did not realize at first that she was talking about Sitting Bull. As he got older, he understood, but he and his sisters were told to keep the stories in their heads and hearts, lest people treat them differently if they knew about the family's celebrated ancestor. In 1992, an aunt told LaPointe that the time had come, and so he embarked on a campaign to tell what he knew about Sitting Bull. Hearing this new information several years later, the Smithsonian got in touch with LaPointe. Meanwhile he began writing a book, and in 2009 it was published. It's difficult to counter over a century of accepted history. Prior to his publication of the book, Sitting Bull's history had been written by white historians using accounts from Native Americans who knew Sitting Bull as well as accounts from soldiers and government officials. Some of these accounts were informed by Sitting Bull's enemies, and these relationships were either overlooked or not understood at the time the histories were written. LaPointe's narrative derives from his own family stories about his great-grandfather, an oral history passed down in a kind of mosaic. In some respects the old history and his retelling of it are not so different. But there are certain major divergences, and one in particular casts an entirely new light on a part of Sitting Bull's story that has been told for decades everywhere.

Sitting Bull's band was the Bad Bow of the Hunkpapa tribe, and, like the other bands among his people, and of the Indians across the plains, its members traversed the vast terrain in pursuit of buffalo, sometimes crisscrossing the paths of their enemies, engaging in battle, and sometimes, after the *wasichu* arrived, encountering settlers and soldiers and mountain men and miners, engaging in battle on new fronts, and commingling with the new pilgrims. They did not want war with the interlopers; they sought to defend their territory, waging offensive moves when it became clear that the newcomers did not intend to honor agreements, preferring to acquire or seize what was valuable, at any cost. Quite simply, the light-skinned arrivals were greedy—and, in fact, the term *wasichu* originally meant "those who take the fat," and was used by the Lakota to describe the kind of person who takes all of the buffalo fat, a desirable part of the buffalo that the Lakota shared.

Sitting Bull was the second of four children, the only son, born to Her Holy Door Woman and Returns Again. He was not yet given the name by which the world would know him; he was first called Jumping Badger, following Lakota culture, a name involving something his father had seen or experienced. He was different from other boys his age. "Where the others were adventurous, eager, and often reckless," writes LaPointe, "Jumping Badger always held back, thinking before he leaped. If he had lived in this century, he would have been considered a gifted child and would have been praised for his self-discipline and for always analyzing everything before he acted." But his own people, LaPointe says, regarded his behavior as "hesitant" and "feeble," and they called him Hunkesni, which meant "slow-moving" or "weak." Later, his biographers called him "Slow," perhaps hearing the shortened version from their own sources or not getting the exact translation.

In Lakota culture, young boys were sent to live with a trusted uncle for instruction in the ways of the tribe. For Jumping Badger, this figure was Four Horns, the brother of Returns Again. As a medicine man, Four Horns knew that the boy was ready to listen. At the age of seven, he did something that is recounted in nearly every portrait, suggesting that he was not just a good student, but making the kind of decision that is often ascribed to ancient holy men. He had constructed a bow and arrow, and it was perfect. One day, the most gifted bow and arrow maker in the band arranged a test for those boys who were between six and ten years old. "Go hunting," he said, "and bring me a beautiful bird." On the trail, Jumping Badger saw a Bullock's oriole at the top of a tree and aimed. At the same time, another boy saw the bird and shot an arrow. He missed, his arrow was tangled in the branches, and he was upset. Jumping Badger shot the arrow out of the tree, and when it landed it was broken. The boy wanted to fight, but Jumping Badger offered his perfect arrow instead. The boy accepted. Later, back at camp, the boys spoke of how a fight was averted and the peace was kept. The bow and arrow maker gave Jumping Badger his own fine bow and arrows as a reward.

Three years later, Four Horns wanted to test the boy's tracking and hunting skills and took him on his first buffalo hunt. This was not just a matter of securing food for his family and tribe, although that was a factor. The buffalo was the lifeblood of the Lakota, satisfying its physical and spiritual hunger and serving in every other way. Such knowledge was given to the tribe in the way that sacred knowledge is passed on or manifested in certain individuals through a vision, and this vision in its intent is no different from any other vision that comes to any other people as a map for living, and it is repeated, one to the other, and generation to generation, to tell the story of how to walk on this land.

"A very long time ago, they say, two scouts were out looking for bison; and when they came to the top of a high hill and looked north, they saw something coming a long way off, and when it came closer they cried out, 'It is a woman!' and it was." This is Lakota medicine man Black Elk speaking, and the story came to him when he was a young boy, perhaps around the time that he participated in the Battle of the Little Bighorn. He is telling the story to the poet John G. Neihardt, who wrote it down in the 1930s, hoping to make a written record of Lakota beliefs.

When the buffalo were gone, Black Elk would become a member of the Wild West, like Sitting Bull, traveling the world to see how the white man lived, and lamenting after Sitting Bull's death that the sacred hoop was broken. But now, in his cabin on the plains, he continued his story.

> Then one of the scouts, being foolish, had bad thoughts and spoke them, but the other said: "This is a sacred woman; throw all bad thoughts away." When she came still closer, they saw that she wore a fine white buckskin dress, that her hair was very long and that she was young and very beautiful. And she knew their thoughts and said in a voice that was like singing: "You do not know me, but if you want to do as you think, you may come." And the foolish one went; but just as he stood before her, there was a white cloud that came and covered them. And the beautiful young woman came out of the cloud, and when it blew away the foolish man was a skeleton covered with worms.
>
> Then the woman spoke to the one who was not foolish: "You shall go home and tell your people that I am coming and that a big tepee shall be built for me in the center of the nation." And the man, who was very much afraid, went quickly and told the people, who did at once as they were told, and there around the big tepee they waited for the sacred woman. And after a while she came, very beautiful and singing, and as she went into the tepee this is what she sang:

> *With visible breath I am walking.*
> *A voice I am sending as I walk.*
> *In a sacred manner I am walking.*
> *With visible tracks I am walking.*
> *In a sacred manner I walk.*

And as she sang, there came from her mouth a white cloud that was good to smell. Then she gave something to the chief, and it was a pipe with a bison calf carved on one side to mean the earth that bears and feeds us, and with twelve eagle feathers hanging from the stem to mean the sky and the twelve moons, and these were tied with a grass that never breaks. "Behold!" she said. "With this you shall multiply and be a good nation. Nothing but good shall come from it. Only the hands of the good shall take care of it and the bad shall not even see it." Then she sang again and went out of the tepee, and as the people watched her going, suddenly it was a white bison galloping away and snorting, and soon it was gone.

Such was the medicine in which young Sitting Bull was nurtured and such was the medicine that would hang in the air when he filled a pipe with tobacco years later in the company of Buffalo Bill and reporters, puffing on it and passing it around the circle, though this would not have been the sacred buffalo pipe that was reserved for special circumstances and used only by certain people who understood its power and when and where it must be used.

When young Sitting Bull embarked on his first hunt that day with his uncle, the elder told Jumping Badger to follow a smaller herd to the west. An expert rider like many Lakota boys, Jumping Badger rode directly into the middle of the herd with his bow and arrow poised. Zeroing in on a big bull, he shot and felled the animal. The rest of the herd was spooked and ran away. Four Horns had warned Jumping Badger to steer clear of situations like this, in which he could get trampled by an angry, stampeding herd. "Why did you choose the big bull," he asked, "when there was a cow close to the edge of the herd?" "I've seen the cow," the boy said, "but also her calf. If I had taken the cow, her calf would have perished."

Four Horns was impressed by Jumping Badger's compassion, and told him to eat part of the buffalo's liver to thank the spirit of the buffalo for giving his life. Then the boy was told to fetch his mother and other relatives to prepare the meat. As they prepared to return with skinning and butchering tools, Jumping Badger told his mother to cut portions of meat for a widow who lived nearby; there was no one to hunt for her family. The ten-year-old's generosity, and again, his compassion, came to the attention of his elders.

At fourteen, Jumping Badger was fully anointed as a warrior, a thing all Lakota boys prepared for from birth. "He had been born and reared in the midst of war," as Stanley Vestal wrote in *Sitting Bull: Champion of the Sioux*. "When he was little, his mother had often dressed his baby feet in tiny moccasins before she went to sleep at night, because they might have to run out of the tent and hide if an enemy attacked. He had learned to fear the hoot of the owl, which might signal prowling foes—perhaps Crow Indians—who would cut a small boy to pieces if they caught him. Wounds, and tears, and wild rejoicings, war dances, victory dances, with all their lively pantomime of battle, ambush, and sudden death, were part of his daily life." Even his uncle had once been left for dead on the battlefield.

One day, Jumping Badger joined a raiding party along with Four Horns and his father, Returns Again, who by then had taken the name *Tatanka Iyotake*, or Sitting Bull. It is said that Returns Again communicated with four-legged creatures like others of his own kind. Around the time that Jumping Badger had killed his first buffalo, Returns Again was hunting. His group had camped for the night and a big white buffalo bull appeared at the edge of the fire. It reared up on its haunches, bellowed, and stomped down on his front hooves, four times, and then disappeared into the night. Returns Again explained to the others that the reason the buffalo bellowed four times was to give four names to the tribe, and these names would be given to individuals. The names were Buffalo Bull

Sits Down (Sitting Bull), Jumping Bull, One Bull, and Bull Stands with Cow. They were a gift from the buffalo nation, Returns Again said. "From this day forward I will be known as *Tatanka Iyotake*."

The Lakota raiding party found a band of Crows in a valley, along with many horses. They closed in and then charged the camp, surprising their enemies. One of the first to reach the Crow was Jumping Badger, who counted coup—or laid a special coup stick on one of the warriors—using the weapon given to him by Four Horns. It was his first successful wartime contact with the enemy, and Jumping Badger's father embraced the boy and said, "Today you are a warrior. You are now a man."

Later, when the band returned to camp with fine horses taken from the Crow, *Tatanka Iyotake* offered a feast, and "there was dancing and eating and telling of heroic deeds," writes LaPointe. "Finally *Tatanka Iyotake* asked for silence." He proceeded to recount his son's accomplishment and then asked warriors to bring horses into the center of camp. By way of Lakota custom, he gave the horses away, honoring his son's bravery. One last horse he kept, a magnificent bay, and then to his son, he said: "I place this eagle tail feather in your hair as a symbol for your first coup. I give you this fine bay horse, a warrior's horse, and this shield. May they serve you well." The shield was round and made of buffalo hide, and there was a black thunderbird in the center. Two semicircles ringed the thunderbird, one red and one black. These were Lakota colors indicating two of the four directions—red for the south, the southern sky, font of warmth and growing, and black for the west, where the sun sets and the day ends, the source of thunder and rain. The boy carried the shield for the rest of his life.

Tatanka Iyotake then dipped his hand into a pot, withdrew it, and covered his son with black paint. "This is my son," he said, "and on this day he is no longer naked, for he is a warrior of the Bad Bow band of the Hunkpapa Lakota Nation. From this day forward, I shall be Jumping Bull and this warrior's name shall be *Tatanka Iyotake*." Sitting Bull had taken the stage.

Later, when he became a superstar, a reporter would mock the name, calling him "Sedentary Taurus." But apart from certain mountain men and various individuals here and there, the *wasichu* did not understand the nature of the native alliance with animals, other than the fact that the only way to defeat him was to seize or destroy his ponies, thus dismounting him, and to wipe out the buffalo, the source of his food and shelter. In the passing of the name to the boy, the spirit had entered and the animal's message would be carried. "The buffalo never turned back, never gave up, kept on going ahead, whatever the danger, whatever the weather," Stanley Vestal wrote. "In winter, it moved against the wind, even in the bitterest blizzard, seeming to welcome opposition. Once it started, in a given direction, nobody could head it off. It was all endurance, headstrong courage, persistence, and strength." In other words, it stood its ground, and in fact, it was the ground—it embodied the very earth, patient, calm, carrying us all; when roused, a force that would cast its burdens off without mercy. Over the years, some would note that Sitting Bull himself resembled a buffalo; he had a big head and broad shoulders . . . he carried the Lakota burdens and it showed.

A year later, another feat would be added to Sitting Bull's story. A band of Flatheads or Crow, depending on the source, ambushed some Lakota warriors, showering them with arrows and bullets. Sitting Bull "ran the line," riding between the two armies to become a moving target for arrows and bullets fired by the enemy. At the end of the line, a musket ball hit his left foot, entering at his toes and exiting at the heel. By drawing off fire, he may have saved others. The damage never healed and he walked with a limp for the rest of his life.

There was a celebration for him later that day, but he could not participate in the victory dance because of his injury. He was given a red eagle feather for his act of bravery. Over the years, there would be many others; each would have entitled him to wear an eagle feather. But he rarely did, preferring just the original two—the first from his coup against the Crow and the second, representing his teenage battle wound. To the end of his years, with a few exceptions (his appearances in the Wild West, for example, in which he wore a full war bonnet), that's how he was generally pictured.

In 1851, Sitting Bull married the first of his five wives. Polygamy was common among the Lakota; although Sitting Bull never had five simultaneously, there were times when he had two, one of whom died in childbirth in 1857. Two years later, Sitting Bull's father was killed during a hunt with Sitting Bull and his band. While moving their camp from the headwaters of the Cannonball River to higher ground called Rainy Butte, they were attacked by a large Crow raiding party. The ambush was mounted with knives, and amid the fighting one of the Crow warriors came face-to-face with Jumping Bull, then sixty-one. Jumping Bull raised his bow, but it was blasted from his hands when the enemy fired his gun. Then the warrior rushed him with a knife. Sitting Bull's father couldn't reach his own weapon before the Crow began hacking into his neck and abdomen. Finally, he plunged the knife into the top of Jumping Bull's head, so forcefully that the blade broke.

Other members of Sitting Bull's band ran toward the fight, just as the Crow jumped on his horse and fled. Sitting Bull gave chase and caught the Crow. With his lance, he took the attacker off his horse and dismounted as well. Then he "worked the Crow over with his knife," Bill Yenne writes in *Sitting Bull*, "leaving his father's assailant in a mass of bloody bits." Other members of the band chased the Crow for miles, killing many. On the run, the Crow left three women and a baby, who were taken captive by the Hunkpapa. Many wanted to kill the prisoners in retribution for the killing of Jumping Bull. But Sitting Bull intervened. It was Jumping Bull's time to die, he said, and getting rid of his killer was enough. The women and child were returned to the Crow at the end of that summer. Sitting Bull himself commemorated the moment when he avenged his father in his hieroglyphic autobiography, a series of pictographs he made while imprisoned at Fort Randall. Jumping Bull was buried south of Cedar Creek, near the current border between the two Dakotas. Sitting Bull passed his father's name on to an adopted brother. "According to the way it was described in the oral tradition," Yenne wrote, "Sitting Bull's father no longer needed it."

As he entered the time of his young manhood, Sitting Bull began to have encounters with animals that have become touchstones in his story. Said to have a remarkable voice, he often sang of these meetings. According to Robert Utley's biography of Sitting Bull, he was especially absorbed by birds. He imitated their songs and understood what the meadowlarks say. Years later, one came to warn him of his death. He also had an affinity for wolves. One day while traveling along the Grand River, he came across a wolf that had been wounded by two arrows. "Boy," cried the wolf, "if you will relieve me, your name shall be great." Sitting Bull removed the arrows, cleaned and dressed the wounds, and sent the animal on his way. Then he composed a song about the experience: "Alone in the wilderness I roam/With much hardships in the wilderness I roam/A wolf said this to me." He dedicated the song to the wolf tribe.

Another oft-told story involves the time that Sitting Bull saved a horse by talking to it with kind words. After his band crossed the Yellowstone River and camped on the north bank, there was a storm and the river was not passable. A young woman became distraught, finding that her favorite riding horse had been left on the other side, where it neighed and pawed the ground. Several volunteers offered to retrieve the horse, but the current was too swift. Sitting Bull walked upstream half a mile and stepped into the river, fighting to get to the other side. Exhausted, he crawled up the banks on the south side and approached the horse. "Grandchild," he said, "I have been sent to come to your rescue. Do not run away from me. Somebody is waiting for you on the other side." Then he rested and regained his strength. "Grandchild," he said again, "do your best to permit me to guide you across. If you and I reach the other side safely, I shall have the tribe make a dance in your honor." Horse and man plunged into the torrent, with Sitting Bull on the animal's back. They were carried downriver and safely reached the north bank. Sitting Bull was greeted with songs of praise and later his band performed what came to be known as the Sacred Horse Dance.

According to Robert Higheagle, who once lived in Sitting Bull's camp, he was also said to have been a thunder dreamer. "He painted his face with lightning," he said, and only those who have had that dream could adorn themselves in such fashion. A thunder dreamer would have dreamed of a thunderbird, a raptor that was an eagle or falcon, and such a dream meant that he had power to call up certain weather. Once, Sitting Bull stayed up all night on a hilltop, singing "Against the wind I am coming/Peace pipe I am seeking/Rain I am bringing as I am coming." Some say that a drought soon ended. Such a power could not be denied—personally or by his tribe—as he told a reporter from the *New York Herald* who interviewed him in Canada in 1877. It was his first such discussion with a newspaper correspondent, and it was lengthy. Among the various interviews that Sitting Bull would provide, it continues to serve as the most revelatory, offering profound clues as to his very nature—clues that were generally not understood at the time, or simply ignored. "I began to see when I was not yet born," he said, "when I was not in my mother's arms, but inside of my mother's belly. It was there that I began to study about my people . . . I was so interested that I turned over on my side." He recounted learning about smallpox that was killing his people and he suggested that it was while in the womb that he learned from the Great Mystery that some day he would be a big man.

With the encroaching *wasichu*, there came more warfare on the plains. On July 28, 1864, the biggest battle on the northern plains unfolded. This was the Battle of Killdeer Mountain, in which General Alfred Sully attacked a large party of Lakota including Sitting Bull and his band encamped in a trading village, in retaliation for the raids on settlers that had led to the bloody Dakota War of 1862. The tribes that were assaulted had not been involved in the Dakota War, but that didn't matter; they were on the plains and within reach for an act of vengeance. Thousands of cavalry troops advanced on the Indians, firing bullets as the tribes attempted to hold them off with bows and arrows. Late in the battle, a disabled Dakota named Bear's Heart asked to participate. Sitting Bull and other leaders consented and he was placed on a horse-drawn travois and sent down the hill into the fray. His horse was killed and he was too, as he sang his own death song. Soon, cannons ripped into the embattled Indians, and after suffering many casualties they fled south into the Badlands. The cavalry overran the encampment, burning tons of buffalo meat and killing horses and ponies that were left behind. One infant was shot. But some had discovered Bear's Heart, and they fired their guns in tribute.

The warfare of 1864 was instructive for Sitting Bull. Having skirmished with the cavalry across that summer, he observed that "the white soldiers do not know how to fight. They are not lively enough. They stand still and run straight; it is easy to shoot them. They do not try to save themselves. Also, they seem to have no hearts. When an Indian gets killed, the other Indians feel sorry and cry, and sometimes they stop fighting. But when a white soldier gets killed, nobody cries, nobody cares; they go right on shooting and let him lie there. Sometimes they even go off and leave their wounded behind them."

As a result of the summer campaigns of 1864, there was collateral damage for a party of settlers heading across the plains at that time. Sitting Bull would later emerge as the man who saved a young white woman who became a famous kidnapping victim, penning a book called *Narrative of My Captivity Among the Sioux Indians, with a Brief Account of General Sully's Indian Expedition in 1864, Bearing Upon Events Occurring in My Captivity*. It was a brutal account of her capture and life with natives, and she included details of the scalping of her nine-year-old niece as she tried to escape. Her book was a bestseller and one of the first in a series of lurid "captivity narratives" that riveted the country during the Indian wars and advanced all manner of speaking tours and careers. Some of the kidnap victims could never readjust to white society and went berserk; others returned to live with Native Americans.

By 1867, it was becoming clear that the Lakota were increasingly besieged and required new leadership—men who were younger than, say, Four Horns, Sitting Bull's uncle. Four Horns called all of the bands together, along with some Cheyenne and Yanktonai, to discuss his plans. He recommended that his nephew, thirty-six-year-old *Tatanka Iyotake*, become chief of the tribe. It was believed that he was advanced in his thinking and action for someone that age, wrote his great-grandson Ernie LaPointe. The tribe also agreed that the number two position be filled by Crazy Horse. "Four chiefs went to Sitting Bull's tipi and escorted him out," LaPointe wrote. "They brought a buffalo robe with them and had him sit on it. Then they carried him to the council tipi for the ceremony."

Four Horns said that there was now a new chief and that it was up to this chief to see that the Lakota were fed and defended. "When you tell us to fight, we will raise up our weapons," he said to Sitting Bull. "If you tell us to make peace, we will lay down our weapons. We will smoke the *Cannupa Wakan* [sacred pipe] so *Wakan Tanka* will bless our decision." Then Sitting Bull was presented with a special bow and arrows and a rifle. He was given a headdress of eagle feathers trailing to the ground, and each feather represented a coup by the warrior who presented it. He was given a magnificent white stallion, lifted onto its back, and paraded around the camp, followed by warriors "dressed in their finest and wearing their eagle feathers proudly." As he was led around the camp, Sitting Bull sang a song. "I humble myself when my people speak my name/So said *Tatanka Iyotake*."

On June 12, 1885, a Friday afternoon, the Atlantic Express arrived at the train depot in Buffalo, New York. Major Burke emerged, followed by Sitting Bull and his entourage. A reporter from the *Buffalo Courier* was waiting. "He is ours," Burke called out. "I have captured him." Sitting Bull seemed to have stepped out of a frontier diorama. He was wearing a full war bonnet with forty large eagle feathers and a buckskin tunic trimmed with beads. He carried a bow and arrows and a peace pipe trimmed with ribbon. There was a medicine bag at his side and he wore a crucifix around his neck. The party boarded an open carriage and headed for the Driving Park. Buffalo Bill was waiting.

CHAPTER FIVE

In Which Sitting Bull and Buffalo Bill Join Up in the City of Buffalo, and Tatanka Iyotake *Reunites with Annie Oakley*

Some friendships form quickly and fade just as fast. Others last for a short period of time, an hour, say, or a day, but even they may be as deep as the kind that lasts for a lifetime. And then there are those in which mysterious forces, the hand of the Creator perhaps, necessity, desire, brings two people together, even former enemies, in an alliance that seems unlikely, and in the end, not at all. Such was the join-up of Sitting Bull and Buffalo Bill, "Foes in '76, Friends in '85," as a photo caption would say of the pair, each an icon to himself, together a powerhouse of mythology and might and sparks.

The men had much in common. Both were fathers, husbands, brothers, sons. Both were celebrated, surrounded by admirers and those who embodied the other side of admiration, jealousy; both were known to everyone and no one, in the end, misunderstood, trapped in a persona, worn down by their gifts.

Both were men of action, fearing not a rumble nor a personal assault; they were warriors in service of their people and their time, not unlike Montezuma and Cortés in some ways, Montezuma who carved out hearts with obsidian and ate them, and dreamed of the newcomer's arrival atop a horse, and Cortés, who performed the assigned dance, lusting for sparkles in the ground and sending greyhounds to devour those in the way. But unlike Montezuma and Cortés, there was one thing that made them blood brothers, took them way beyond a show biz alliance, and that was the buffalo, to which they both owed their lives and paid tribute with their names. Two sides of the buffalo coin they were. William Cody had killed thousands of them—about three thousand to be exact—while he hunted as an employee of the railroad, taking the plentiful animals from the land to feed workers along the Iron Road, leaving their carcasses and organs to rot where they were felled and skinned. He won his name in a contest because he shot more buffalo on one day than the other guy, and from then on, that's how Cody was known. The name allied him with the animal that was synonymous with the Great Plains, although he was really no friend to the buffalo—until late in life, after he had witnessed or known about some terrible things, and he had a change of heart and tried to save them. On the other hand, Sitting Bull was kin to the buffalo (along with the other creatures of the plains); when he killed one or several, he uttered a prayer, and then his people were called in to take the animal, and they carved it up, later making use of not just the meat, but the hide, the horns, the hooves, the spleen, the sinew, and when he danced under the sun, staring at it until he nearly went blind, the dance was in concert with the buffalo, whose skull looked on and whose bones were all around him, and pierced his skin, and he asked for continued blessings for his people and through the pathway of the dancing and sacrifice and the buffalo and all other facets of the circle, there was life.

"PTE" the Lakota called the buffalo. It crossed the Bering land bridge during the Ice Age on its way to America as horses were heading in the opposite direction, populating the rest of the world and returning to their homeland thousands of years later and meeting up again with the buffalo on the plains. The Indian, the horse, and the buffalo formed a triumvirate that became the symbol of the frontier, drawing people to its heart, stirring up a fever that caused people to pay large sums of money for train trips across the plains, picking off the slow-moving buffalo through the windows.

In 1883, as the Wild West show began, Sitting Bull had come in from Canada and at Fort Buford was permitted to go on one more buffalo hunt, the very last one before the curtains closed. The railroad had divided the vast herds in half—the northern and southern herds—and by then both populations had dwindled. After that, cows replaced buffalo on the reservations, and every month a steer would be released and resident Indians would be permitted to kill it in a mock version of their hunts. There was never enough meat and, of course, this strange form of early canned hunting did not satisfy the Indians' other needs. For instance, they were not permitted to hold Sun Dances, the most important ceremony of the year, or any number of other rituals. Their medicine bags were confiscated and so were their pipes (though there is many an account of facsimile medicine bags being presented to authorities while the real thing was hidden away). And they were not allowed to leave the agencies without special permission, which was hard to acquire. In short, they were prisoners, with few ways out. One escape hatch was the Wild West, a spectacle that employed not just cowboys and Indians, but elk and horses and buffalo as well—not that the animals wanted a job, but they too became reenactors in a frontier drama that was over but would never close.

It is not known what Sitting Bull thought about beginning his Wild West career in a city called Buffalo (itself probably named after the animal, though that is not known for sure either). A smart man, he must have known that this was the English word for what he called "pte," and he had surely heard it many times from interpreters, most prominently, perhaps, when he embarked on that final buffalo hunt, for it was a noteworthy adventure known at the time it happened as being the last one that he and his people would be permitted to embark on and thus there was much ceremony. We can further surmise that he may have seen the word at the train depot or elsewhere, or that someone even joked en route about heading to Buffalo, of all places, "Hey, chief, get it? Do you know where you're going?" or that the reporter waiting for him on the depot probably was introduced, in translation, as representing the *Buffalo Courier*, and that he understood, most likely and before he arrived, that William F. Cody, whose show he was joining, was a famous figure nicknamed "Buffalo Bill." But if he did make those assumptions, would they have caused him pain or a sort of strange amusement at one more folly of the *wasichu*? A reaction he must have had, but it is lost to the ages, and at that point you could say that having witnessed and been part of one of history's most rapid reversals of fortune, he may have simply thought, "It figures." Yet in a little while, he would be meeting up with a new herd of the four-legged, small though it was, for they were part of the Wild West, and from then on, he would be touring with them.

On the day that Sitting Bull arrived in Buffalo, he traveled along Michigan Avenue in a parade of carriages with his in the lead. One of the men who accompanied him was the reporter from the *Buffalo Courier*. The interpreter William Halsey was also there.

Let us recall that one of the reasons Sitting Bull had joined the Wild West and had traveled with other troupes before allying with this one is that he wanted to learn how the white man moved in the world. He wanted to learn his ways, to find out about the things that were the foundation of his dominance. Had he known there were so many white people, he would soon say upon visiting cities of the Midwest and East, he would have understood that his war could not have been won. Yet now that it was over, one of the things he most wanted was for his children to flourish in the world that had overtaken them. To that end, he played several roles, not that he was acting or presenting a false front or pretending to be a person that he was not. Certainly, he was an ambassador of sorts, not in the glad-handing way, for that would have been untrue, but he was also a representative of his people, and as such there were specific things he would be conveying. You could say that he was a man on a mission. To that end, he was also a kind of spy in a strange land; given his attunement to the natural world, he would have continued this walk in cities and towns, absorbing details of life and behavior and how the newly constructed centers of human endeavor worked upon ground that had once supported other tribes. So it must have been with a sense of puzzlement and curiosity that he entertained the questions of the reporter from the *Courier*, who probably confirmed things that he already knew and indicated that the distance between the two cultures would not be bridged in words, at least in this first interview.

"Have much pleasure and much fatigue," Sitting Bull said, according to the report that appeared on June 13, the next day, evidently in response to a series of unreported queries. "Great difference between prairie travel on horse and foot and on the wagons drawn by the vapor horse. Major Burke very kind, all persons very kind. Think all the pale-faces feel kind to the Sioux soldier. Believe they know why he held his braves and all his people to starve rather than submit to what was wrong. Believe the pale-faces respect him for the hard fights and do not wish to hurt him because he had to kill the pale-faces when he was fighting." He continued in this vein, adding that he always spoke the truth to the white man, but was always deceived. Still, in his heart, he had no wish for blood, and he knew the power and brain of the white man. He was sorry the white man was not as honest as he was full of brain power, and he recognized the *wasichu*'s inevitable supremacy.

"I hope that the red man has enough self-respect and the white man enough honesty left to make the end of the controversy a peaceful one," he said. It was to that end that he had agreed to come and see "the great scout and warrior, Buffalo Bill," and was pleased to be in the old campground of the Great White Father, hoping to meet him in Washington. "If he would listen," Sitting Bull said, "I have something to say. I would not ask for something he cannot give." All he wanted, he explained, was for a wide prairie where he could live with his tribe in safety. And he hoped that the pale-faces would let him die in peace, and that his people could bury him undisturbed.

In retrospect, this last remark was significant, almost wrenching, in fact, suggesting a certain concern, you might say, or prescience, given Sitting Bull's ability to see and feel the past and the future, for discussion of what might happen to him in death is not something that appears elsewhere in the historical record. Another, more thoughtful reporter, might have wondered why the Lakota warrior expressed such a concern, and pressed him a bit further. Perhaps the reporter wanted to, but shied away for various reasons; the statement was a striking one in the most fundamental of ways, and it's quite possible that the reporter thought about it later, especially when Sitting Bull was assassinated and interred. In any case, the interview quickly moved on, with the reporter asking about the Little Bighorn—which still obsessed the country. Sitting Bull raised his hand and warned him off. "That is of another day," he said. "I fought for my people. My people said I was right. I will always answer to my people. The friends of the dead pale-faces must answer for those who are dead."

To break the spell of this apparently awkward moment, the interpreter offered cigarettes and they all had a smoke. As the carriages continued down the avenue, Sitting Bull took note of the size of the horses pulling vehicles such as brewers' conveyances. These would have been much bigger than the fast and fleet ponies his people rode, bigger even than the more robust cavalry horses he had encountered in battle; they were plow and draft horses, after all, and for a man who had an alliance with the four-legged, these must have been quite a wonder. Soon, Buffalo Bill would be giving him his own horse, and for the first time since his surrender two years earlier, he would be permitted to dress in full war regalia and ride the animal that had been stripped from his tribe. In doing so, he would re-create a moment that was contained and paid for—yet eternal. It was where he lived, after all, along with Buffalo Bill and the cowboys of the Wild West, who joined him in staged acts of glory and defiance, the endless version of the American dream.

What was Sitting Bull thinking as he approached the Driving Park? Recall that he was oh so gaily dressed when he emerged from the train, with his war bonnet of eagle feathers and owl feathers dipped in crimson. He wore a buckskin tunic trimmed with intricate beadwork and it was said that his medicine bag was the finest specimen of handicraft ever turned out by the Lakota nation. His black hair was braided in long scalp locks, the reporter noted, and the two main plaits were twined with strips of otter skin. He wore a brass chain with a crucifix around his neck, and buckskin pantaloons trimmed with black and white beads; on his feet were moccasins decorated with elaborately worked porcupine quills. He carried a long calumet trimmed with ribbon, and a bow and arrows in buckskin cases festooned with beads. On his face, there were a few traces of vermilion pigment that he had applied several days earlier, probably for his journey out of the plains.

Sitting Bull and his party arrived at the park as the day's program was under way. Buffalo Bill was presenting his shooting skills on horseback, and that scenario was followed by an Indian attack on a stagecoach. Then came pony races, followed by another attack, this one on a settlers' cabin. "Sitting Bull seemed much interested," reported the *Courier*, "and gave vent to frequent monosyllabic utterances of approval. A number of people connected with the show pressed forward to get a good view of the famous redskin." Among them was the "clever and adept feminine markswoman Annie Oakley." Given her iconic status in the American story, the language may seem restrained, but she was not yet a superstar. At the time of Sitting Bull's arrival, she herself had been part of the Wild West for just a few months. She and Sitting Bull had met the previous year in St. Paul, as previously mentioned, striking up an immediate friendship in which Sitting Bull would take note of her skills and give her a nickname that guaranteed her immortality. Now they fell right into conversation, with Annie asking Sitting Bull a number of questions about a red silk handkerchief and some coins that she had sent him after they went their respective ways. "I got them," he said via the interpreter. "But I left them at home for safety. I am very glad to see you. I have not forgotten you and feel pleased that you want to remember me."

"GREEK MEETS GREEK" was the headline for the interview with Sitting Bull the following day, perhaps referring to gods or heroes. Then came the florid subtitle, "A Thrilling and Romantic Encounter Between Redskin and Pale Face Chieftains," with the most important news of the moment in the next subtitle, one line below: "The Sioux Warrior Sitting Bull and Buffalo Bill Bury the Hatchet at the Driving Park." Given the nature of this development, one might have expected it to be on the front page. But it was on page four. The front page was everything that Sitting Bull had already experienced about white culture. It was plastered with ads. For instance, in the left-hand personals column, there was a solicitation for "voice building" with an instructor named Franklin; there were ads for laundry services, a coffee substitute from a homeopathic pharmacy, and several refrigerators. Second from the left were more ads; there were Turkish mats for sale, shirts made to order, and chandeliers and gas fixtures "at popular prices." Third from the left but not in the middle where news began were ads for "amusements." "First-Class Comic Opera at the People's Prices" was going on at the Court Street Theatre, and at Bunnell's Museum, Miss Katherine Rogers was starring in "Leah, the Forsaken," a popular play written in 1863 about a Jewess who violates 17th-century German law and falls in love with a Christian farmer.

Most prominent among the ads was this announcement:

BUFFALO BILL
"HE IS KING OF THEM ALL."—GEN. E. A. CARR
THIS AFTERNOON POSITIVELY LAST PERFORMANCE.
AFTERNOON ONLY.
RAIN OR SHINE.
BUFFALO BILL'S WILD WEST.
RECONSTRUCTED, ENLARGED AND IMPROVED.
DOUBLE ATTRACTION, FIRST AND ONLY APPEARANCE OF THE
WORLD RENOWNED SIOUX CHIEF SITTING BULL.
WE FULFILL EVERY PROMISE—CODY AND SALSBURY.
MUSIC FURNISHED BY THE FAMOUS COWBOY BAND
ADMISSION 50¢ CHILDREN 25¢

Times for the show followed, along with transportation information. "Carriages admitted free" was the ad's last line.

In 1946, *Annie Get Your Gun* opened on Broadway, starring the zaftig Ethel Merman as the petite and unassuming sharpshooter

Annie Oakley. The show was about Annie's time in the Wild West, and of course featured Buffalo Bill and Sitting Bull, and even a person playing a dancing horse. Merman had been singing and performing musical comedy in Manhattan clubs for years, and then Hollywood came calling, followed by Broadway. She had a powerful voice that has been much copied and parodied over the years, but however camp it has become, her rendition of "There's No Business Like Show Business" from this musical is both her signature and a Hollywood anthem. The scene from the play in which she belts out this song, and the scene from the movie version of the play, starring Betty Hutton doing the same, is shown at film industry tributes everywhere, permanent features of the show biz landscape. Yet few people are thinking about Annie Oakley when footage of Ethel Merman is rolled out at Academy Award openings. That's a shame because, although the Irving Berlin song stands on its own, the heated lyrics actually tell us much about the experience of being a performer on Buffalo Bill's stage, a birthplace, after all, of American theater. As one of the stanzas goes:

> *There's no business like show business like no business I*
>   *know*
> *You get word before the show has started that your favorite*
>   *uncle died at dawn*
> *Top of that, your pa and ma have parted, you're broken-*
>   *hearted, but you go on*

The stars of the Wild West had lost everything, seen it all, and combinations thereof, and Annie Oakley was no exception. Nowadays, there are certain ways to escape such circumstances. Often it's through sports; a person excels at one and becomes professional, going on to earn large sums of money and live a life of monetary comfort and public admiration. For others, it's through the military; join and follow the path out of a town, a situation, a life. For yet others, no skill or service is required; all that's needed is fame. In the nineteenth century, a primary escape hatch was comprised of animals, birds, and natural resources—anything that was in the air, in the ground, or on it. Annie Oakley literally shot her way out of poverty, hunting countless small animals to feed her large family of seven brothers and sisters during her childhood, and later selling them to restaurants that served game. Quite simply, she lived in a bloody era and circumstances forced her prowess with guns. But that alone would not have made her an adored icon. To paraphrase a childhood friend, she had a "fine unexplainable personality" that captivated the world.

Like many pivotal characters in frontier history, Annie was born in Ohio. Her Quaker parents, Jacob and Susan Moses, met in the hills of western Pennsylvania. According to family lore, Jacob fell in love with fifteen-year-old Susan, asked for permission to marry her, and then took her away on a horse. They married in 1850, and had three daughters. In Holidaysburg at the end of the eastern division of the Pennsylvania Canal, they had a small inn. One night in 1855, a guest knocked over an oil lamp and the inn burned down, leaving the family homeless. Jacob packed up his family and headed to Ohio, at the time a western frontier fabled for its endless possibilities. Jacob and Susan settled on a small rented farm in Darke County, about eighteen miles north of Greenville, in a village called Woodland. Ohio was already a hot spot in the Indian wars. Greenville was a horrific location in the country's westward march, with General "Mad" Anthony Wayne building a fort there and launching his bloody campaign against Indians in that region. In 1794, it culminated in the Battle of Fallen Timbers, the last conflict in the Northwest Indian War, during which natives siding with the Crown were destroyed. This included Tecumseh and the Shawnee who tried to fend off the Americans, on foot, in the southeastern part of the state until Tecumseh was killed in the War of 1812. He was widely regarded as a warrior and statesman of great power—and thus, in that strange way Americans have of honoring those who have been destroyed, was invoked in the middle name of General William Sherman, Civil War hero and Indian fighter.

When the Moses family arrived, the region was relatively quiet. Woodland had no general store and the post office was half a mile away. Jacob's plan was to eke out a living from the land, like other settlers. He cut down trees and built a cabin and constructed a little farm. In the cabin, Susan gave birth to Phoebe Ann on August 13, 1860; she was the sixth daughter, soon to be joined by a brother. One of Susan's daughters had already died in infancy. Phoebe Ann's sisters called her Annie, and, as Shirl Kasper wrote in *Annie Oakley*, "she grew into a small child, strong despite her size, with thick, dark hair and eyes that people noticed, for they were blue-gray, large, and bright with direct gaze." She was not interested in playing with her sisters and their rag dolls, and instead preferred the company of her father and her brother, John, who was two years younger.

On the farm, the family butchered their own cows and tanned the hide to make shoes. "They smoked ham, pickled beans, and tucked away apples before the winter set in," as Kasper wrote. "Annie spent hours wandering through the woods, listening to the birds and tracking rabbits. The woods were full of hickory nuts, walnuts, and wild cherries. Roses grew unchecked, and the wild ducks and geese flew free."

It was in the Ohio woods that Annie learned to shoot. She had learned to make cornstalk traps from her father, and by the time she was seven, she was trapping quail and rabbit for dinner. Her father had brought an old Kentucky rifle from Pennsylvania, and according to legend there came the day that eight-year-old Annie took it down from its spot above the fireplace and fired her first shot. "I still consider it one of the best shots I ever made," she said. "I saw a squirrel run down over the grass in front of the house, through the orchard and stop on a fence to get a hickory nut." She ran inside, climbed on a chair, and took the rifle down, carrying it outside and resting the barrel on the porch railing. Then she aimed. "It was a wonderful shot," she said, "going right through the head from side to side."

Annie's brother was upset that she used the rifle, reported Frazer Wilson in the *History of Darke County, Ohio*, and he put a double load in it and handed it to her, hoping the kick would scare her away from shooting again. Throwing up his hat as a target, he was surprised when Annie shot right through it. And she never stopped. "My mother was perfectly horrified when I began shooting," Annie once said. "She tried to keep me in school. But I would run away and go quail shooting in the woods or trim my dress with wreaths of wild flowers."

In 1866, Annie's father died in the brutal manner of so many who were vulnerable to the elements. On a winter's day, he had set out on buckboard to take his corn and wheat to the local mill, about fourteen miles away. It was snowing and within hours a blizzard set in. At midnight, the family heard wagon wheels creaking toward the cabin. "Mother threw the door wide open into the face of the howling wind," Annie recalled. There was her father, upright in his seat, with the reins around his neck and wrists. His hands were frozen and he could not talk. A doctor was called, but it was too late. Annie's father died of pneumonia several weeks later—just like Buffalo Bill's.

This was the beginning of a harrowing phase. Susan Moses moved her family to another farm. Annie's oldest sister, Mary Jane, died of tuberculosis. Her mother sold Pink, the family cow, to pay for doctor and funeral expenses. Then she took on nursing jobs for $1.25 a week, devoting her practice to pregnant women.

But it was not enough to sustain her family, and she sent her youngest child, Hulda, who had been born in 1864, to live with another family and work for them—a common practice of the era. In 1870, when Annie was ten, her mother sent her to the county poor farm, a kind of dumping ground for the elderly, the orphaned, and the insane, which often included women who just could not abide the expectations of the day. The repository was also known as the Infirmary, and it was in Greenville, by then a town of rapidly expanding commerce, with three rail lines, four roads, and two newspapers. There was even a public square around the old fort, and lots of stores along the borders. The plan for Annie was that she could live at the Infirmary in exchange for helping the children. "Many persons incapable of attending to their own wants were housed at the Infirmary," a local historian wrote, "and a shortage of rooms compelled the children to associate with these unfortunates, whose habits of life and language were not intended to exert that influence for good that should always surround the child."

One day, a local farmer dropped in at the Infirmary, looking for a companion for his wife and baby. Poor children were often farmed out during those days and she moved in with this man and his wife and baby. She would never identify them and when it was all over, referred to them as "The Wolves." Basically, she was a slave. "I got up at 4 in the morning," she said, "got breakfast, milked the cows, washed dishes, skimmed milk, fed the chickens, rocked the baby to sleep, weeded the garden, picked wild blackberries and got dinner. Mother wrote for me to come home. But they would not let me go. I was held a prisoner." She was also physically abused, which she briefly notes in personal writings, mentioning scars and welts on her back. One night, she recalled, the farmer's wife threw her into the snow, barefoot, because she fell asleep while darning. She would have died if the farmer had not come home and let her into the house. On a spring day around 1872, she fled "the Wolves" and ran away—back to the poor farm.

The new superintendent and his wife realized that Annie deserved more than a life among the general population of the Infirmary, and they let her stay in their quarters. "Mother couldn't stand to see her placed with the other children," the superintendent's son said years later. She went to school with the official's children, and it was an amicable arrangement. The kids even gave her a nickname, "Topsy," after the happy character in *Uncle Tom's Cabin*.

The superintendent's wife taught Annie to sew, and she made dresses and quilts for the inmates. She also learned embroidery, and deployed fancy stitching on the cuffs and collars of the dark dresses that the orphans wore. During her time with the Wild West, her affinity for children was quite apparent, and many have suggested that it began in this time. It was something she shared with Sitting Bull. Her years at the Infirmary would also become manifest in other ways. While touring with Buffalo Bill, she made her own costumes. She didn't have to, but was proud to do so.

At the Infirmary, it wasn't long before she was placed in charge of the dairy, where she milked the cows and made butter for the kitchen. She got a raise and saved her money. One day, she received another offer, asked to be a mother's helper in a private home near Greenville. She tried it for a while, but she was lonely and scared, and not able to communicate with her own mother. So she went home.

En route, she made a stop that turned out to be a critical one on her journey out of Ohio and around the world. She was probably fifteen years old. On the corner of Main Street and Greenville's public square, she headed into the grocery store owned by G. Anthony and Charles Katzenberger. She knew that the brothers traded with hunters and trappers for wild turkeys and rabbits, giving them flour, wheat, and ammunition in exchange. And they had bought game from her in the past. Now she had a new plan. Once again, she would be hunting and trapping in the north county woods. Would the Katzenbergers like to purchase game that she shipped to their store? They said yes, and Annie got her gun.

"I donned my linsey [dress] and hied me back to the deep, quiet woods," she wrote. "Oh, how grand God's beautiful earth seemed to me." Yet, she was in for a surprise. Back at home, she discovered that she had a new stepfather, Joseph Shaw, and he had built a new cabin for her mother, brother, and sisters. It was a modest dwelling, but for once the family situation was a loving one. Annie's mother seemed happy. There was an orchard, garden, and cellar, and she was planting, harvesting, and storing food for the winter. The three oldest daughters were married and gone, and now Annie was the eldest daughter at home, joining a sister and new arrival, a half-sister, and her younger brother, John, who had tried to trick her with her father's rifle. Annie's shooting abilities made her a major source of support for her family.

When it came to guns, she was a natural. "I guess the love of a gun must have been born in me," she later said. And she took great delight in refining her gift, heading to her beloved woods whenever she could. She would wear an outfit that became her trademark: a short, sturdy dress with knickerbockers, as Kasper described it, and heavy mittens with a trigger finger stitched in. Her boots were copper-toed and she sported long yarn stockings. She tramped through the forest, hunting and setting traps. She watched the animals and learned how they lived and moved. Quail were fast and she was too. But she was fair. She did not shoot sitting game, once telling a reporter that "I always preferred taking my shot when the game was on the move. It gave them a fair chance, and made me quick of eye and hand." There is nothing more simple, she told another reporter. But she added that "you must have your mind, your nerve and everything in harmony. Don't look at your gun, simply follow the object with the end of it, as if the tip of the barrel was the point of your finger."

Annie's stepfather, a mail carrier, began making two trips per week to Greenville, taking her game and exchanging it with the Katzenbergers for food and supplies. The game was sent to fine restaurants in Cincinnati, where there was an ongoing demand. According to legend, hotelkeepers loved the quail and rabbits that Annie killed because they had been shot clean, through the head, and guests never complained about finding buckshot in their meal. True or not, Annie's shooting expertise is so much a part of American myth that it was celebrated in a song called "Anything You Can Do" in *Annie Get Your Gun*. There's a duet between Annie and Frank Butler, the handsome trick shooter from Ireland who became her partner in theater, and her manager and husband. "I can shoot a partridge with a single cartridge," Frank croons. "I can get a sparrow with a bow and arrow," Annie sings back.

By the time Annie and Frank had the shooting match that led to their marriage—and that song—Annie had done so well with her hunting that she was able to pay off the $200 mortgage on her parents' house. The Katzenbergers liked her so much that they gave her a serious gun, a Parker Brothers 16-gauge breech-loading hammer, along with one hundred brass shells. This kind of gun was an advance in the manufacture of firearms; the shooter would not have to carry a powder horn or a ramrod, or be concerned with rain, which could dampen gunpowder and render it useless. Also, the new gun permitted the shooter to load shells at home and insert them into the barrel while on the hunt. Now, "Annie shot more game than ever," Kasper wrote. "She wrapped them in bunches of six and twelve." She had become a full-on "market hunter."

There were no hunting limits at the time. According to "The

Story of American Hunting and Firearms" in *Outdoor Life* magazine, there was so much game that anyone with a muzzle-loader
could kill two or three thousand prairie chickens a year for the mar-
ket. Around the Great Lakes, it was not uncommon for a hunter to
kill 150 to 200 white-tailed deer in one autumn, and receive $15
or $20 per deer. It was good money, more than the average lum-
berjack, farmer, or miner could earn in one year. Many years after
Annie had become famous, Charles Katzenberger showed her his
old account books, which listed the amount of game he had bought
from her. "I won't say how much," she said, "as I might be classed
as a game hog, but any man who has ever tried to make a living
and raise a family on 27 acres of poor land will readily understand
that it was a hard proposition." In 1891, a retrospective of Annie's
career in *The Guardian* reported that by the time she was in her late
teens, she had shot so much game and won so many turkey shoots
that she was barred from entering them.

In 1881, Frank Butler arrived in Greenville with some friends
for a shooting match. They were on a nationwide circuit of con-
tests. "I got there late," he later told a reporter, "and found the
whole town, in fact, most of the county out ready to bet me or
any of my friends to a standstill on their 'unknown.' I did not bet
a cent. You may bet, however, that I almost dropped dead when a
little girl in short dresses stepped out to the mark with me." It was
Annie. "I was a beaten man," he continued, "for I was taken off
guard. Never were the birds so hard for two shooters as they flew
from us, but never did a person make more impossible shots than
did that little girl. She killed 23 and I killed 21. It was her first big
match—my first defeat."

It was the beginning of a lifelong love affair and partnership.
Before he left town, Frank invited Annie to a theater to see his
act. Among other things, it involved Frank shooting an apple off
the head of his poodle, George. George then picked up a piece of

apple and laid it at Annie's feet. When Frank left to join the circus, he continued courting her, via letters from George, a box of candy from George, and finally a poem from Frank, called "Little Raindrops."

There's a charming little girl
She's many miles from here
She's a loving little fairy
You'd fall in love to see her
Her presence would remind you
Of an angel in the skies,
And you bet I love this little girl
With the rain drops in her eyes.

The pair married in 1881 or 2; the record is vague, due to a first marriage of Frank's that may or may not have been legally dissolved when they appeared as husband and wife. At the time, Frank was traveling with the Sells Brothers Circus, along with his partner, John Graham. They had a shooting act known as "America's own rifle team and champion all around shots." They dressed like dandies, in tall black boots, tight pants, and coats with tails. They shot an apple off each other's head. Frank would fire while bending over backward, and John shot with his rifle upside down between his legs. Around 1882 or 3, Annie left Ohio and joined the men on tour. One day when John became ill, Frank asked Annie to hold objects while he shot. It was his custom to miss the first couple of shots, and then hit the mark. But on this day, he kept missing. Finally a spectator staggered to the ring. "Let the girl shoot," he said, pointing at Annie. Annie hadn't practiced that particular shot. But she picked up a gun, fired, and hit the target on her second try. "The crowd went into an uproar," Frank said, "and when I attempted to resume my act I was howled down." He made Annie his new partner, and around that time she began calling herself "Annie Oakley," after the town where she and Frank had the shooting match. But according to Sitting Bull's great grandson, the name was mistranslated. Its meaning was actually "Little Person Who Does Good Things." As often happened, the first translation stuck, and it is as "Little Sure Shot" or "Little Miss Sure Shot" that Annie became known (though to Cody, she was "Little Missie")—and in any case, it was Sitting Bull who described her thusly.

It was an inspired "brand," in today's vernacular, and it certainly helped Annie along her road. Would she have attained stardom without that billing? It's hard to say, but Sitting Bull had zeroed in on something that was very American: when it came to guns, she did not hesitate. She fired and her aim was true and people went oooh and aaah and wanted more. For her, shooting was an act of defiance; in taking on the challenge of hitting difficult marks, she was rising to an occasion. It was also an act of assertion, for in pulling the trigger, there was no going back, and in that moment, in the intersection of that latitude and longitude, was her glory. With that nickname and those characteristics, Little Miss Sure Shot was bound to be a superstar, for it is inside the act of pulling the trigger that America resides. Mysterious are the forces that lead us to one another, at certain times, for certain reasons, and looking back on that era, it would seem that Sitting Bull's meeting with Annie Oakley in St. Paul was written on the winds, for without that nickname she would have been billed differently, and quite possibly different things would have happened. After receiving the name and Sitting Bull's friendship, all she needed was one more turn of the wheel.

It happened later that year. While traveling with Frank in the Sells Brothers Circus, the pair arrived in New Orleans. It rained throughout December, and the circus was closed after two weeks. Annie and Frank were jobless, although due to start again with the circus, but not until April, when Annie's salary would be increased. Stranded in Louisiana, they were looking for work until springtime. Meanwhile, William Cody and his Wild West show had arrived, just as the Sells Circus was closing. Sometime during mid-December, Cody headed to the Sells lot and met Annie and Frank. They asked for a job, and Cody turned them down, explaining that his show was heavy on shooting acts, including the famous Captain Bogardus and his four sons. Annie and Frank went north for the winter, playing theaters in other cities.

Cody opened in New Orleans, but was nearly destroyed by the aforementioned flood, trying to reorganize after the sinking of his steamship and loss of animals and equipment. Captain Bogardus lost his guns and quit the show, taking his sons with him. Word traveled quickly on the shooting circuit, and Annie immediately wrote to Cody, again asking for a job. "At first," Annie later recalled, "Colonel Cody entertained a grave doubt as to whether I"—a woman of 110 pounds—"could withstand the recoil from a shot-gun." To prove that she could equal Bogardus and his shooting, she agreed to a three-day trial. If Cody wasn't happy, she would leave the show, and that would be that. Her performance pleased Cody, and in 1885, she and Frank joined the Wild West in Louisville, Kentucky. Annie, now twenty-five and a solo act, opened the new season in April, smashing glass balls and clay pigeons on the wing Bogardus-style, but with her own flair, and of course, as a woman—the only white female member of the show. "Little Miss Sure Shot" had taken the stage.

With Buffalo Bill, she and Sitting Bull were a trio of misunderstood souls. In an era during which people spoke not of their hardships and reporters who recounted their lives thought not to ask, such a thing was hardly expressed and given the circumstances of their lives, we can imagine how deeply their experiences reverberated and were channeled into their time together in the Wild West.

They were projection screens after all, revered for their warrior ways, aspects both real and imagined, their hunting and shooting prowess, the way they sat on a horse, greeted a crowd, fired a rifle, scalped an opponent. Together they represented an America that all knew but few had witnessed—they were survivors who had lived through shock and awe to show you what happened. Together they shared the truth of America and they alone knew it, along with the cast of the Wild West, and without the show, they might have followed the path of their contemporaries who were not cast members—players in lesser shows or drunks in alleys, ordinary people leading ordinary lives, farmers or settlers or miners, cast-offs confined to reservations or a vanishing frontier, never to shout, holler, or ride again.

On the day of his arrival, the *Buffalo Courier* reported that Sitting Bull waited in his carriage in the afternoon sun "with characteristic Indian patience," watching the day's acts. He may have been heartened to see Annie Oakley displaying her shooting skills, to the thunderous applause of twelve thousand spectators. Finally, word came that Buffalo Bill was ready to meet him. He indicated assent and the carriage moved along the track toward the grandstand. People spotted Sitting Bull and began cheering loudly. Suddenly the carriage was stopped. Up the track, standing motionless, was Cody. Major Burke stepped down from the carriage, followed by Sitting Bull, his interpreter, and a reporter. Major Burke approached Bill, and heartily shook his hand. "I am here, governor," he said. "I've got him. Come and shake hands. He's a fine fellow. See, he is coming." Cody hesitated and step forward briefly. So did *Tatanka Iyotake*. There was a strange pause, according to the *Courier*, and then "the famous redskin and the equally noted white hunter, pressed by the interpreter and Major Burke, advanced, and

Buffalo Bill, drawing himself up and assuming a very striking and really handsome pose, held out his hand." They grasped hands and eyed each other for several seconds, with the Indians, cowboys, and Mexicans of the Wild West lined up along a fence and looking on. So too were spectators watching from carriages and the grandstand, "with breathless interest," as "the novel interview" unfolded.

Their grasp continued and became more forthright, "and both seemed to say to the other, 'I can trust you.'" Major Burke then pointed to Cody and said, in Lakota, "Ea ton she Weechaka To kia," which meant, "This is the white chief." Then, gesturing to Sitting Bull, he said, "Dakota Weechiata ta-tape," which meant, "The Great Dakota Sioux King." Sitting Bull tried to smile and he looked at the throngs around him. Buffalo Bill was momentarily disconcerted, but with "vigorous effort, he straightened himself up to his full height." Then he turned toward the concourse in the grandstand and addressed the crowd.

> Ladies and gentlemen of Buffalo. To me this hour is a most peculiar one, as on your beautiful fairgrounds, I meet a warrior whom I [once] attacked [along with] the active army forces of the government, fought a personal conflict with in the campaign of 1876, but he evaded us most successfully. Without egotism I can point with pride to my own record, if you will excuse the use of the only phrase I know to explain it as an Indian fighter; but though I have never been insensitive to the abstract [notion of] civilization, as our progress is called . . . [I think of myself as] the red man's friend. . . . The man who stands before you today is a great warrior; his deeds, divested of our personal feelings to the victims of his success, occupy the blood-red pages of the nation's history. He, from his standpoint, fought for what he believed was right, and made a name for himself to be known forever.

The man I now introduce to you is Sitting Bull, the Napoleon of the red race, who has journeyed thousands of miles
to be present with us today.

There is no description of the crowd's reaction to this speech,
and we do not know if it was rehearsed. But from Cody's body
language upon his meeting with Sitting Bull, we can guess that he
was shaken and humbled—after all, he had to pull himself up to
his normal height after being initially reduced—and that in this
moment, and the physical shaking of hands, and the general sizing
up of a person that happens quickly as many things transpire—the
exchange of scent and other less obvious signs—an understanding
was hatched, a communication between the men was passed, regardless of Cody's words, which were remarkable unto themselves.

After the speech, Buffalo Bill and Sitting Bull got into a carriage and were taken to a clubhouse, where they were joined by
Sitting Bull's party. They rested for a while, "partaking of modest
refreshments in the form of pop and sandwiches," and then they
adjourned to camp, where a hearty dinner was served. Sitting Bull
ate moderately, but Crow Eagle, Crow's Ghost, and Iron Thunder
"disposed of truly enormous quantities of broiled steak, potatoes,
coffee and bread." Then there was a meeting between the newly
arrived Sioux and the Pawnees and other Indians in camp. At first,
there seemed to be some sort of hesitancy or jealousy (and later the
Lakota became the preferred members of the Wild West), but this
soon wore off. "Sitting Bull was the recipient of a large amount of
hero worship from those of his own race," said the *Courier*. "After
passing round the calumet of peace, the whole party went to the
sleeping tent provided for them and usually occupied by Buffalo
Bill and his aides."

They settled down, and then "the victor of the Little Bighorn"
reclined on a couch of blankets, without his war bonnet and tunic,

wearing a "boiled shirt of civilization"—meaning it was formal and starched—"and his buckskin pantaloons, quietly smoking a good cigar given him by Major Burke and listening to the talk of old John Nelson, who speaks Sioux fluently, and who has passed nearly half a century among the redskins." The next day, Sitting Bull would join Buffalo Bill and Annie Oakley and the cast of the Wild West in the arena.

CHAPTER SIX

In Which an Indian and a Wasichu Certify Their Alliance
Across the Medicine Line

A new passion play was unfolding, with touchstone moments for a burgeoning nation reenacted shortly after they had occurred. The moments were violent and involved guns and hatchets, and in the end there were heroes and villains and everyone wanted to meet them. And so they converged in giant outdoor arenas in Buffalo, Burlington, Boston, Philadelphia, Saginaw, Columbus, and beyond, witnessing the national birth time and time again as a cowboy band played on, choir to the sacred rite. "Westward the Course of Empire Makes Its Way" proclaimed a mural at the U.S. Capitol, a twenty-foot-long celebration of pioneers and covered wagons at the Continental Divide, all facing a setting sun above the Pacific Ocean as a pilgrim atop a peak pointed the way, surrounded by images of Moses and the Israelites and Lewis and Clark—prophets all, now merged in the name of fate in a new world. It is said that the name of this painting had great meaning for William Cody; it was oft repeated at the time, a solitary line from an influential poem of the era, "Verses on the Prospect of Planting Arts and Learning in America." He well may have seen the mural during one of his visits to Congress, and even if not, its images and sentiment were brought to life in his grand rite and spectacle. Buffalo Bill's Wild

West—"Larger and Greater than Ever" with the addition of "the renowned Sioux Chief, Sitting Bull," his name in ads only slightly smaller than the name of the show itself—came to celebrate and teach, and the lesson had a cast of all-stars and lesser icons and animals and it even featured a "literature wagon" on the premises, selling all manner of the psalms and scriptures and fables that comprised the show. Everywhere you looked there was myth and story, and even as you picked up a dime novel about Buffalo Bill or an account of the Little Bighorn, the immortals were right there before you, in full dress and war paint, right out of another dimension.

Why, Sitting Bull even had his own staff! as newspaper ads announced with a touch of whimsy in advance of every engagement. It included "White Eagle and 52 braves; the one-legged Sioux spy; Frisking Elk; the great markswoman from the Western border, Miss Annie Oakley; largest herd of buffalo ever exhibited; grand Indian buffalo hunt, known as the Surround; the phenomenal boy shot, Johnny Baker; Mustang Jack, jumping over a horse at 16½ hands; Buck Taylor, the king of the cowboys, in novel equestrianism, lassoing wild cattle, and many others such as a shooting whiz who aimed his weapons at marbles, half dollars and nickels."

The primary attraction of course was William Cody, who seemed to fulfill a national need for one man to step forward from the stage of Manifest Destiny and own it. Central casting couldn't have imagined a better actor: he was oh so handsome; his long flowing hair rendered him both rugged and ethereal—a quasi-religious figure with a Winchester, delivering the national dream, galloping out of the magic dust and into the arena, astride a magnificent horse.

True to the spirit of the West, the arena in each town was outside, an outdoor driving park, to be precise—sprawling raceways built on the outskirts of cities at the end of horse car and rail lines, designed originally for the burgeoning spectator sport of harness racing. The tracks were surrounded by grandstands and private boxes; fans could also align themselves against railings around the racing ovals, or plant themselves on nearby railroad embankments. Over time, the driving parks evolved into fairgrounds, adding stables and corrals and other structures. They became a point of debarkation for Barnum and Bailey circus trains, and when the Wild West came to town, they could easily accommodate the thousands of fans who converged at each show. There was also plenty of atmosphere for a presentation that worked best under a wide-open sky, with its buffalo stampedes, renegade stagecoaches, cowboys leaping atop bucking broncos, and trick shooters firing away at glass balls flying through the air—without the possibility of gunshot sparks starting a fire inside a building or buffalo running into a crowd because there was no escape. It is no wonder that, for instance, in August of 1885, the *Toronto Globe* reported that the "biggest, wildest, most exciting outdoor show that the city had ever seen" took place at the Woodbine Park and Racetrack with the arrival of Buffalo Bill's Wild West.

Newspapers across the U.S. deployed similar language to describe what happened whenever Sitting Bull and Buffalo Bill were in town. In fact, the multicity tour that they embarked on in the late summer and early fall of 1885 set new records for the Wild West, playing to a million people and earning over $100,000, an amount that more than made up for the losses incurred during the New Orleans flood that literally sank Cody's show. In today's parlance, Cody had been convinced that making the A list star Sitting Bull a major attraction would guarantee ongoing success and fascination, and he was right.

And yet, Sitting Bull did not "participate" in the show, in the sense that other Native Americans did; he was Sitting Bull, after all, "the Napoleon of the Great Plains," "the Moses of his people," and in the manner of all royalty through time, it was enough for him simply to appear. At each venue, he would ride through town in the parade, right behind Buffalo Bill, wearing his war bonnet, and then generally once around the ring, as an honored guest in a carriage, and then he would fade back into the mists and the show would go on.

Fans were starstruck, even those who hated Sitting Bull in their belief that he had killed Custer. All wanted to see these giants of the frontier, and express their admiration or rage, to participate in history shortly after it had been made, or even revisit scenarios of which they had been a part. After the show, many could actually meet their idols. In one instance, when the Wild West played Columbus, officers of the Seventeenth U.S. Infantry who were based there visited Sitting Bull at his tent. Recognizing one of the men, he smiled, jumped up, and said "How How!," and then shook hands with a Lieutenant McMartin, who returned the greeting through the interpreter. "This young man," Sitting Bull said to reporters, "rolled cigarettes for me at Fort Randall." McMartin rolled another, lit it, and handed it to Sitting Bull. As he smoked it, McMartin explained that he had been in charge of Sitting Bull when the chief was confined to that fort. Often enough, there were arrangements for groups of women and children to visit the cast in their village, and on Sundays religious-minded fans could even follow them to church (attended by white and red man alike)—the beginnings of what is still, today, in frontier tourist towns that thrive on myth and reenactments, an attraction known as "cowboy church." The visits were an anointing of sorts, and young men wanted to join the "show folk" who were disparaged in temperance-minded quarters and run away with the circus and all of its painted, wild ponies. Women were transformed, for a moment or two; they wanted to leave town with Buffalo Bill, and we know that regardless of where they met him, some did. "Women on the plains have prayed for him," said *Outdoor Life* magazine, "have called that name as the one thing between them and suicide."

When Sitting Bull and Buffalo Bill arrived in Montreal in August 1885, they had been traveling together for several weeks. Montreal was the biggest city in Canada, a burgeoning center of trade and commerce with its own tribal rivalry—this one involving the British and the French, who had vied for control of the territory since the aboriginal Iroquois had been vanquished. Fueled by its own rivalry, it was the perfect place for the staging of a photograph that would become iconic and memorialize an alliance between the former enemies, Sitting Bull and Buffalo Bill.

Of their own stature, each man was a figure of great admiration in Canada. While feted in many American locales and later in cities around the world, Buffalo Bill was welcomed as if a native son in Montreal, given a "magnificently illuminated" commendation by the mayor and members of Parliament at a ceremony attended by thousands. "The celebrated bison hunter," reported *La Patrie* on August 17, "was congratulated for having given our people such a remarkable, true-to-life idea of life in the Far West and the expansion of civilization in those faraway lands. . . . [The mayor said that Buffalo Bill's show] was a veritable contribution to the science of natural history and its creators deserved praise for having presented it in such a suitable way from every aspect. Mr. Cody has garnered legitimate fame and merits all the honor he has received."

The newspaper also noted that one W. H. Murray commended Cody and his troupe as well. This was remarked on because "Adirondack Murray," as he was popularly known, was a kind of celebrity about town, and other towns, including on his home turf of New England, where he had built a reputation as a strong wilderness advocate, writing bestselling books that had rendered him the "father of camping." It sounds silly now, but at the time the idea of spending weeks away from work or the drudgery of home in a land where all such things were once integrated by its original inhabitants and the frontiersmen who followed had become novel. It was as if Sitting Bull and Buffalo Bill hadn't already been "camping" for years. Later, Adirondack Murray would pose with Sitting Bull and Buffalo Bill in one of the lesser-known photos taken in Montreal, a fortunate white man who got to appear with the two icons on the continent who most embodied the idea of wilderness. Shortly thereafter, he opened a restaurant in the Yukon, perhaps hanging the image in a window.

Like Buffalo Bill, Sitting Bull was regarded with much reverence in the land of the Grandmother. It was there that he had made a last stand of his own before returning home, and when he visited Montreal with the Wild West he was greeted like a returning hero. All along the streets of Wellington, McGill, St. James, Catherine, and Pointe-Saint-Charles, crowds cheered the parade. "The first performance was held in a summer downpour," wrote Walter Havighurst. "Annie Oakley did her shooting through a curtain of rain and splashed her horse through standing water. But the crowd cheered wildly and the sky brightened. Before the final rout of Indians from the settler's cabin, sun streamed down and the wet ponies shone like paint." Later the cast was taken to Lachine on the St. Lawrence, where LaSalle had dreamed of heading for China in a canoe caravan. "Sitting Bull was presented to a group of Iroquois chiefs," Havighurst noted, "and the whole party, red men and white, boarded the steamer *Filgate* for a swift and swirling trip through the rapids. Back at the dock in Montreal, they inspected the spanking new steamers *Sarnia* and *Sardinia*." Later they would go the studios of the world-famed photographer William Notman and pose for the iconic pictures.

It is not known if Major James Walsh of the North-West Mounted Police visited with Sitting Bull when he was in Canada. Sitting Bull had forged a deep alliance with Walsh and others while there, and it was north of the Medicine Line that Sitting Bull had learned to write his own signature in English, as opposed to the ledger drawings he would also make, featuring the lance and shield and buffalo on its haunches that was his stamp of identity. Later, when he would sign his autograph for fans, there was speculation in certain quarters that he was some sort of fraud, not "Sitting Bull" at all, but that was hardly the case, and to set the record straight on many things, Walsh had arranged his first interview with a white journalist, on October 17, 1877, several weeks after Sitting Bull had met with an army commission which came to Canada, seeking his return.

The reporter was Jerome Stillson of the *New York Herald*, who had also covered the commission hearings. Through his groundbreaking coverage and subsequent interview, we can gain insight into Sitting Bull's mind-set a little over a year after the Little Bighorn, and understand how far the wheel had turned by the time he joined the Wild West and posed for the Notman photographs eight years later. Stillson was clearly in awe of Sitting Bull, although the florid language of his coverage was not atypical of the era. To help Stillson try to understand Sitting Bull, Walsh intervened here and there, adding Lakota context to questions that took no account of it. Without such sensitivity, this first interview with Public Enemy Number One might have been much different.

"At 3 o'clock," Stillson's first report begins, "Sitting Bull entered, followed by Spotted Eagle and the rest," referring to his delegation. "Now for the first time was visible to white men since the beginning of the Indian Wars the most noted Indian of the period, and now was made real [James Fenimore] Cooper's often derided vision of the Indian face. . . . His features, like Goethe's made music to the senses. He wore a quiet, ironical smile. His black hair streamed down along his beardless and swarthy cheeks over clean cut ears, not burdened with ornaments." Sitting Bull sat down on a buffalo robe near a wall and lit his pipe.

"This commission that has come to interview me," he said, "can go to the devil." It was the very first comment attributed to Sitting Bull in the newspapers of the day—and bear in mind that it came one year after his tribe's great victory at the Little Bighorn.

Among the commissioners was General Alfred Terry of the U.S. Army, one of the men who had led his soldiers onto the Big-horn battlefield when it was all over, discovering the carnage, all the dead men and horses, all the men mutilated except Custer and Myles Keogh. Now, at the commission north of the Medicine Line, General Terry told Sitting Bull that the president wanted to make a lasting peace. He would like all hostilities to come to a close and that all the people of the United States shall live in harmony. "If you will return to your country," he continued, "and hereafter re-frain from acts of hostility against its government and people, a full pardon will be given to you for all acts committed in the past." Of course, you would be subject to the rules that applied to all Indians now living at the agencies, Terry explained to Sitting Bull, and you would have to give up your guns and horses.

Why should I walk a thousand miles back to the Dakota Ter-ritory on foot? Sitting Bull asked. Terry replied that the president would not consent to the Hunkpapas' return "armed, mounted, and prepared for war." Sitting Bull then launched into a reply of defiance, and his words add great resonance to the alliance that he would later make with Buffalo Bill.

. . . We have done nothing. It is all the people on your side who started . . . making trouble. We could go nowhere else so we took refuge here. It was on this side of the line that we first learned to shoot, and that's why I came back here again. I would like to know why you came here. I did not give you my country, but you followed me from place to place, and I had to come here. . . . Look at me. I have ears, I have eyes

to see with. If you think me a fool, you are a bigger fool than
I am. This house is a medicine house. You come here to tell
us lies, but we do not want to listen to them. I don't wish
such language used to me, nor any such lies told to me in my
Grandmother's house. Don't say two more words. Go back
where you came from.

The meeting disbanded, and later that evening Sitting Bull
spoke with Stillson. At first he was reluctant to do so, but Walsh
convinced him that it could help his cause. "The reporter," he said,
"was a great paper chief who talked with a million tongues to all
the people in the world. This man is a man of wonderful medicine;
he speaks and the people on this side, and across the great water,
open their ears and hear him. He tells the truth; he does not lie.
He wishes to make the world know what a great tribe is encamped
here on the land owned by the White Mother. He wants it to be
understood that her guests are mighty warriors." Sitting Bull said
he would grant the interview, but only after dark, and the only
people who could attend were Major Walsh, two interpreters, and
a stenographer.

At 8:30 p.m., several hours after the talks with the army commission had concluded, "The most mysterious Indian chieftain who
ever flourished in North America was ushered in by Major Walsh,"
wrote Stillson. "He locked the door behind him. . . . Here he stood,
his blanket rolled back, his head upreared, his right moccasin put
forward, his right hand thrown across his chest."

Stillson stood up and approached Sitting Bull, offering both
hands, and Sitting Bull grasped them. "He was about five feet ten
inches," he wrote. "He was clad in a black and white calico shirt,
black cloth leggings, and moccasins, magnificently embroidered
with beads and porcupine quills. He held in his left hand a foxskin
cap, its brush dropping to his feet. . . . His eyes gleamed."

After a moment, he said, "I am no chief."

"You are a great chief," Stillson said, "but you live behind a cloud. Your face is dark; my people do not see it. Tell me, do you hate the Americans very much?"

"I am no chief," Sitting Bull said again.

"What are you?" Stillson asked.

"A man," he replied.

Puzzled, Stillson turned to Walsh. "He means to keep you in ignorance of his secret if he can," the major said.

His position among his bands is anomalous. His own tribes, the Hunkpapa, are not all in fealty to him. Parts of nearly twenty different tribes of Sioux, besides a remnant of the Hunkpapa, abide with him. So far as I have learned, he rules over these fragments of tribes, which compose his camp of 2,500, including between 800 and 900 warriors, by sheer compelling force of intellect and will. . . . He is supposed to have guided the fortunes of several battles, including the fight in which Custer fell. That supposition, as you will presently find, is partially erroneous. His word was always potent in the camp or in the field, but he has usually left to the war chiefs the duties appertaining to engagements. When the crisis came, he gave his opinion, which was accepted as law.

"Is Sitting Bull a medicine man?" the reporter then asked. "Don't for the world," Walsh said, "intimate to him that you have derived the idea from me, or from anyone, that he is a mere medicine man. He would deem that to be a profound insult. In point of fact he is a medicine man, but a far greater, more influential medicine man than any I have ever known. He speaks. They listen and they obey. Now let us hear what his explanation will be."

"You say you are no chief?" Stillson then said to Sitting Bull.

"No!" he said.

"Are you a head soldier?" the reporter asked.

"I am nothing," Sitting Bull said. "Neither a chief nor a soldier."

"What? Nothing?"

"Nothing."

It was an answer that was coy and truthful. A term or phrase could not begin to explain that he was part of a world where all were related, the two-leggeds, the four-leggeds, rocks, trees, the creatures of the wing . . . yes, there were many who followed him, and yes, there were many who did not, but to a man who was seeking a name for all of this, such a thing could not be conveyed.

Stillson then asked why the great chiefs who were in Canada with him looked up to him. "Oh," Sitting Bull said, smiling proudly, "I used to be a kind of a chief. But the Americans made me go away from my father's hunting ground."

"You do not love the Americans?" Stillson asked. "I saw that all the warriors around you clapped their hands and cried out when you spoke. . . . If you are not a great chief, why do these men think so much of you?"

"Your people look up to men because they are rich," Sitting Bull said. "Because they have much land, many lodges, many women?" The reporter said that was so. "Well," Sitting Bull continued, "I suppose my people look up to me because I am poor. That is the difference." This sort of thing, a voluntary commitment to poverty, was a point of pride in the Lakota community.

"What is your feeling toward the Americans now?" Stillson asked. Sitting Bull touched his hip where his knife was, an interesting bit of body language, perhaps a tell of sorts. "Listen," he said, and then put his right hand on Stillson's knee. "I told [General Terry and his men] what my notions were—that I did not want to go back there," and he reiterated that he had no intention of relinquishing his guns or horses. "Don't you see that you will probably have the same difficulty in Canada that you have had in the United States," Stillson wondered. "The White Mother does not lie," replied Sitting Bull. And then the reporter asked about the "great lies" that are told about Sitting Bull. "White men say that you lived among them when you were young; that you went to school; that you learned to write and read from books; that you speak English; that you know how to talk French?"

"I have heard some of these stories," Sitting Bull said. "They are all strange lies. What I am I am . . . I am a man. I see. I know. I began to see when I was not yet born," he explained, and it was a story his brothers and sisters knew well. "When I was not in my mother's arms," he continued, "but inside of my mother's belly. It was there that I began to study about my people." Stillson then touched Sitting Bull on the arm, but Walsh jumped in. "Do not interrupt him," he said. "He is beginning to talk about his medicine." Walsh's statement was correct, and it must have offered a kind of reassurance, much needed quite possibly in this, his first interview with a representative of the other side, that Walsh himself was a true friend; here was a *wasichu* who knew him so well that he could almost finish his sentences.

And it must have been further assurance that the land of the Grandmother was, for the moment, his home. And so Sitting Bull continued. "I was still in my mother's insides when I began to study about my people," he said. "God gave me the power to see out of the womb. I studied there, in the womb, about many things. I studied about the smallpox, that was killing my people—the great sickness that was killing the women and children. I was so interested that I turned over on my side. The God Almighty must have told me at that time that I would be the man to be the judge of all the other Indians—a big man, to decide for them in all their ways." It was a statement that revealed much about Sitting Bull's path and fate and burden, and while it may not have resonated that way for Stillson, who may have thought it to be aggrandizing, though he did not say so, he pressed him on the matter. "And you have since decided for them?" he asked. "I speak," Sitting Bull said. "It is enough."

It was soon time to ask Sitting Bull about "the most disastrous, most mysterious Indian battle of the century—Custer's encounter with the Sioux on the Bighorn—the Thermopylae of the Plains," Stillson wrote. He showed Sitting Bull a map of the battlefield and Indian encampments (including his own, which Sitting Bull confirmed) and troop movements, and Sitting Bull also confirmed the point of Reno's attack and the hilltop rise where Custer and his men made their last stand. It quickly became apparent that this conversation was the end point of the interview, as Sitting Bull got up to leave.

"Do you have the stomach for any more battles with the Americans?" Stillson asked. Sitting Bull said that he did not want any fight. "Not now?" Stillson continued. Sitting Bull then "laughed quite heartily," Stillson reported, and then said, "No, not this winter."

"Are your young braves willing to fight?" the reporter asked.

"You will see," Sitting Bull said.

"When?" was Stillson's reply. "I cannot say" was Sitting Bull's. And then came another request. "I have not seen your people," Stillson said. "Would I be welcome at your camp?"

Sitting Bull stared at the ceiling for a few moments. "I will not be pleased," he said. "The young men would not be pleased. You came with this party [the Terry delegation] and you can go back with them. I have said enough."

And then Sitting Bull wrapped himself with his blanket, shook hands with Stillson, and headed for the door. There, he stopped, put on his cap, and said "adieu" to the reporter. His first newspaper interview was done.

Five years later, perhaps suspecting the trouble that lay ahead, Walsh was reluctant to see his friend depart. Yet he was in a difficult spot. Sitting Bull's Canadian exile had not been without problems. Primarily, there was an overriding one: his band was going hungry. Buffalo herds were depleted up and down the Great Plains, and the Lakota were competing for sustenance with the indigenous tribes of Canada. Sometimes they crossed back into the United States when they were hunting, and then they would cross back to Canada. The land of the Grandmother may have provided sanctuary while Sitting Bull and his followers were on the run, but it was now withholding support, acquiescing to its powerful neighbor below the Medicine Line, who wanted Sitting Bull to return. Quite simply, it was time for the Hunkpapas to go home.

Now, for a time, four months to be precise, through his association with Cody, he was free of political concerns. In the Wild West, Sitting Bull lived a version of the life he once had on the Plains. He was indeed a king, as newspapers described him, and as Cody well knew. Yet he was not always greeted with the awe and reverence with which kings are usually met. While often cheered by throngs, especially in Canada, below the Medicine Line there was also hissing and booing as he entered the arena atop a gray horse at the beginning of the gaily bedecked procession.

This was ritualized, a response to the heroes-and-villains nature of the Wild West, though in some cases brutal and not devoid of anti-Indian fervor. Yet it was a far cry from the previous year in St. Paul, which took Sitting Bull and a troupe of Lakota to the Eden Musee in New York and then on to other cities, where he would have some of his first experiences as a celebrity. In St. Paul, someone fired a shot at Sitting Bull as he and the tour manager were leaving the theater. In Philadelphia, he was lured into a strange and potentially deadly public relations trap. When his party arrived at their hotel, the editor of a local paper asked for his photograph, guaranteeing prominent coverage. The tour manager provided the photo, and sure enough, the next day, a Sunday, there was Sitting Bull, splashed across the front page. But his picture was accompanied by something much darker.

He was denounced in uppercase letters followed by exclamation points, and the newspaper enumerated his "crimes." It restated the horrors of the Custer massacre, and accused him of disemboweling men, women, and children. Years of official presentations of Sitting Bull as a savage red man who was doing the devil's handiwork would not be unraveled in a single tour, and the frenzied editor went on to ask the citizens of Philadelphia to boycott "the monster" and "to assemble and hang him" as well. Shortly thereafter, the venue that was featuring his show canceled it. The Indians left town and headed for Brooklyn, but by then there was bad publicity everywhere. The show was a failure. Other newspapers closed in, railing against the government for allowing Sitting Bull to leave the reservation. In the heat of a presidential election, the Indians were ordered back to Standing Rock.

Now, while on tour with Cody, he was besieged by reporters. Yes, they wanted to discuss Custer, but perhaps when Walsh had told Sitting Bull years earlier that the man from the *New York Herald* "talked with a thousand tongues," he had conveyed that Sitting Bull's very words could reach the four directions, beyond his own people across the Plains, all the way to the Grandfather possibly, and who knows where else? Now, in the Wild West, it was time to fulfill the next part of the thing he had learned in the primordial waters of his mother's belly—that one day he would be a big man. Some said that Cody's path had been foretold too, by a gypsy. "Your child will be a boy," she told his mother. "You should give him the world. He will be famous. His name will be known to all—young and old, rich and poor. People will love and praise him. He may even be president of the United States."

Behind the popularity of the Wild West was a net that had been cast wide and far, fueled by a machinery of fame and advertising that was finely tuned and carefully considered. The results were weighed and adjusted, and each tour became a kind of frontier focus group for the next one. Weeks in advance of an engagement, laborers would converge on a location, plastering it with Wild West posters, or what was referred to as "paper"—lots of it. In some years, according to Paul Reddin in *Wild West Shows*, "a half million sheets went into storefronts, on buildings, on fences, on specially constructed billboards, and in any number of other conspicuous places." There were posters for every conceivable venue and space, from small window-size posters to gigantic ones that were nine feet high and nearly 150 feet long. Cody himself was closely involved with advertising, befriending the designers and producers of the posters, "and making certain that the finished product reflected his ideas," Reddin wrote. "Some conveyed a single western scene, others an act or personage from the show, and others a variety of western images and acts," including, as described by a publicist at the time, "Indian Massacres, wild horse bucking, dare-devil riding, and hair-raising Indian dances."

Much of the time, there was but one solitary figure on the posters, and it was Cody himself. Buffalo Bill was the Wild West, and with every poster plastered to every wall or doorway, the idea was restated, and even this routine affixing of announcements became an event. Children would converge at the site, seemingly out of nowhere, and the men who pasted the paper to walls would spin tales of adventure on the road. Sometimes, the kids would wangle a free pass for the show in exchange for pitching in and tacking up posters. Rock stars were in town, and a pass was a big deal, not just because celebrities were involved, but because tickets were expensive. At a time when a typical working man earned between a dollar and a dollar fifty a day, and two dollars would buy a week's groceries or a pair of shoes, the cost of entry to the Wild West was two dollars for a family of six—at fifty cents per ticket for adults and twenty-five cents for children. An outing to see Cody and his cast was not unlike a trip to the baseball park today, a significant and meaningful expense that a family saved for weeks in advance.

Once a location was primed, advance men followed, and they bought ads in newspapers. The notices had evocative headlines such as "The West at Your Doors" and "Practically a Tour of the Frontier"—the latter of which might not have been so intriguing without strategic placement of the adjective "practically." In addition to the ads, there were stories cooked up by publicists and distributed via magazines called "couriers," and the stories in turn were picked up by reporters who seem to have quoted them verbatim—a forerunner of the kind of modern coverage that is so prevalent today, whereby news outlets simply restate what they hear at press conferences or from certain people, no questions asked, or repeat material from press releases without citing the source. The Cody publicity enterprise was a masterwork in promotion, one that seems to have sent forth seed pods in the methodology of how to attract attention.

But one other thing factored into the success of the show and it was nothing that could be concocted by a publicist. It was something that other enterprises of a similar nature did not have, and that was magic. Much was swirling around this epic spectacle of a vanishing America; in the dust and thundering hooves and flying manes and tails there was a portal, open as long as the show was in town, and it led right to the national dream. Some of the most powerful figures ever to take the stage represented the dream and were the dream, and when it was in your town, your front and backyard, it was an American prayer in action and resplendent, presenting the longings and the history, real and imagined, of a nation that loved freedom, made a fetish of it, while at the same time, it had to squelch and control it. In short, America was still forming, and it had formed, and here was its DNA for all to see, hear, and feel.

The reporter from the *New York Herald* may not have understood the concept of "medicine man," but it did not matter, for there was indeed a medicine man upon us and his name was Sitting Bull. He did not have the right to vote, but he could make it rain. He was not a dictator or a man who used threat of force, but when he had called for the horse tribes to assemble in the greasy grass for the battle that sealed his fame and fate, scores of his kin and kind trekked in from the four directions, simply because the town criers had spread the word and it came from him. Those who attended the Wild West would not have had knowledge of such matters, but such were the elements of his force field, and they were in play.

Buffalo Bill, through the magnetic strength of his own personality as well as how people perceived him, could make a lot of things happen too; his show was a strange and dazzling and idiosyncratic conjure, a serious act of alchemy that spun off in a thousand trajectories, presenting screaming wildmen with tomahawks in face paint and glorious regalia and fearless cowboys who mounted crazed mustangs and stayed there until they got calm, and the whole parade fell in line behind Cody himself, a national true north regardless of location and what he was actually doing at any given time.

And of course there was Annie Oakley, Little Miss Sure Shot herself, a feminine killer, a dead-eye who skipped onto the field in a dress, blowing kisses, demurely. She wiped out no animals in the Wild West, though people knew she could, and had, and how they loved to see her send those bullets whizzing right past her dog's head and into a bull's-eye, and later, when she took a break from Cody's show and joined up with another circus, she would shoot live birds released from a trap, so many that she was told to stop, and at some point she rejoined the Wild West, and of one thing, her fans were convinced: here was a woman who liked to shoot and she was as serious as any frontier bad man.

Let us also tip our hat to another star of the show, sometimes *the* star, pictured front and center on program covers, stampeding, emblazoned with Cody's image, and listed as an official cast member along with the cowboys and Indians in the text of the programs, and given its historical due.

"The buffalo is the true bison of the ancients," its official biography said. "It is distinguished by an elevated stature, measuring six to seven feet at the shoulders, and ten to twelve feet from nose to tail. Many there are under the impression that the buffalo was never an inhabitant of any country save ours. Their bones have been discovered in the superficial strata of temperate Europe; they were common in Germany in the eighth century. Primitive man in America found this animal his principal means of subsistence, while to pioneers, hunters, emigrants, settlers, and railroad builders this fast-disappearing monarch of the plains was invaluable." The portrait concluded with a characteristically self-congratulatory but truthful statement: "Messrs. Cody & Co. have a herd of healthy specimens of this hardy bovine in connection with their instructive exhibition, 'The Wild West.'"

In 1892, after a performance in the Wild West during its London tour, a cast member named Long Wolf came down with pneumonia. Not wanting to be buried at sea, he asked his wife to leave him behind. Buffalo Bill helped them locate a plot and then the show left port. Shortly thereafter, he died, and decades later, in the twentieth century, a woman in Worcestershire read a story in an old book about his life, death, and burial "in a lone corner of a crowded London cemetery, just at the end of a smoke-stained, Greco-Roman colonnade, under a poplar tree." She visited local cemeteries and looked for a wolf emblazoned on an old tombstone. After finding it, she tracked down Long Wolf's descendants in South Dakota. They traveled to London to bring him home. When his body was exhumed, the bones of a young girl were also found. These belonged to Star, long rumored to have been buried in England.

The three Lakota who had come to claim Long Wolf carried off his remains in a ceremonial procession, bedecked with feather headdresses and followed by a pair of black horses pulling a casket in a wagon draped with American and Lakota flags. A few weeks later, he was reburied at Wolf Creek, east of Pine Ridge, and a herd of buffalo appeared on a bluff overlooking the ritual. They had been repatriated sometime earlier. In 1999, something else from the Wild West was returned. This was a ghost shirt, the item of apparel said to repel bullets from the white man. It had been taken from a warrior at Wounded Knee, carried to Glasgow in 1891, and sold by a man who said he was in charge of relics from the Wild West, along with a baby carrier and a pair of boy's moccasins. The shirt was bloodstained and had bullet holes. A Cherokee Indian visiting Scotland saw the shirt in a gallery at an exhibit called "Home of the Brave." He contacted the Wounded Knee Survivors Association and negotiations for the shirt's return began. It was finally returned to the Lakota at a ceremony at the massacre site on a summer afternoon. Once again, some buffalo appeared on a hill and witnessed the occasion, and yet one more time, they would appear on another rise several years later and watch the return of wild horses. "I have been told," said Crow chief Plenty Coups in 1930, shortly after bounty hunters had gunned down hundreds of ponies, "that the white man, who is almost a god and yet a great fool, does not believe that the horse has a spirit. This cannot be true." In the Wild West, it was not true, and the triumvirate was complete: man, horse, and buffalo, together again in the Dreamtime.

Yet at its core, the show was an equestrian extravaganza. This was the original concept, and as Cody's partner, Arizona John, made a point of telling reporters in Chicago shortly before Sitting Bull joined, the show's full name, Buffalo Bill's Wild West, was copyrighted, lest anyone try to use it without permission. But more importantly, for anyone who did reprint the name for commercial use, it must be followed by its official description, which was this: "The Wild West, or Life Among the Red Men and the Road Agents of the Plains and Prairies. An Equine Dramatic Exposition on grass or under canvas of the Advantages of Frontiersmen and Cowboys." Often the show's equine stars received more visitors than Cody or Sitting Bull, with fans rushing "backstage" to their corrals; in 1886, when the Wild West was presented to Queen Victoria, the *English Metropolitan* welcomed the frontier horses with breathless prose in an article entitled "Mustangs, Horses, Mules, Some 250 Animals, 166 Horses." "These are not remarkable for height or the ordinary points of thoroughbreds, but they possess staying powers that an English racer does not," the paper said. "They are suitable for riding unshod over rough country for many miles together. . . . Bronco horses, mustangs, or buck jumpers are to be seen here—animals that have never been, and never can be tamed; whose kick is death, and upon whose back no man could remain for a moment."

In every city and town all of these elements converged to make the Wild West a thing to behold. It began with a grand procession, people flanking it on either side and swarming in between the mounted cowboys and Indians, the prancing horses, the hangers-on as it paraded down the main avenue, and there came Sitting Bull and Buffalo Bill and Annie and all the rest. The show consisted of a series of scenes suggesting or depicting frontier signs of the cross: Sitting Bull making a circuit of the arena, in his war bonnet of eagle feathers, sometimes in a buggy, other times warrior-style on a war pony, looking neither right nor left, not waving or expressing any gestures, issuing no battle cries or utterances, still and quiet, responding only to the announcer Frank Richmond telling the crowd, "Here he comes! The Napoleon of the Plains! Chief Sitting Bull, ladies and gentlemen!" and he did what he had promised, making this one appearance, around the track, and then exiting without gesture or farewell—a rare moment of exposure that only added to his mystery and evoked no further verbal assaults, should they be in the works; and then there came Cody reenacting the scalping of Yellow Hand with an Indian playing him, the run-away Deadwood stage with the Grand Duke in it, a buffalo stampede and hunt or "surround," which demonstrated how Indians would circle and circle the animal until there was nowhere for it to go and then they would close in as it became tired and frightened, or if they were in the wilderness, run the herd off a cliff on sites that were known as "jumps," and which to this day still bear the markings.

A highlight of the show was "the girl of the Western plains," as announcer Frank Richmond called out, "and her incredible feats with pistol, rifle, and shotgun." Annie Oakley would run to a gun table while glass balls sailed upward, and then, hoisting a rifle, she would swing it to her shoulder and squeeze the trigger. The balls shattered in the air and the crowd made the right noises and then in galloped a cowboy, wielding targets from a leather thong, and Annie would mount a buckskin, grab a pistol from the ground, and quickly shatter the target. "And now," the announcer said, "with the target behind her, seeing its reflection in the blade of a hunting knife, Miss Oakley will pierce a playing card held in the attendant's hand." She fired the rifle and the card fluttered to the ground.

The grand finale of each show was the "Attack on the Settler's Cabin," a scene that was an explosive stand-in for the burgeoning new America. A settler had just returned from hunting, and his wife stepped out the door to welcome him home. There was a shout in the near-distance, and then the settler would turn to confront an Indian racing toward the house in feathers and war paint.

The hunter "raised his rifle," wrote Louis Warren in *Buffalo Bill's America*, "and fired," watching as the intruder fell into the dust. Then there was "an outburst of cries and screams and suddenly the lonesome cabin became the center of a swirling mass of mounted Indian warriors, guns blazing. The settler and his wife retreated through the door, their children loading and firing guns through the windows." But there were too many Indians, and they were getting closer to the cabin. "Their war cries were terrifying, the roar of guns and smoke filled the air." In a moment, their home would be destroyed.

Suddenly there was another yell and there came Buffalo Bill and a posse of whooping, shooting cowboys, converging with their guns. "A fierce fight ensued," Warren wrote. "Indians and cowboys dropped from saddles, their bodies thudding into the dust. Finally, the last of the Indians rode out of sight. As the settler family emerged from the cabin to thank the scout and his cowboy militia, another sound rolled over the home." It was almost literally a roar, a voracious cacophony coming from the audience, everyone now standing, clapping wildly, and stamping their feet. Cody had saved the day and all was well on the frontier; the moment of not backing down and standing your ground and defiance entered into, the birthplace and address of America.

Fittingly, it was in Boston that the Wild West presented one of its most memorable shows. The July engagement of 1885 occurred just a few weeks after the nation celebrated its 109th birthday, no doubt a singular event in the city that was the cradle of the American Revolution. The fever of that celebration was quite possibly heightened by advance knowledge that Cody was coming, and stirred again by the actual arrival of the Wild West. The show's publicists concocted a publicity bonanza that was one for the annals.

On July 20, 1885, the *Boston Post* previewed the appearance in

a special report, announcing that "arrangements [have] been made
to illuminate the grounds by electric lights"—a feature that was
indeed unusual for that era, but the language about "arrangements
having been made" was kind of inspired, suggesting complicated,
behind-the-scenes maneuvering that rendered the makings of the
show almost as big as the show itself. The paper also noted that
"excellent music will be furnished by the famous Wild West cowboy band, who perform some very pretty solos." The unnamed reporter may or may not have known for himself that the music was
excellent, but of course who doesn't love a cowboy band, especially
one that is highly recommended?

One week later, on July 27, the Wild West opened, and the
Post continued its glowing notices, reporting that ["Mr. Cody's]
ponies, horses, jackasses and elk are finely trained. The marvelous
feats performed by this company have surprised those who have
considered themselves adepts; and all who have witnessed their
performances have been delighted."

Sometime during the week, Sitting Bull had an unexpected
reunion with a veteran of the Little Bighorn. This was Sergeant
John Ryan, who had served under General Reno, and lived in
nearby Newton. He was introduced to Sitting Bull, according to a
report in the *Arkansas City Republican* on August 15, 1885, probably picking up syndicated accounts from papers in Boston. At first,
Sitting Bull was reluctant to converse. But Ryan produced a blood-
spattered cavalry guidon and asked if Sitting Bull had ever seen a
flag like it. "Yes," the chief said, his interest now piqued. "When?"
Ryan asked. "When we had the fight and killed Custer's men," said
Sitting Bull through the interpreter, "we got a number of them.
Where did you get it?"

Ryan explained that he had seen an Indian riding up and down
in front of cavalry lines during the last battle on the second day,
and he was carrying this flag. Along with another soldier, they

repeatedly fired at him with their long range rifles, finally dropping him off his horse. "When night came," Ryan said, "I went out and brought the flag in."

But what made the Boston engagement truly memorable was a barbecue in which local scribes could dine with the Indians, eating grilled beef—with their hands!—just like Sitting Bull. It was an event concocted by Arizona John, not only Cody's partner but his publicist extraordinaire. He had laid the groundwork for coverage weeks in advance as the show toured, meeting privately with reporters and editors, courting them and telling them stories about the show's stars.

"A pleasant feature of the afternoon was the wild west dinner served in one of the tents," said the *Post*. Reporters and other guests sat cross-legged around a tent, "sampling delicious roasts cooked to a turn on a spit over the open fire." Each man made his own utensil, whittling a fork from a stick "a la cowboy," allowing for the enjoyment of "a pleasant repast." Through his interpreter, Sitting Bull regaled visitors with campfire stories, speaking of the pleasure derived from his travels and "his intercourse with so many white men who he was constrained to believe were his friends." Use of the word "constrained" may have been a translator's call— or not; it may have had a slightly different connotation in the nineteenth century than it does today. In any case, the reporters' experience made news, as planned—and like "cowboy church," may well be the forerunner of modern-era wilderness experiences in which tourists pay well to camp with cowboys and go to their cookouts, with ranch hands singing under the stars.

Dinner with Sitting Bull was not the only orchestrated publicity event presented by the Wild West in Boston. Thousands of spectators had just seen what may have been the best performance of the week, according to the newspaper; it was just as the ad had said: "all promises fulfilled!" The production featured the trademark program content, but this time the cowboys put on a new and especially noteworthy presentation, with the famous horseman Tom Clayton leaping aboard the celebrated horse Dynamite, and Mustang Jack closing out the cowboy act with a standing jump over a horse that was sixteen hands high.

Yet there was one more surprise to be had. After the show, reporters received another invitation. They were asked to follow Buffalo Bill and his associate Nate Salsbury into "the tent of the chiefs," where they saluted Sitting Bull and his colleagues and sat cross-legged on the ground. Sitting Bull filled the peace pipe, lit it, took a few vigorous puffs to make sure that the tobacco was flowing, and stood up, passing the pipe to each reporter. Each took several puffs, pronouncing the experience "good." Yes, it was a ritualized and oft-repeated proclamation that was clearly occurring for the benefit of reporters. But unbeknownst to them, a pipe ceremony was one of the underpinnings of Lakota tradition. In the old days when such ceremonies were not hidden or outlawed, medicine men would talk to the pipe, like a relative, "encouraging it as it gave itself to us to smoke," in the words of latter-day Lakota healer Joseph Eagle Elk. They would explain that the tobacco was alive, and one must speak to its spirits. So yes, of course, there was a publicity-generating ritual under way, but it carried great import, which perhaps some of the reporters could feel (though they may have made light of it later, reporters being reporters, but no matter).

And so Sitting Bull sat down and passed the pipe to the other chiefs, and as they smoked he made an unexpected announcement. Nate Salsbury was about to become a member of his tribe, and Sitting Bull was giving him the name of "Little White Chief." What the reporters made of this, we do not know, but we can surmise that Salsbury knew the honor was coming, for it was planned and yet had its own kind of potency, reverberating somehow, in some way, at that moment and perhaps for a long time elsewhere in ways that remain unknown. Salsbury then addressed the other chiefs, "expressing his satisfaction at being adopted and pledging eternal friendship to the tribe." Sitting Bull said he'd give Salsbury a pony if he were at home, but all he could offer was the pipe—vessel of peace and other mysteries that he passed out to many during his travels across the land, quite possibly even with silent humor, for recipients often thought they were the only person who had been so honored, but Sitting Bull—as we have seen—could deliver a joke and knew otherwise.

Now, in the tent of the chiefs, there was handshaking all around, and by way of saying "congratulations" the word "How" was uttered by Indians and white men alike. Nate Salsbury was a member of the tribe, perhaps the first white man adopted by it, fulfilling his new name, or at least a part of it, the part that referred to his skin color. Later that evening, the grounds at Beacon Park were illuminated by "a large number of calcium lights," just as the ads had promised, "used in the manner that footlights are utilized in a theatre." Yes, it was show biz all right, but we can imagine that a man who had long been a kind of solo operator now had formidable allies, an extended family even!, for the Indians, as Cody would sometimes tell reporters, were men of their word, unlike white men, who signed treaties and made promises and then broke them. Quite possibly, Nate Salsbury, a cynic who put much effort into contriving things, may have found himself content, if only for a moment. As for the matter at hand, there followed a lot of publicity; coverage of the barbecue and adoption of Nate Salsbury was reprinted in many newspapers, and reporters in other venues clamored for an audience with Sitting Bull. And what red-blooded American didn't want to eat grilled meat with his hands?

Short of a meal, a moment or two with Sitting Bull would suffice. On September 12, 1885, the Wild West played in Grand Rapids, Michigan, and there followed an article entitled "Sitting Bull," with the subtitle "A Half Hour in the Tent of the Great Sioux Chief—He Talks About the Campaign Against His People." Once again, the show's publicists had escorted a number of reporters into Sitting Bull's tipi, where he was lounging with friends. According to the *Grand Rapids Leader*, "an intelligent half-breed" was acting as interpreter. "Sago, tatanka—I—yotanda, ne kata-kush—stom a-che a-che Sioux wee-chasta ya tape," a reporter said, launching the conversation. That meant: "Good day, Sitting Bull, I welcome the celebrated chieftain of the Sioux." It was a curious greeting, coming from a man who was a guest in another man's tent, but perhaps it was a welcome to his city. "Sago! How! Niche ha po taw!" came the reply, which translated as, "Good day. How are you? Come in."

And in they filed, as Sitting Bull appeared to register happiness at hearing words in his native language, "his countenance lighting up with a smile of welcome and gratification." From then on, the reporter pored over every detail of his clothing and face; he was, after all, a man who had seemingly just stepped off the warpath.

As the reporter regarded him closely, Sitting Bull may have wondered if the questions about Custer were coming, behind the friendly gesture of speaking in his native tongue, for that was one thing that most representatives of *wasichu* publications wanted to know. How strange it must have been to oversee a great victory, then witness the conquest of his people and be honored as one of the last—and feared for a killing he did not commit. Yet here he was, one more time, a celebrated and vanquished figure about to be asked for his account of the battle that wiped out a national hero and rendered him a fugitive, a prisoner, and finally, a performer. Now part of the engine of fame, he rode the wave.

You could see his smile through the thick red ocher covering his features, the *Leader* recounted, and, after the initial exchange of greetings, the reporters reclined on Indian blankets next to him, while he sat on a reclining camp chair. His feet were curled under it, "encased in beaded moccasins of a pretty design." He wore dark wool trousers, a vest with a fancy pattern, a "boiled" shirt with flamboyant sleeve buttons at the wristbands, and around his neck there was a tawny silk scarf, pinned with a gold pin that "could have been improved with a little soap and water." On the middle finger of his right hand, he wore a "large, cheap prize package cameo ring" and around his neck, a brass chain with a crucifix—some said that this was a gift from the black robe he met after his return to the United States, Father de Smet; others with darker motives said it had come into his hands in a nefarious fashion. His features were massive, the reporter said, and his skin was "of a copper hue." The reporter noted his braided hair, as had others who met him on the road. There were accoutrements such as his bonnet of eagle feathers and owl plumes, hanging above Sitting Bull's head; a medicine bag—always of interest to scribes—"said to be the most complete thing of the kind in existence," and several bows and arrows. Sitting Bull's "first lieutenant and man Friday," Crow Eagle, reclined next to him on a blanket. His "countenance indicated more of the savage and less intelligence than the Bull, and it was also hidden by a coat of red paint." He smoked a cigarette with apparent dedication. A third Indian sat nearby, and he expressed thanks when a reporter passed him a cigarette case with "several rolls." For at least half an hour, the inquisitors spoke via the translator with Sitting Bull alone, and he responded in "a deep, down-cellar, cyclone pit voice, guttural in the extreme, and freely interspersed with significant gestures." At one point, an elderly woman among the visitors pushed forward, and "gazed long and earnestly at the Indian king, with an expression as if she would like to ask after the condition of his immortal soul."

After a while, Sitting Bull finished his cigarette and began smoking a cigar. But he was not satisfied. Crow Eagle then reached for the pipe and filled it with a "strong, peculiar-smelling tobacco."

He lit it and took a couple of whiffs, passed it to Sitting Bull, who did the same. The pipe made the rounds. Soon it was time for the official interview to begin; pleasantries had been exchanged, and now the reporter wanted to get to know him.

The questions aren't included, but judging from Sitting Bull's answers, we can see that he presented a quick summation of his biography in response to boilerplate queries that are still an industry reporting standard. Where are you from? When did you meet Buffalo Bill? What do you think about the Wild West? Reporters may have seen bits and pieces of Sitting Bull's personal story in other newspapers, but it certainly was not widely known, and elements of it, if not the whole thing, may have seemed a kind of revelation at the time, filled with facts and milestone recitations that opened a window onto a lost way of life. "I am 50 years of age," he said, perhaps in that stilted manner because of the translation. "My father's name was Jumping Bull, and he was chief of the Sioux. When 14 years of age, I went on my first warpath against a neighboring tribe. I distinguished myself for my bravery."

All in all, the *Leader* continued, "The general expression of the face indicated good nature, latent fierceness, great firmness of character, considerable savage curiousity, much craftiness and great intelligence. He looked something like the portraits of Daniel Webster and he appeared a statesman every inch." And then, a strange blow was smuggled in, perhaps because the newspaper was in Michigan, Custer's home state. "Taken all together," the reporter said, "he was as mild mannered a man as ever cut a throat or scalped a helpless woman." The statement went well beyond inquiring about Custer, and we can wonder if Sitting Bull asked for interpreters to read him the reports that followed his interviews. Expecting little from the white man, he would not have been surprised. But the statement was so wrong that it might have taken a toll—and although public, it was delivered in the shadows.

And on the show went. En route there was another adoption ceremony; this time Sitting Bull adopted Annie Oakley as his daughter, after having adopted her as a member of the tribe, like Salsbury, when he had first met her in St. Paul a year earlier. Annie was about the same age as his daughter, he told her, and it was his daughter who had made the moccasins that he wore on the day of the Battle of the Little Bighorn. She had died not long after the battle, he said, and then, giving her the special moccasins, he asked if Annie would take his daughter's place? What she felt at that moment we do not know, but recalling it later in her autobiography, she wrote that Sitting Bull had fought justly at the Bighorn, "for his people had been driven from their God-given inheritance and were living upon broken promises." After the ceremony, she began referring to Sitting Bull as her "adopted father." He often visited her in her tent, where before and after shows he watched as she would sit and crochet and sew as she made her own costumes—and was said to be quite fastidious in this enterprise. Often, she would read from the Bible; such readings Sitting Bull would have heard before from missionaries, and there would be more coming his way. Both figures took much comfort in the company of the other, and later Annie would bear witness for her friend, speaking of his generosity toward the poor young wastrels he would encounter on the road, always giving away coins and always saddened that America was not taking care of its own. In doing so, she presented a side of Sitting Bull that might have been lost to the ages, for his willingness to help these orphans of the street was not much remarked on or recorded by others.

When the tour got to Washington, D.C., Sitting Bull's long-held wish to meet the Grandfather was close to realization. On June 24, newspapers reported that he met with Interior Department secretary Lucius Lamar, who formally issued a decree stating that Sitting Bull and those accompanying him could continue to travel across the country with Buffalo Bill, as seeing the country and its vast population and resources would benefit the Indians—a strange statement that overlooked the resources of which Sitting Bull was already quite familiar, in particular the "yellow metal" or gold, that peeked out of the sacred lands in the Great Plains, irresistibly calling the *wasichu* to come and get it. Now a statesman in a new phase of his life, Sitting Bull expressed gratification for the kindness that white people had extended to him on tour, and he also said that the more he could see of their peaceful intentions, the better. Later, Buffalo Bill, Sitting Bull, and his delegation headed to the War Department for a meeting with General Sherman and Adjutant General Richard C. Drum. The Indians were in full costume, their faces embellished with red and yellow, and eagle feathers in their hair. In General Sherman's office, they engaged in little conversation, but all, except Sitting Bull, seemed to be quite taken with the paintings of army and Indian life on the walls. In particular, there was a buffalo scene that captured their attention; in the words of the *Evening Star*, "it caused them much pleasure." Soon they filed out, past corridors lined with awestruck clerks, after which they checked in with General Drum for a brief introduction. A little while later, they headed to the State Department, where they were shown a copy of the original Declaration of Independence. It would not be until 1924 that Indians became citizens of the United States, protected under all of the rights delineated in the Constitution.

As for Sitting Bull's meeting with President Grover Cleveland, a desired goal of this trip, the record varies. Some second- and third-hand accounts say that the men met and shook hands, and that warrior to warrior, the event indicated to Sitting Bull that he had the respect of the head chief of America. But in newspaper coverage of the Washington meetings, there is no mention of any contact with the president, although several years later, in 1888, Sitting Bull and Gall and John Grass traveled to the capital and did in fact meet with President Cleveland. They were there to discuss the fate of the Standing Rock Agency, where they lived. Once again, the government wanted to carve up the land. Sitting Bull opposed the plan, but lost that battle.

When the Wild West arrived in Philadelphia during the summer of '85, the question of Indian rights became front and center, resulting in a strange confrontation with Sitting Bull and several representatives of the Indian Rights Association (IRA), who had arranged for a visit. Such matters were very much a topic of discussion in Philadelphia; the group had formed there in 1882, joining other organizations that had come on the scene earlier in New England and Brooklyn. The IRA's mandate was to make sure that treaties were enforced—seemingly, an honorable task. Yet it wanted to advance assimilation in such a way that obliterated native culture. According to its credo, "farming is superior to hunting; alcohol is evil; idleness is the ultimate evil, and Christianity is the cure." Upon completion of this work, the group's founder wrote, "the Indian will cease to exist as a man, apart from other men . . . his empty pride of separate nationalism will have been destroyed." In its place, greater blessings will arrive, primarily "an honorable absorption into the common life of the people of the United States."

Whether Sitting Bull knew of this mandate is of no consequence, for it would soon become very clear. At their meeting with him, the members of the IRA launched into a discussion of the Little Bighorn. "Ask Sitting Bull if he ever had any regret for his share in the Custer massacre," they said to the interpreter. For the sin of murdering the American hero, he must "flee from the wrath to come." Sitting Bull jumped to his feet, according to Nate Salsbury, who witnessed the bizarre encounter. He then thrust his fingers into a questioner's face. "Tell this fool that I did not murder Custer," he shouted. "It was a fight in open day. He would have killed me if he could. I

William F. Cody, Buffalo Bill, about twenty-nine.

First Scalp for Custer, illustration depicting Cody brandishing the scalp of Yellow Hand, which he took following the Battle of the Little Bighorn.

An Old-Time Buffalo Hunt, painting by Charles M. Russell, 1898.

An 1895 poster for Buffalo Bill's Wild West and Congress of Rough Riders of the World performing in an arena featuring electric lights.

Annie Oakley, c. 1899.

Sitting Bull c. 1882. His signature was apparently added later for this souvenir card.

Autographed portrait of Sitting Bull with peace pipe, circa 1884.

The Paiute prophet Wovoka, sometime after the Ghost Dance era and Wounded Knee.

The Ghost Dance by the Ogallala [sic] *Sioux at Pine Ridge Agency*,
drawn on the spot by Frederic Remington, published in *Harper's Weekly*,
December 6, 1890, nine days before Sitting Bull was killed.

Fort Yates photographer George W. Scott staged a reenactment of Sitting
Bull's arrest and then memorialized it for the record. Shortly after
Sitting Bull's murder, the cabin was dismantled and shipped to Chicago,
where it was rebuilt and displayed at the Columbian Exposition in 1893.

11

95 | The Detroit Free Press | EXTRA

DETROIT, MONDAY, DECEMBER 15, 1890

CHIEF SITTING BULL KILLED

Chief Who Lead Sioux In Battle of the Little Big Horn Is Shot By Indian Police When His Warriors Try to Stop His Arrest At His Village On Grand River

Chief Sitting Bull was shot to death today after his warriors tried to prevent his arrest by Indian Police. Eight Indians, including Sitting Bull's son, Crowfoot, were also killed, as were six of the police. After the battle of the Little Big Horn, Sitting Bull escaped to Canada, but returned to the United States after being promised a pardon. He then appeared in Buffalo Bill's Wild West Show, but lately he has been urging the Sioux not to sell their lands.

Since Sitting Bull's return to the U. S. the strange religious craze of the Ghost Dance has spread among the Indians, who believe that a Messiah is coming to free them from the oppression of the white man.

Chief Sitting Bull

CT.C.G.   PTD. IN U.S.A.

See Scoop No. 96 — GERONIMO SURRENDERS TO GEN. MILES

The death of Sitting Bull received front page coverage in newspapers around the country.

Sitting Bull's son Crow Foot. He was killed with Sitting Bull in 1890. Photograph taken by D.F. Barry, date unknown.

Vice President Charles Curtis receives a peace pipe from Chief Red Tomahawk, slayer of Sitting Bull, at the United States Capitol on June 29, 1921. Curtis was part Kaw Indian—the first Native American to hold the office of Vice President.

Big Foot, Minneconjou chief, after the massacre at Wounded Knee, where he was found frozen in the snow.

Indian chiefs and U.S. officials, Pine Ridge, January 16, 1891, shortly after Wounded Knee. The group includes Cody (sixth from left, back row) and Kicking Bear, an early visitor to Wovoka, who returned to the Lakota with information about the Ghost Dance.

Buffalo Bill and his horse taking a bow after a 1915 performance with the Sells-Floto Circus. The horse could have been Isham, saved for Cody by his friends just before it was auctioned off to pay bills, or the horse that he had given to Sitting Bull and then reacquired, variously described as white or gray.

have answered to my people for the dead on my side. Let Custer's friends answer to his people for the dead on his side." Recalling the incident years later, Salsbury referred to the rights-minded men as "worthy cranks."

What reserves did Sitting Bull draw on at such a time? In today's parlance, he was not the kind of guy who would walk away from a bar fight. We know from the record that he was close to having one with the God-fearing men who told him that Custer's last stand would be avenged. Yet brawling while on tour was obviously precluded; he was traveling with Cody for other reasons, after all, and an altercation might have sent him back to Standing Rock. Perhaps it was his animal allies who came to him in these private moments, as they had at other times in his life. They were right there in the flesh too, in the stables and corrals that were part of the Wild West, and perhaps he drew on the power of his four-legged brothers and sisters who had always advised him. Perhaps he drew on all of this medicine and more; we can imagine that he recalled a song from his youth, a song of the wolf, who had come to him for aid, and in this song he became its vector. As he sang its song, the wolf made a promise in return, and through Sitting Bull forever after ran a current of this encounter:

Whatever I want, I always get it.
Your name will be big, as mine is big. Hau! Hau!

The song echoed what he had heard in his mother's womb—that he was destined for greatness—and such things were necessary for a man who was cast in a role that was honorable and fraught, and so, as visions and visitations had foretold, he remained on this path, and on tour he was soon back in Canada, "the medicine house," as he had told army commissioners, on safer ground where he would be treated in a fitting manner.

In Toronto, and later elsewhere, Cody spoke on behalf of the Indians during an interview with the *Globe* titled "The Bill and Bull Show" following the Wild West performances on August 23, 1885. "I never shot an Indian but I regretted it afterwards," he said. "In nine cases out of ten, when there is trouble between white men and Indians it will be found that the white man is responsible for the dispute through breaking faith with them. When an Indian gives you his word that he will do anything he is sure to keep that word, but it is different with white people. The white men were responsible for the Sitting Bull war, which was really caused by miners invading the Sioux reservation [in the Black Hills] in search of gold."

In the same interview, Sitting Bull spoke fondly of his old friend Major Walsh, and then mentioned that on the reservation at Standing Rock his family of sixteen received rations once a week but they were usually gone in two days. A U.S. government agent who was traveling with the cast quickly intervened. This was only because Bull "invariably fed all the hungry members of his tribe," he said, "who swarmed into his house whenever he had rations."

"I'm too old to adopt the ways of the white man," Sitting Bull responded, and added that his children might be taught economy and frugality but, as long as he had anything to eat he would live as he always lived, and feed anybody and everybody who came to his door hungry whether they were white men or Indians.

The interview was an unrehearsed song-and-dance in the best of ways, pure of heart and intent, a dramatic routine in which two superstars exchanged opinions and views of the other by way of a reporter—and thus each learned things that they may have been unable to say without an intermediary, or perhaps they did, in their own way, in private and therefore known only to themselves. But through this exchange, a portrait of the two men emerges, perhaps the portrait behind the photograph soon to be taken; we see them as rivals, friends, and members of different tribes. And the more they talk, the more it becomes clear that their paths were indeed foretold.

In Montreal, Sitting Bull was besieged by young fans. They would hang around his tent, follow him onto the grounds, sometimes imitating his gait, described by a reporter as "bowlegged and limping," and he would buy them Cracker Jack and candy. But it was more than young fans who sought his attention backstage. By all accounts, he was sought out by admirers wherever he went. In posing for the famous series of photographs with Buffalo Bill at the Notman studios in Montreal, he must have been relatively confident that he would not have to face intrusive individuals inquiring about Custer or threatening him with damnation for his sins as he emerged from the session. But that is a low bar, as they say; in Canada, he knew he was in the Grandmother's arms, and Lakota culture, after all, was a matriarchy.

The man who would take the photograph that memorialized the alliance between Sitting Bull and Buffalo Bill is hardly recognized today—not outside of Canada, at any rate. But William Notman was the first Canadian photographer known internationally. He emigrated to Montreal from Scotland in 1856 and set up a commercial photography studio that became a roaring success. His first commission was photographing the construction of the Victoria Bridge across the St. Lawrence River, which Sitting Bull would cross as a celebrated guest during an orchestrated event when he returned to Canada with Buffalo Bill. Queen Victoria so appreciated Notman's photographs of the bridge construction and opening and other iconic Canadian scenes that she made him "photographer to the Queen." During that era, photographers such as Edward S. Curtis and D. F. Barry attained prominence for making photographic portraits of Native Americans and making sure that their images were not lost to the ages. Notman was taking pictures of everyone and everything—and earning a good living while doing so. If you were celebrating a milestone, you contracted with Notman for the portrait. If your class was graduating at Yale or Harvard, you hired Notman for the portrait (he had set up seasonal studios at various American universities). If you wanted a record of your marriage, you arranged it with Notman, and if you were the Canadian government and you wanted images of the landscape for the archives or pictures related to forestry or mining, you set it up with Notman or his surrogates.

Little is known of the preparations that were made for the visit with Notman, or, for that matter, of who exactly contacted him and what was said, and if the idea had been percolating for a while (or not). But there is intrigue surrounding the session which memorialized the two icons. Did Notman happen to be in town at the same time that the Wild West was booked for Montreal? Or was that arranged in advance? Or perhaps he had contacted Cody or his advance people with the idea of a joint portrait of Buffalo Bill and his most celebrated star; after all, Sitting Bull had been generating more coverage in Montreal than Cody and it would have been the natural thing to do for a man who made his living by making photographic portraits, sometimes of celebrated figures. Of course there had already been many photographs of Buffalo Bill, and some of Sitting Bull, but none of the pair together. The idea was sure to be a publicity bonanza, and however it was hatched, something was clearly in motion in advance of the portrait, it seems, as Sitting Bull apparently headed to Notman's studio with two sets of clothing, each of which was used in different photographs from that session. In one photograph of Sitting Bull alone, of his head and shoulders, he is in a white shirt and vest with a bandolier across his chest and two feathers in his hair. In the other, with Buffalo Bill, he is in full dress, wearing what he wore in the show, as did Cody. The fact that Sitting Bull brought two clothing changes with him would suggest that he liked the idea of the session with Notman—and maybe even was something of a dandy or a little bit vain; certainly those are not traits out of character for a man who symbolized an empire, regardless of the fact that its time had come to a close. He knew what was at stake on the day of the photo session, and Cody too was well prepared for the moment. Dressed to the nines, with his Winchester in tow, he and Sitting Bull arrived at the Notman studio on an August afternoon. They were accompanied by several other Indians. Adirondack Murray, the "father of camping," would join them.

Judging from the tones of light in the photographs, it was probably bright and sunny on the day that they were taken, according to the former curator of the Notman Museum, Stanley Triggs. The skylights in the studio faced north to get soft light. As an assistant helped set up the shot, the two men posed against a painted background, one that Notman had used in other portraits. "It looks eastern," Triggs tells me in a phone conversation, examining the photos that are rarely inquired of nowadays. Yet the background's origin is of little consequence; not much is visible, and the men are front and center in a prominent way. "Sitting Bull just stood there," Triggs recounts, recalling museum records. "He was not posing. Apparently Notman had trouble with Sitting Bull because he wanted a more pleasant look on Sitting Bull's face." Buffalo Bill of course was clearly posing, assuming a well-known attitude with ease. It would have taken about one-tenth to one-twenty-fifth of a second for the photograph—the one that has entered the annals—to be taken, and while Notman was taking it, and the other images, an assistant would have been going back and forth into the darkroom, checking on them. We can imagine Sitting Bull and Buffalo Bill holding their positions, both men frozen in the moment, neither betraying any thought or feeling (though perhaps Cody said something witty while waiting for the images to develop between takes). Notman would have shown the results to Cody and Sitting Bull, and clearly, some of them met their satisfaction. One in particular would become a hallmark of the Wild West, the image dramatically entitled "Foes in '76, Friends in '85." The slogan instantly became part of the show, with the photo made into cabinet cards and widely sold and distributed, and even after Sitting Bull left, it continued to be used as an invocation of Cody's ongoing alliance with Native Americans.

So there the two men stood, clutching a Winchester—"the gun that won the West"—and, in a lesser known role years later, caused Sarah Winchester, the wife of its progenitor, to go mad because this gun, the one that made her family rich, killed so many Indians that she wanted no part of it and gave her fortune away, and then tried to purge the famous mansion named after the gun and where she lived of its aboriginal ghosts.

It must now be noted that there was another photograph taken by William Notman, or credited to him, when the Wild West was in Montreal, one that is of lesser fame, to be sure, but nonetheless significant. I refer to a picture of a newborn buffalo calf in the corrals of the four-legged Wild West menagerie. The calf is with its mother and Cody is nearby. It's not an especially well-composed photograph, does not romanticize the animals or capture them in a transfigurative moment such as mid-stampede or while they are charging or making eye contact with the photographer. The buffalo and its mother are just there, recorded casually, seemingly as an afterthought. The rest of the herd that traveled with the Wild West is nearby, out of frame, because they were kept with their kin, along with all creatures in this spectacle. To Sitting Bull and the other Indians on tour, the birth of a buffalo while touring would have been noteworthy, though not strange; life goes on, of course, but they knew the buffalo had vanished and seeing that it was procreating even as they were in captivity would probably have registered. They may have made no public mention of it, for such a manifestation was not meant for chatter. Yet some may have acknowledged it in some way, remarking on it to cowboys in the troupe, for instance, or a cook, or maybe it was the other way around; it is Cody in the picture after all (and he may have strode into the frame because Notman was recording the image), and Cody himself may have told the Indians of the birth, and maybe he even relayed the news to Sitting Bull (though if so, that's something Cody would have mentioned in his many autobiographies). I imagine Sitting Bull getting word one way or another, for there was probably little that escaped his attention when it came to matters of tribal interest, then perhaps walking the grounds at dusk after the show, pausing at the corral fence or the gates, reminded of his Sun Dance just before Custer was felled. The ritual was now forbidden on the reservation and its underpinnings were the buffalo, and now here he was, in a show that permitted him and his kind to live the Lakota way again, and the buffalo was back, one of them was anyway, and they were prisoners together on the White Man's Road, and people paid good money to cheer and jeer them and buy their photographs. As the sun set and fires were lit in the Wild West camp and tourists who had gone backstage to mingle with Indians and even touch them were heading home, Sitting Bull might have headed back to his tipi, his choice to travel this road affirmed by the birth of the buffalo calf, a thing that was in accord with spirit, and his alliance with Cody would bode well for all people—bittersweet though it was.

In October of that year, the Wild West headed to St. Louis, where Sitting Bull would make his final appearance. Arizona John took him on a tour of the city's hotels and restaurants, and at one of them, they ran into General Carr, a famous fighter of Indians, perhaps the most famous of them all, the man who had pursued Sitting Bull and his people in the Badlands to their exhaustion and doom. Here was a figure who loved his work; once he had said that he would rather be a cavalry officer than czar of Russia. Now, the wheel had turned yet again for both men; as they made eye contact across a hotel lobby, Carr rushed through a crowd, happy to see his battlefield nemesis. Sitting Bull said nothing. It was time to go.

On October 11, reporters gathered in the rain outside Sitting Bull's tent. The final show had concluded, and the cast was packing up for the winter. Everyone wondered if Sitting Bull would return to the Wild West. And what would he tell his people of his time on the road? "The wigwam is a better place for the red man," he said at the time. "He is sick of the houses and the noises and the multitudes of men." Then he headed to Annie Oakley's tent. "She was putting away her costumes and guns," Havighurst reported. Sitting Bull had brought presents—"a quiver of finest arrows, beaded moccasins, a feathered headdress. They stood together for a moment, and then Annie followed him into the rain. Sitting Bull looked off into the western sky and spoke."

"What did he say?" Annie asked the interpreter.

"He says it will be a cold winter."

Later, they all dined in the cook tent and the band played "Auld Lang Syne." At some point Salsbury arrived, thanking the cast on behalf of himself and Cody for such a successful season, and bidding them farewell until springtime.

Before Sitting Bull headed for the Dakota Territory, Buffalo Bill took him aside. There was something he wanted to give him. It was a horse—the one that he had ridden during the four months that Sitting Bull had been in the show. For a man who had to give up his horses when he returned to the land of his birth, this was a most symbolic gesture. The tribes had been stripped of their ponies during the wars against them; there were massacres in which thousands had been gunned down in cavalry attacks. The ponies represented freedom, and on foot the tribes were at a disadvantage—at war and on the hunt, as they well knew. Without the thundering four-leggeds, they were diminished. Somewhere during the course of his time in the Wild West, Sitting Bull had given Cody a gift as well. It was a bear claw necklace, a presentation that was also of significance. It symbolized might and strength, for the bear was an ally of the greatest warriors, the first animal to be the object of shamanic adoration. There was little if any fanfare around either of these gifts, for in the end Sitting Bull and Buffalo Bill knew that they were joined in ways that could not be publicized or spoken of. They shared something that was written in their blood perhaps, in the blood of the buffalo, whose name was linked to theirs; in the Wild West, they were brothers in arms and now as the frontier was closing, had closed, they were brothers as they went their separate ways, never having disclosed, to our knowledge, resentments and points of admiration to one another, now conveying such matters to strangers. So here we find Buffalo Bill, a few months after Sitting Bull had left the Wild West, talking with a reporter in Minnesota. Sitting Bull was a great general, he told the scribe. *Tatanka Iyotake* had heard such praise many times in many places, from making an entrance as a performer to meetings with army opponents. But Cody also told the reporter something he may never have heard— that no white man could convince his people to follow him as they starved, which is what Sitting Bull did for months, and even years, until he and his people could no longer bear it.

Arriving in Nebraska a few days after saying farewell to the Wild West, Sitting Bull was greeted not as a returning hero in the local paper or even just a celebrity, for all of his travails and triumphs. In fact, it was as if the reporter had not only never been to a performance of the show, but had no awareness of the chief's stature elsewhere in the country, and around the world. Or perhaps he knew it well, and was overcome with jealousy and resentment. "Sitting Bull and His Band of Dusky Stars Return from a Summer's Engagement," announced the *Bismarck Tribune* on October 16, 1885. "Sitting Bull and his band of dingy dudes who have been swelling among the giddygawks of the orient during the summer months in connection with Buffalo Bill's Wild West monstrosity, returned to the city yesterday and will leave this morning for their home at the Standing Rock agency," the newspaper said in on page three. "Sitting Bull, the chief of the bloodstained savages, and the greatest attraction because he has the most horrible record in the butchery of the innocent whites, never appeared more imposing and never sent the cigarette smoke swirling from his nostrils of his expansive nose with greater satisfaction." This was what Sitting Bull faced in the world of the *wasichu* when he returned to the Great Plains. It was nothing new, and home was where he had been called.

A year later, the Wild West would transform into another version of itself, the international one in which a panorama of American history was presented, scene by scene, from the primeval Ice Age when mammoth and saber-toothed tiger roamed the land, to Lewis and Clark and their meeting with Sacajawea and how she guided them into uncharted territory, where they encountered buffalo and badgers and natural wonders and came face-to-face with the red man and returned to tell others of their adventure, and finally to Custer and trappers and miners and farms and ranches and the end of the dream. The Wild West became a theatrical manifestation of all the great players in our story and how they moved and clashed across our purple mountains and redrock canyons and mesas and prairie that led to the Milky Way and its oceans of stars to which we were all tethered, whether or not we knew it, but we did know it because we all had the yearnings and the desire. And on the Cowboy Band played, soundtrack of longing and delight, music that accompanied the American conquest, which bears the national sin and triumph.

CHAPTER SEVEN

In Which There Comes a Ghost Dance, or, a Horse from Buffalo Bill Responds to the Assassination of Sitting Bull, and Other Instances of the Last Days of the Wild West

It started, you could say, in Nevada, land of the perpetual mirage, once-and-future repository of all-or-nothing bets, supplier of gold and silver and other shiny metals to anyone who comes and gets it. It was passed on from the sands to a man whose birthplace was right there on them, baked into him in such a way that it all seemed so natural, so true. He was an obscure Paiute Indian named Wovoka. He was a prophet perhaps, a shaman to those he had healed or witnessed as he opened the clouds. He was Steve Wynn before casinos, he was Jesus Christ incarnate (and he had the scars to prove it), or maybe he was just some guy in a gulch with a sign. Many followed his words—and only one would escape the hail of bullets that came after, wearing a shirt that Wovoka said would protect him.

Now Wovoka had his good points and his bad, and he was a product of his time, as we all are, and he was a product of all time, as we all are too. But something happened on New Year's Day of 1889, and it was a thing that elevated him above his brothers, a thing that reverberated across the land and across many tribes, a thing that would lead to the assassination of Sitting Bull and thereafter the death throes of the great peoples of the northern plains. You see, on that day Wovoka "died" and had a vision. In it, God came to him and decreed that he was the messenger among Indians. If the Indians danced a dance that God taught him, a miracle would soon follow. A great cloud kicked up from the stomping of the earth would cover the earth, burying the white man forever and restoring the Indian to his former glory. Dead friends and relatives would return, along with the buffalo and all the other animals that had been killed by the white man. The present would vanish and be remembered only as a passing nightmare. But before that time came, the white man would try to quell this dance. To stop the bullets that would come from his guns, those who danced the dance must wear medicine—or ghost—shirts. "Paint the shirts with thunderbirds, morning stars, and other sacred symbols," God told Wovoka, and that was what he told those who sought his counsel. "Take this message to my red-skinned children and tell it to them as I say it."

The message contained other details, instructions about how to arrange the dance, when to have it, the nature of the resurrection and how lovely it would be for those who beheld and brought it to bear. It was all so alluring and full of hope, and the details rendered it palpable, a path that could be broken down and followed step by step, and, like all codes that come our way during times of darkness, it passed through the afflicted, moving some of them to ecstasy and trance, to don the protective shirts festooned with sacred symbols and dance the dance of ghosts.

They swayed and wailed by the thousands, and authorities took notice. They were alarmed, fearing that a dance such as the one being performed could incite who knows what, and they wanted to squelch it, just as the prophecy said. Some among them knew that conditions for Wovoka's children were dire, so urgent that they did not see any other path, and even one of the conquerors, a prominent *wasichu*, spoke of these conditions for the record, a rare victor who signed off on a truth that has long since been forgotten. The statement came from General Nelson A. Miles, commander of army troops in Dakota, whose winter campaign following the Battle of the Little Bighorn had forced the surrender of many Indians, including Crazy Horse and his followers. He presented this statement to the secretary of war in 1891, shortly after the cataclysm at Wounded Knee, which occurred under his command and effectively marked the end of the Lakota era on the Great Plains. As he himself said, the statement was an agreed-upon narrative involving countless witnesses who, in the repellent language of bureaucracy, had "opportunities of knowing." What they knew was that the Indians were trapped in a cage and starving, and this is how he said it:

> The causes that led to the serious disturbance of the peace in the northwest last autumn and winter were so remarkable that an explanation of them is necessary in order to comprehend the seriousness of the situation. The Indians assuming the most threatening attitude of hostility were the Cheyennes and Sioux. Their condition may be stated as follows: For several years following their subjugation in 1877, 1878 and 1879, the most dangerous element of the Cheyennes and the Sioux were under military control. Many of them were disarmed and dismounted; their war ponies were sold and the proceeds returned to them in domestic stock, farming utensils, wagons, etc. Many of the Cheyennes, under the charge of military officers, were located on land in accordance with the laws of Congress, but after they were turned over to civil agents and the vast herds of buffalo and large game had been destroyed their supplies were insufficient, and they were forced to kill cattle belonging to white people to sustain life.

The fact that they had not received sufficient food is admitted by the agents and the officers of the government who have had opportunities of knowing. . . .

The unfortunate failure of the crops in the plains country during the years of 1889 and 1890 added to the distress and suffering of the Indians, and it was possible for them to raise but very little from the ground for self-support. . . .

The Indians could not migrate from one part of the United States to another; neither could they obtain employment as readily as white people, either upon or beyond the Indian reservations. They must remain in comparative idleness and accept the results of the drought—an insufficient supply of food. This created a feeling of discontent even among the loyal and well disposed and added to the feeling of hostility of the element opposed to every process of civilization. . . .

They signed away a valuable portion of their reservation, and it is now occupied by white people, for which they have received nothing. They understood that ample provision would be made for their support; instead, their supplies have been reduced and much of the time they have been living on half and two-thirds rations. . . . The disaffection is widespread, especially among the Sioux, while the Cheyennes have been on the verge of starvation and were forced to commit depredations to sustain life. These facts are beyond question, and the evidence is positive and sustained by thousands of witnesses.

It was amid these conditions that Wovoka's message was cast and it spread eastward through the deserts of Nevada and then to the south, up and down mountains and arroyos, perhaps carried by the winds and the sands and all manner of tributaries, picked up by the chattering creatures of the land and the air, who passed it on to the two-leggeds, who soon answered the call, traveling in caravans to seek an audience with the messiah. What was going on? they wondered. Was this fellow on the level or just another gimmick put forth by the *wasichu*? They had to find out for themselves, for they were now grasping at straws, and after all, there was always the chance that salvation was at hand. First to arrive was a delegation from the northern Arapaho and the Shoshone in nearby Wyoming. Along with a member of the Gros Ventre tribe in Montana, they visited the messiah in May of 1889, and returned to their tribes with the good news. Soon, it spread to the Cheyenne in Montana and the Sioux in the Dakotas, and in the fall of that year, Porcupine, representing the Cheyenne, and Short Bull and Kicking Bear, representing the Sioux and both having participated in the Battle of the Little Bighorn, among other clashes with the *wasichu*, traveled with other members of their tribes to Nevada for an interview with Wovoka. It was a frontier echo of the three wise men journeying through the desert for Bethlehem two thousand years earlier, searching for a man who later proclaimed himself a savior.

When it was all over, the famous cowboy Tim McCoy, star of early Hollywood westerns and his own Wild West show, traveled to the Pine Ridge Reservation in South Dakota to visit a friend. This was not unusual; many cowboy actors had made close acquaintance with Indian actors who were then appearing along with them in the new wave of movies emanating from Tinseltown and celebrating the West, a way to make a living as Buffalo Bill's shows succumbed to the movies. At his friend's log cabin, McCoy was introduced to two guests, a pair of elderly Sioux warriors. As he told his son years later in the book *Tim McCoy Remembers the West*, they were dressed in white man's clothing, along with reservation-style hats and moccasins. The men were Short Bull and Kicking Bear, and McCoy knew that they had battled Custer and met Wovoka. As a longtime student of the frontier, he wanted to hear their stories. They "drank coffee and smoked from Short Bull's pipe," he said, "a fine piece with a well-chiseled catlinite bowl and a stem richly decorated with intricately arranged orange, yellow, red, and green-dyed porcupine quills."

"You went to see the great Paiute Medicine Man," McCoy then said to Short Bull, who puffed on his pipe and caught his eye. "What did he say?"

Short Bull explained that he and his compadres had visited with the Arapahoes Yellow Calf and Sage at Wind River in Wyoming before journeying on to meet the prophet himself. They knew more than the Sioux, and filled them in about the Ghost Dance. "But we wanted to know more," Short Bull said, so they rode west.

"What happened on your journey?" McCoy asked Kicking Bear.

At first suspicious, and then encouraged by his friend whose cabin he was visiting, he began to tell his story, with some hesitation.

"The Messiah had scars on his hands and feet," Kicking Bear said, "and told us he was the same man who had come down to see the white man a long, long time ago. But the white man stuck him on a tree. Those scars were the places where they had nailed him to that tree. Wovoka said he had died and gone back to his father, but now he was here on earth to help his children, the Indians."

"And what else did he say?" McCoy asked.

"He told us to live in peace, that the white man would be gone after one more year and a spring"—April or May of 1891—and then he told the delegation of Cheyenne and Sioux inquisitors about the necessity of the dance and the shirts that were to be worn and how all would be well in the end. This was the message that Kicking Bear and Short Bull brought back to their people, and when it was all over there was a dispute as to who exactly said the shirts would repel bullets. Had Kicking Bear embellished Wovoka's instructions because he was the more bellicose? Why was Wovoka claiming that he never said anything about the shirts? The queries mattered not: there was the promise of a return to the old ways, a restoration of all that was good and pure, and when the delegation of Cheyennes and Sioux returned to Standing Rock, the dancing began.

Now it so happened that in 1889 Sitting Bull had been living at Standing Rock since his departure from the Wild West show four years earlier. Specifically, he had made his home at Grand River, apart from the main cluster of homes on the reservation. He had taken up the ways of the white man, learning to till and farm the land, living in one of the square houses—a shape that was anathema, not round like a tipi, one more representation of the *wasichu*'s disconnected approach to being on and with the land—that was required of all reservation residents, and encouraging his many children and grandchildren to become educated in the manner of the conquerors. He had expressed the desire for his descendants to flourish in the changing world when he turned himself in at Fort Buford in 1881 and throughout his four months on the road with Buffalo Bill. By this time, he was an icon, both to his people and the white man, months away from reaching the status of an immortal due to forces that were about to converge at his doorstep. Since his engagement in the Wild West, he had acquired even more fans around the country, and reporters in his region or from major New York periodicals filed dispatches about life on the reservation, chronicling his response and the response of other tribal members to the unfolding developments regarding federal policy toward the recently vanquished tribes.

Back east, there was a burgeoning Native American rights movement, some of whose members had verbally accosted him in

Philadelphia with Buffalo Bill. This campaign was organized by abolitionists from the Civil War, society matrons, and religious folk who were appalled by the treatment of Indians as treaty after treaty had been ignored and the original residents were now living in squalor on what was until very recently their own land. These concerned citizens came together in various groups, lobbying in Washington, D.C., for fair treatment of Indians, taking up collections, and spreading the word. One of the most significant groups was the National Indian Defense Association (NIDA), which published a widely read periodical called *Council Fire*. Members of the organization included not just white people, but prominent Indians such as Red Cloud, Circling Bear, Black Shield, and Thunder Hawk as well, and their voices were heard through the newsletter.

Some NIDA members dedicated their lives to trying to right the wrongs that had been mounted on the Indians, such as Alfred Meacham, a lawyer and advocate for temperance from Iowa. With a keen sense of justice, he traveled to California in the 1870s, taking up the cause of the Modoc Indians during their final days, ultimately nearly dying after being scalped in an altercation in the lava beds of Alturas—now a national park—where the Modocs were making a last stand against the army.

When Meacham was found, he thought he was dead; his wounds were dressed, and, he later wrote, the surgeons told him he might survive because he was a teetotaler. Upon his recovery, he accompanied Captain Jack, a Modoc chief involved in the fight and convicted of murder, on his final walk to the gallows. With the Great Spirit as his witness, Meacham promised the chief that "with malice toward none, and charity for all," he would continue to battle for Indians. He resumed his travels around the country, advocating for Native Americans, often asked by the federal government to act as an intermediary with the tribes. "My right to tell 'the other side,'" he said before each talk, "is certified to by Modoc bullets in my maimed hands and mutilated face." When asked how he could speak on their behalf after what had happened, he said he was not pleading for the Indian, but for humanity.

On January 1, 1878, Meacham published the first issue of *Council Fire* in Philadelphia. "After years of repeated importunities by the friends of the Indian," he wrote, "I have consented to establish a journal devoted to his interest, assured that my own race are willing to do right whenever convinced of the right, and that the other stands to bury the tomahawk and scalping knife forever, whenever justice is guaranteed to them. . . . [And so] we light THE COUNCIL FIRE:

> *May it burn until every Indian on the continent of America has been recognized as a man . . . until he has been admitted to citizenship . . . and until the last savage council fire in America shall have died out forever.*

As the last of the prominent Plains Indians to have surrendered—or returned—Sitting Bull continued to have gravitas in the outside world, even as some in his own community had grown increasingly jealous of his stature. His situation was not unlike that of certain celebrities today, around whom swirl acolytes, detractors, hangers-on, and all manner of individuals who seek a piece of the adored figure. Such a condition is appealing and a prison, as someone like Sitting Bull well knew. The product of a warrior culture in which feats of daring were enshrined, he was familiar with being admired. Yet as we know, he was a humble man who did not draw attention to himself. Quite simply, it came with the territory. In his later years, he was drawing ever inward, weary of all the battles—and still, a force to be reckoned with, even if because of what others projected his way. His position as an American superstar following his time in the Wild West only added to the growing animosity between him and Major James McLaughlin, the government agent in charge of Standing Rock.

To quell increasing tension on the reservation, McLaughlin had an interesting plan. It had to do with the actual standing rock from which the reservation took its name. The rock resembles a woman with a child on her back—and in fact, it is more than a resemblance; it appears to be a petrified woman with child. It was so lifelike and startling that even McLaughlin subscribed to the origin story of the sacred rock that the people at Fort Yates revered and had kept since ancient times. "It was the common property of the Teton Sioux," the major wrote in his memoir, *My Friend the Indian*, "but it lay for years in the section occupied by the Lower Yanktonai, and that band was the protector of the rock." McLaughlin proposed that the rock be carried from its location five miles from Fort Yates and set up on a pedestal overlooking the Missouri on a rise known as Proposal Hill. It was called thusly because it was where young men and women did their courting as they strolled above the riverbank.

A great council was called to discuss the idea, and it was accepted. After much consideration, the Indians chose Fire Cloud, a member of the Blackfeet Nation, to perform the dedication ceremony. "Fire Cloud had been a hostile," McLaughlin wrote, "and his peculiar virtues were intensely Indian and therefore not of a character to appeal to whites." But he was considered a powerful spirit worker, and the major said that he had never heard pleadings and prayer as eloquent as Fire Cloud's when the spirit so moved him. The stone was readied for dedication and Fire Cloud prepared himself as well, purifying heart and body. On the day before the ceremony, he painted a woman on the rock, following its contours, using many colors and making stripes whose meaning was known only to medicine men. That night, the rock was wrapped in a blanket, and the following day, Indians and whites who manned the fort gathered for the unveiling. "Sitting Bull was there," McLaughlin wrote, "his spirit apparently tamed, and he a peace advocate for the first time in his life." That statement was partially true; while we do not know the state of Sitting Bull's spirit at that moment, he was indeed there.

McLaughlin began the ceremony, telling everyone that it was fitting for the rock to be preserved and kept above the Missouri. That way, travelers who saw it from afar would know that the Sioux lived and were protected in the land that was their fathers'. Standing at the rock, Fire Cloud gave a moving invocation, asking the Great Spirit for a lasting peace across the land, among Indians and whites and among the Indians themselves as well. He also asked for a blessing upon the rock and the place, and that the rock "be regarded as a pledge for eternal cessation of warfare." Sitting Bull and his people gave "guttural assent with many Hows," McLaughlin wrote, "which sounded like Amens." Fire Cloud then asked the Great Spirit to bless his red children and make their crops prosperous, withholding the hail that had destroyed their fields in the previous year. He concluded by saying that those among them who did not have clean heart and hands should stand abashed and humbled before the woman of the Standing Rock and the Great Spirit, and he called on everyone to repent and lead clean lives from then on. McLaughlin performed the unveiling, removing the blanket. Fire Cloud added a few more painted symbols to complete the medicine. For a brief time—moments, hours, perhaps even days—the spirit of peace invoked by Fire Cloud presided over "the land of the Teton Sioux to the west of the Missouri."

But it was not long before the situation at Standing Rock was roiled by the arrival of a paleface from the tribe of East Coast bohemians. Her name was Catherine Weldon, or, as she was eventually renamed by Sitting Bull, Woman Walking Ahead. She had been married twice (widowed and divorced) and had a son. At heart, she was an artist, and she had wandered Long Island, painting Indians. To date, those paintings have not surfaced and, like other women of her era, she was not encouraged to pursue this endeavor. Her income came from her family and although she indulged herself with fine things, she also used her money to help Indians. A member of the NIDA, she wanted to do more than just speak up for the tribes, and so one day she left the confines of city life and headed to the plains to seek the most famous of them all, Sitting Bull. Moreover, in a time when women often found more freedom in the West than they did among forward-thinking members of their own communities in the East, she sought a way of life that would nourish her as an artist and a woman with a son and no husband.

Weldon was not the first white woman to have made such a westward journey in search of communion with Native Americans. Prior to her arrival at Standing Rock, there was Mary Collins, a missionary, writer, and Indian advocate who planted herself in the Dakota Territory in 1875. Inspired by a Sabbath school teacher to help Indians, she came with considerable talents and skills. She was well educated, with an MA from Ripon College; she was an accomplished horsewoman; she knew something about medicine and the law, and soon learned to speak Lakota. All of this helped her forge friendships with Indians at Standing Rock, and she often spoke on their behalf at lectures around the country. Closest of all was her friendship with Sitting Bull; she nursed his children and helped him with many tasks. According to one of Sitting Bull's primary biographers, Stanley Vestal, Collins "knew him better than almost any other white person at the agency." She made ongoing efforts via regular church services to convert Indians to Christianity, and Sitting Bull considered Collins a relative.

Whether Mary Collins was still part of Sitting Bull's family when Weldon arrived, and if so, whether she considered Catherine Weldon a rival for Sitting Bull's attention or favor, we do not know.

Collins was a missionary through and through, with no seeming greater design other than to help foundering Indians by way of various pathways and spiritual conversion. Yet she did not like the NIDA and what it represented, and may have resented the group's intrusion into her world. However, from the time of Weldon's arrival in 1889, her first departure shortly thereafter, her return in 1890 and final departure soon afterward, she seems to have been the primary white female in Sitting Bull's life—and throughout her tenure on the reservation, there was speculation of a romance between the two, with some newspapers referring to her as "Sitting Bull's White Squaw." It is noteworthy that in his final days, as it became clear that the gates were closing, both Catherine Weldon and Mary Collins would try desperately to save him in ways that befitted each. Their last-ditch efforts were dramatic, cinematic even, and not heeded by Sitting Bull. And how else was he to have reacted? He was a man of heightened instincts, one who had recently learned from a meadowlark—one of his key allies—that he would soon be assassinated by some of his own people. The four-leggeds and winged creatures had always been right; the buffalo, for whom he had been named, had provided him with a good life. Now they were gone and it was his time. But for a while, there seems to have been a moment of grace in the months that Catherine Weldon spent with Sitting Bull and in fact he gave her a new name.

It had all started with a series of letters that Catherine wrote to Sitting Bull from her apartment in an artists' enclave in Brooklyn. Her apartment on Baldwin Street was near the Brooklyn Bridge, and it may have been at the opening of the bridge that her interest in the Lakota was heightened. On May 24, 1883, the bridge opened to much fanfare. The parade included many dignitaries, various spectacles of the day such as elephants provided by P. T. Barnum, and a band of Native American students from the Carlisle School in Pennsylvania.

One day, as the Lakota Luther Standing Bear wrote in his book, *My People the Sioux*, members of the band were told they were going to New York City to play before thousands of people. Their clothes were to be neat and clean in order to create a good impression. The students drilled every day. When the time came, they boarded a train and headed to Philadelphia, and from there took a boat to New York. They assembled in a park, and the captain asked Luther Standing Bear if he could lead the band. He told him he would try. "We were instructed to keep playing all the way across the bridge," Standing Bear wrote. "When the parade started I gave the signal, and we struck up and kept playing all the way across the great structure. So the Carlisle Indian band of brass instruments was the first real American band to cross the Brooklyn Bridge, and I am proud to say that I was their leader."

Perhaps Catherine Weldon was among the spectators who had gathered to pay tribute. As a woman who was drawn to Native Americans, she may have been particularly struck as the Carlisle Band crossed the structure, playing an American anthem, noting their skill and wondering about what music they had been forbidden to play once they arrived at the Indian school. As a member of the NIDA, she may have read the first issue of the *Council Fire*, which included an account of the arrival of three boatloads of Sitting Bull's followers at Standing Rock two years earlier. Now here were members of his tribe participating in a ceremony heralding one of the great feats of modern engineering.

Four years later, in 1887, with the Indian wars nearly over, the government turned to other tactics. The Dawes Act was introduced by liberal senator Henry Dawes. Before passage of the act, the Lakota Indians had been living on the Great Sioux Reservation, under the jurisdiction of various federal agencies. It was a fragment of the land that the Sioux had once called theirs, but it was one half of what is now South Dakota. The idea was to divide this land into six smaller reservations (named for already existing communities)—Standing Rock, Cheyenne River, Lower Brule, Crow Creek, Rosebud, and Pine Ridge. As Eileen Pollack wrote in her book *Woman Walking Ahead*, "The sum of these reservations would be less than the whole. On each reservation, each family would be allotted 160 acres. The total of these plots would be smaller than the expanse the tribe had held in common." In addition, the nine million acres left over after the division would be sold to white homesteaders for fifty cents an acre. An outrage today, the plan was heralded by many politicians of all parties, as it promoted the belief that the best hope for the survival of the Native American was to live like the white man on self-contained parcels of land that he could own and farm, and through this commitment gain citizenship and then vote. As Pollack notes, the only Americans who opposed the Dawes Act were the National Indian Defense Association—and the Indians themselves. As a member of the NIDA, Catherine Weldon was one of the voices most strongly opposed to the legislation.

There was one roadblock to passage of the act. The 1868 treaty that established the Great Sioux Reservation stated that any change to the reservation must be approved by three fourths of the adult male Indians who lived there and were on the official census rolls. Federal commissioners headed west, seeking assent from each of the six agencies. On July 23, 1888, they arrived at Standing Rock. Sitting Bull would not see them—for weeks. The commissioners blocked the Indians from tending their livestock and crops. Upon return to Washington, one of them tried to push the act through without the Indians' approval, but by then there was sufficient outrage to stop him. In October, the federal Bureau of Indian Affairs brought Sitting Bull and sixty other chiefs to the capital to work out a new agreement, putting them up at the Belvedere Hotel, and taking them on a tour of the Smithsonian, where they viewed Indian paintings by George Catlin—the artist who had taken Native Americans to Europe decades earlier in the first traveling Indian spectacle. At the conference about the Dawes Act, the secretary of the interior increased the government's offer for the Lakotas' land; now it was one dollar per acre. To everyone's surprise, Sitting Bull was ready to negotiate, or so it seemed, upping the ante to one dollar and twenty-five cents. The meeting was adjourned so that Congress could ponder the counteroffer.

Having learned of Sitting Bull's latest travails, Catherine Weldon wrote him a series of letters, some of which included lists of fair prices for Dakota land and maps of the plans to carve up the reservation. "Showing the Indians maps was no small act of subversion," Pollack wrote. "The whites counted on the Indians not to understand exactly how much land their tribe could lose if the big reservation were divided into smaller ones, each smaller reservation divided among its members, and the rest sold off to whites."

In 1889, after the Dakotas had been granted statehood, commissioners in Washington agreed to Sitting Bull's price. But the Indians refused to sign, and a new federal delegation traveled to the plains, hoping that in-person appeals would secure signatures at each agency, saving Sitting Bull and his followers at Standing Rock, the most intransigent group, for last. Weldon arrived at Standing Rock while the commissioners were at the other agencies, with a rigorous and rugged itinerary in mind: she wanted to travel to each reservation—miles apart over paths that in some cases were not even dirt roads—with Sitting Bull, rallying the other chiefs to hold their ground.

Such a journey would not have been her first, or even her second, into the deep northern plains. To get to Standing Rock, she had already taken a train from Brooklyn to Bismarck, stopping several times, and finally taking a ferry and then a stagecoach, which then took her to a small settlement near the Cannonball River, the northern border of the reservation, where she was staying. She had met some of the native residents of the little town during a previous trip. "I had long ago contemplated a visit to Dakota, to visit some Indian friends," she wrote later to Red Cloud, Oglala headman at Pine Ridge, with whom she regularly corresponded. "Some are at Cannon Ball now, some at Standing Rock and some at the Yankton Agency. I was glad to get away from the busy world to breathe [the] air of Dakota once more & to see the faces I liked to look upon." At the time, Sitting Bull was "almost dyeing," she told Red Cloud, "& was reported even dead." Among the local white community, people were taking bets on when Sitting Bull would "head to the happy hunting grounds," as one wag put it. And certainly, his enemies within his own tribe were counting down. Moreover, the idea was reverberating favorably beyond the reservation. The *Yankton Daily Press* wrote that "the report that Sitting Bull is dying of pneumonia is not generally received with sorrow throughout Dakota." On June 15, 1889, the *Bismarck Weekly Tribune* confirmed his deteriorating condition, reporting that photographer D. F. Barry visited Sitting Bull in his tent, where he was confined. "Sitting Bull . . . is able to set up," he said, "and although he has failed perceptibly during his illness, he is still defiant, outspoken and resolute." Although wanting to continue the battle, Sitting Bull felt that he was at a disadvantage, Barry said, because he didn't have a trustworthy adviser who spoke and read English. "The white is wise in books," he told Barry. "He can read and write and we cannot. We know nothing about books, and the whites have fooled us. Now we are approached with another treaty, but us old men will not sign it. We are not able to deal with your people, but in a few years our young men will know how to handle papers. They are going to school and will soon know how to trade with the government."

Such was Sitting Bull's state of mind as he received letters from Catherine Weldon saying that she wanted to visit. He knew that Major McLaughlin had to sign off on the comings-and-goings of all residents, particularly his own, since he was still viewed as a trouble-maker. Perhaps he thought that with a white woman accompanying him, McLaughlin would provide him with a pass. Or perhaps he did not think it possible at all. In any case, he wanted to meet her. Un-beknownst to him, McLaughlin was already turning Weldon down. Meanwhile, there were numerous attempts to discredit her, including an article that ran in the *Bismarck Daily Tribune* on July 2 of 1889. "SHE LOVES SITTING BULL" ran the headline, with the subhead, "A New Jersey Widow falls victim to Sitting Bull's Charms."

"A sensation is reported from the Standing Rock Agency," the article said. "Sitting Bull has many admirers, and among them is [Catherine Weldon]. During Sitting Bull's recent illness she vis-ited him at his camp, and when he recovered sufficiently to travel she made arrangements with him to convey her in his wagon from Standing Rock to the Rosebud Agency. It is against the rules to leave their reservation without permission. . . . No sooner had Agent McLaughlin refused than [Catherine Weldon] flew into a rage."

But Weldon had not visited Sitting Bull at his camp. Instead, for days, she waited for a response to her various entreaties for him to travel with her to the other agencies, convinced that he was on his way. Indeed, he had responded, but his messages were intercepted or delayed. Finally, Weldon learned from an Indian messenger that Sitting Bull wanted to speak with her, but was too ill to travel. Then one day she received word that Sitting Bull was heading her way. He had just recovered from pneumonia, and as Eileen Pollack recounted, he was "driving forty miles in a rickety wagon over dusty roads in the oppressive heat."

From Stanley Vestal's sparse account of their first meeting, we know that Weldon was "swept off her feet by the old man's charm." He also noted that "she had come to see a great man and was not disappointed. In him she saw the integrity, the wholeness that her baffled heart looked for in vain in that travesty of culture which had frittered her talents away. To her he seemed like a rock in a weltering sea. She did not foresee that she herself would soon be beating vainly on that rock."

We do not know what Sitting Bull thought when they first met. Recall that he was a man who had traveled far during his time with Buffalo Bill, and understood that Catherine had come from a great distance to see him. He knew a little about her from her letters—that she had a son, that she was not married, that she had taken up the cause of his people. And recall too that he was a man of great instinct and perception, and was wary of white people. Most likely, he did not consider Weldon a frivolous person or take her for a liar; if he did, he would not have undertaken his own journey to meet her, especially in a weakened state. The universe, the Great Mystery of Lakota parlance, his own heart, must have been urging him to meet this stranger from afar, and so he did—and because of that, we have a window on his final days. This is not to say that his family and friends could not and did not bear witness. They did. But perhaps Sitting Bull wanted an emissary from the Grandfather's world to watch him exit the stage. Or maybe he was hoping that here was a white person who could do *something* for his people. She was a member of the NIDA, after all, the only Indian organization that allied itself with natives on the subject of the Dawes Act, and they were having an effect. Was there not that crazy *wasichu* who had been scalped but kept speaking up for the Indians, for humanity? Maybe Catherine Weldon could help Sitting Bull's children and grandchildren make their way in the new world, see that they kept some of the old ways as they learned the new. There was nothing much else that the old medicine man could do. And in the end, maybe he just wanted more company, a fan, especially. He was, after all, a superstar, stripped of power before his own people, yet throwing off sparks around the world. Here was a woman who believed in his magic and had succumbed to it, for all to see. And she did not care what others thought of her for doing so. For a while, she helped him, and he helped her, and many assumed that they were lovers.

So disturbing to Major McLaughlin was their friendship that on at least one occasion he would not even see Sitting Bull when he sought permission to leave the reservation for a visit with Catherine at a nearby ranch. He assigned the task of refusing a travel pass to an underling named Louis Faribault, who walked Sitting Bull to the guardhouse and implied that he wanted the pass so he could kidnap Catherine and rape her. "If you take her anywhere in that wagon of yours," Faribault said, "you will end up in the penitentiary."

Upon hearing these "vile insinuations," Catherine later said in a letter to Red Cloud, Sitting Bull's heart ached. He told Faribault that he would have shielded and protected her from harm. To spare Sitting Bull from more trouble, she announced that she was leaving the reservation immediately. Sitting Bull offered to drive her to the Missouri River, where she could board the ferry for Winona, a small town where the public roads began. What these two spoke of en route we do not know. Catherine had been trying to learn Lakota and Sitting Bull had picked up some English over the years, but no matter. Here were two kindred spirits, both trapped by cultural constraints (though certainly one was free to go anywhere), sharing what was very likely a tender moment, heading across the wide-open space that had shaped Sitting Bull and called Catherine Weldon. Perhaps they heard the familiar trill of the meadowlark as they made their way over the rutted trail to the port, or caught sight of ravens on a thermal; maybe there was a passing thundercloud and it smelled like rain, or quite possibly there was a stiff wind blowing across the plains and it might have carried the promise of change and hope. Alas, there were those who rendered what was surely a tender meeting between two spirits from different worlds into something tawdry. Immediately following the short trip, there appeared another scandalous report. According to the *Sioux City Journal*, Catherine had told a local sheriff that she had come from New York to marry Sitting Bull and that McLaughlin tried to prevent their meeting. Again, it was a fabrication. "I never saw nor spoke to this man," Weldon wrote to Red Cloud. "All this is the Agent's work. He fears Sitting Bull's influence and pretends to his face that not politics were his motives for refusing the pass, but my welfare & he took this opportunity to humble the old chief & make his heart more than sad."

With Weldon's departure, many observers figured that the sign-off on the Dawes Act was a done deal. Yet it was not so quick to happen. There was dissension in the ranks at the less hostile reservations, with younger men opposed to approving the treaty changes. But much politicking ensued, with key Lakota figures reversing their positions at the eleventh hour, perhaps succumbing to pressure or suspecting that the game was over, or both. The Dawes Act was finally endorsed, but Sitting Bull never did sign it. Even so, approval of the legislation was an emasculation, and his enemies began to circle. Soon, the government pressured him for capitulation via a visit from his brother-in-law, Grey Eagle, at the behest of Major McLaughlin. Grey Eagle had recently converted to Catholicism, McLaughlin's path, and urged Sitting Bull to follow suit on this and other fronts. According to Stanley Vestal, Grey Eagle came calling with gifts, in particular a log cabin and a number of horses. "Brother-in-law," he said, "we have settled on the reservation now. We are under the jurisdiction of the government now. We must do as they say. We must stop roaming about, and obey them. We must give up these old dances." He was referring to the ghost ceremonies that many were now participating in, hoping to trigger the apocalypse.

"Yes, you are right," Sitting Bull said. "But I cannot give up my Indian race and habits. They are too deeply seated in us. You go ahead and follow the white man's road, and do as he says. But as for me, leave me alone."

"Well, if you're not going to obey," Grey Eagle said, growing angry, "and do as the whites say, you are going to cause a lot of trouble and lose your own life. I have sworn to stand by the government. We have been friends a long while, but if you will not obey the orders of the agent, we shall not be together any more."

From then on, Sitting Bull rarely visited agency headquarters, sending others to pick up supplies and communications, finding comfort ever more in the ways of his youth. It was at this moment that the Dawes Act was signed that the seeds of friendship between Catherine Weldon and Sitting Bull began to flourish.

Was there an unspoken understanding between Catherine Weldon and Sitting Bull that she would return? Did their body language suggest such a possibility? Had Catherine learned how to inform Sitting Bull of her plans for just this occasion? In any case, while she was back in Brooklyn, Sitting Bull seems to have consumed her thoughts. She began selling possessions such as sterling silver items and jewelry and sending him the money. She became fervently involved in the NIDA, attending more meetings and issuing impassioned pleas on the Indians' behalf to congressmen. Soon she was writing to Major McLaughlin, asking again for permission to visit Sitting Bull, and stating her desire to live nearby. "I suppose it is needless to state that I have no intention to become either Sitting Bull's wife or a squaw, as the sagacious newspaper editors surmised," she wrote in her final try for approval. "I probably would not be able to dispose of first class paintings or plush lambrequins or be able to teach modern languages on the prairies. . . . I honor and respect S. Bull as if he was my own father and nothing can ever shake my faith in his good qualities. . . . I regret that at the

present time he is so universally misjudged." Implicit in her letters
was the idea that she would try to bring the finer points of white
civilization to Sitting Bull. With this last entreaty, McLaughlin
agreed that she could return.

It was in May of 1890 that she did, just several months after
she had left. Within weeks, she divested herself of many belongings, packed up several suitcases and trunks, proceeded to Grand
Central Terminal, and headed west again. After a short stay with
her old friends at the ranch near Grand River, she moved in with
Sitting Bull and his two wives, their children, and grandchildren.
This of course triggered more speculation that the two were lovers,
yet she herself never said such a thing, and it is not likely that his
wives would have permitted it. Although it was said that they were
actually very jealous, and soon were chasing her around camp with
butcher knives. Shortly after her arrival, she sent for her thirteen-
year-old son, who by all accounts quickly took to the Great Plains,
succumbing to a life unfettered by convention, learning the ways
of a young warrior from Sitting Bull's boys, and from Sitting Bull
himself, how to ride a pony. As for Catherine, she expressed her
gratitude and devotion in many ways. Upon her return, she presented Sitting Bull with a little golden bull, which he wore as a
watch charm. She also gave him a revolver, a surreptitious act and a
seditious one, as Indians had relinquished their arms as a condition
of surrender and were not allowed to have weapons, though some
still had hidden caches. She immediately pitched in as a domestic
caretaker, washing dishes, sweeping the floors, and cooking for him.
She learned Lakota. She read aloud, tales of Alexander, Napoleon,
and Achilles—martial glory all—most likely translating, or trying
to, as she went along. She also served as Sitting Bull's secretary,
writing letters on his behalf, and continuing to advocate for the Lakota cause. During this time, Catherine began painting a portrait of
Sitting Bull, letting her passion for making art take flight. When it

was over, she had painted four of them—as far as we know, her life's work as an artist, for none of her other paintings have surfaced.

Sitting Bull was devoted to her. He once prevented her from mounting a wild horse lest she be thrown off and suffer a broken neck. He took a keen interest in her son, and eased his way into his family. Finally, true to the rumors that were flying, Sitting Bull asked Catherine Weldon to marry him. He had had five wives so far, and it would not be unusual to add a third to his current two. But as Weldon told it in her journal, she seemed to have been insulted: "Is this the reward after so many years of faithful friendship which I have proved to you?" We do not know why Catherine responded that way, or how her reaction was received by Sitting Bull. Certainly he had experienced a parade of white people who behaved in strange ways over the years. But Catherine had never lied to him and he was a man who honored those who heeded their hearts. She may have been living life exactly the way she had imagined it, away from cities and crowds and people who did not appreciate her true gifts, and perhaps that was enough. She continued her service to Sitting Bull, completing a final portrait and hanging it on the wall of their cabin. Yet there was something that bothered her, and possibly this was why she rejected Sitting Bull's proposal.

Yards away from their cabin, the ghost dancing grew more intense as the days and weeks went by. It was not something that Catherine Weldon liked, as she knew it meant trouble for her friend. Although Sitting Bull did not participate, he gave the dancers his blessings; they were his people, after all. They were starving and their spirits were broken. They chanted and stomped by the hundreds, sending up great clouds of dust, and lo and behold, some of the *wasichu* on the reservation grew fearful and clamored for a halt. Mary Collins, the missionary, had erected crosses in plain sight of the dancers, hoping to ward off evil and show them the way. In response, Sitting Bull had placed buffalo skulls on pikes.

It seemed like angels and demons were arranging themselves and one day as the singing reached a new height and people prostrated themselves on the ground and then were roused, announcing that they had seen their ancestors and the return of the buffalo, Sitting Bull's *wasichu* friend Mary Collins became more alarmed than ever, retreating to her nearby church and banging out "Nearer My God to Thee" on the piano. It was a most peculiar sight: the impassioned devotee of Christ hoping to squelch the cries of the fallen, a lone voice against hundreds, and the dancers, convinced that their ecstatic calls would end their pain, if only they could break through to the Great Mystery—and the demons and angels wrestled with each other until dusk fell and it was time for all to go home.

With white citizens aroused and demanding an end to the ghost dancing, Catherine Weldon advised Sitting Bull to end the ceremonies. He would not. Their disagreement on this issue deepened, and he came to resent her urge to save him. One night, she moved out of their cabin and into a smaller one on his farm. The dancing of the Indians "sounded awful in the stillness," she wrote, "and they kept it up until I could stand it no longer, so I arose and went through the crowd. It was dark, and there was the width of a street between me and Sitting Bull's house. I told Sitting Bull I would go away at daylight if he did not stop it, and he did. The next morning I asked him to have no more dances, as the troops would come and there would be a battle. He said it was not his doings, but the [other] chiefs', and he would be glad if the soldiers would kill him, for he wanted to die. 'If you want to die, kill yourself, and do not bring other people into trouble,' I said." So he told the dancers to move to the foot of a nearby hill, where their sounds would not irritate Catherine.

She tried in other ways to intervene in the dancing, conferring with other influential Indians, and importuning them to call a halt. Even so, some of Sitting Bull's enemies blamed her for the dancing, suggesting that it was her money that was funding the subversive activities and if she left the reservation, things would return to a state of calm. The friendship between the two seemed to have run its course, and on October 22, Catherine Weldon and Sitting Bull made their final drive together, retracing their first passage and heading back to Fort Yates over the rutted terrain. They did not see it as their last time alone, or at least Catherine did not write of the trip that way. But Sitting Bull was dressed for burial, with a black cloth around his head. Perhaps a meadowlark called out again, the great songster of the plains reminding Sitting Bull of his fate, and adding a melodic touch to an otherwise silent journey in the gathering late autumn cold. The buckboard was hauled by the horse that Buffalo Bill had given to him upon his departure from the Wild West show five years earlier, the one he rode during his performances. As they approached the fort, he got down and walked before the horse; if soldiers started to shoot, he wanted to make sure they got him instead of Catherine. But he was not taken captive and he did not have to mount a fight. Instead, the officers shook his hand.

Major McLaughlin knew that Sitting Bull had never been an active proponent of ghost dancing. And he knew that the dance posed no threat to the stability of his agency or the others. Yet he had long wanted to get rid of his old nemesis and regarded fear of this religious outbreak as a cover. Now the timing was right, and in the days following Sitting Bull's return to Grand River, he began laying the groundwork for his arrest, telling reporters and others that the chief was the instigator of the troublesome dance. The reservation was a cauldron of rumors, stoked by facts on the ground, decades of distrust between natives and Indian agents, and intra-tribal rivalries. It was of utmost importance to save face; after all, the situation here involved two warrior cultures with men who wore badges for taking the lives of enemies. In fraught times such as this, all men were on guard, hyper-aware, understanding that a state of siege was at hand. Edges were to be found and maintained, lest a point of weakness become manifest, obscuring the way back. Sitting Bull had spies planted among McLaughlin's staff and the major had his own informants among Sitting Bull's allies. The stage was set and it was time for the final act to unfold. Ever the showman, Buffalo Bill would soon make an appearance, along with an entourage.

On November 17, one week after Catherine Weldon had left, McLaughlin and his interpreter, Joseph Primeau, headed to Grand River to gauge the ghost dancing's fever. When they arrived, there were about one hundred people circling around a pole, crooning, shrieking, and swooning, as another hundred looked on. A woman fainted and was carried into Sitting Bull's tent. Sitting Bull put his ear to her mouth and she whispered of the promised land and ancestors she had seen. Deciding that it was a bad time to intervene, McLaughlin and Primeau spent the night at the nearby home of Bull Head, a lieutenant in the Indian police and enemy of Sitting Bull. At dawn, McLaughlin returned to Sitting Bull's camp as the chief was stepping out of a sweat bath. Sitting Bull looked "very thin and more subdued than I had ever seen him," McLaughlin later wrote. He wrapped himself in a blanket and shivered in the morning chill as McLaughlin made one more pitch against the ghost dance. Sitting Bull made a counteroffer, suggesting that the major accompany him to the other agencies and find the men who had visited the messiah. "I will demand that they show him to us," he said, "and if they cannot do so, I will return and tell my people that it is a lie."

McLaughlin told him that would be a waste of time, and that when he came to Fort Yates on the following morning, as per monthly instructions, he could spend the night and they could continue the conversation. Suspecting that this was a trap to detain him, Sitting Bull never made that trip, sending his friend Strikes-the-Kettle instead, who explained that Sitting Bull couldn't come because one of his children was sick. Twenty other men from Sitting Bull's encampment sent their wives for their rations. Mc-Laughlin immediately issued an order stating that no family could receive supplies unless a male head of the household came to get them. So now, with conditions at Sitting Bull's camp already deteriorating, he and his followers were being starved out. But the dancing continued, even as winter unfolded; true to a prediction of Sitting Bull's, the season had been mild, as if favoring the display.

From then on, there followed a strange series of crossed wires and near-misses, desperate attempts at heading off the inevitable mounted by an increasing number of players. Under the auspices of Kicking Bear and men of influence at the other agencies, some of the dancers had fled to a remote place in the Badlands known as the Stronghold, where they continued their quest. Sitting Bull wanted to join them—not to participate, but to talk to them, see what was what. He needed permission to leave the reservation, and sent McLaughlin a poorly translated and badly spelled note, in which he seemed to threaten the major, allegedly saying among other things that "I will let you know something . . . the Policeman told me you going to take all our Poneys, gund, too . . . I want answer back soon." McLaughlin had read many such notes from Indians over the years, given that they rarely had access to good translators. He could not, and did not, act on all of them; he was a smart man and well knew that often enough the messages were inaccurate. But this one indicated that Sitting Bull planned to leave Grand River and head to Pine Ridge in search of his compatriots. Right or wrong, it was one more pretext for the major to dispatch Sitting Bull. McLaughlin sent a letter ordering him to remain at his cabin. In other words, Sitting Bull was under arrest, and he knew that the Indian police would be coming.

Meanwhile, his old friend Buffalo Bill was being enlisted to head off a possible confrontation. Cody had just returned from a European tour. He was scheduled to testify before Congress at a hearing brought about by advocates of Indian rights who were angered by the fact that several members of the Wild West had gotten sick and died while the show was abroad. They wanted to shut down Buffalo Bill and his enterprise, and such calls would escalate over time. The calls came to nothing because, for the most part, the Indians who traveled with Cody liked doing so, and they were not in favor of giving up their ways and assimilating, which many of the Native American rights proponents advocated. The Wild West or the reservation were two roads being offered, and whenever Cody's scouts came looking for cast members, a number of Indians chose the first one, showing up by the hundreds every spring in Rushville, Nebraska, for sign-up days, dressed in feathers and furs. Now, as Cody debarked at New York harbor on November 24, he received a telegram from General Miles asking him to proceed immediately to Standing Rock, where—as Major McLaughlin had just informed Miles—a tense situation was unfolding. Miles further authorized Cody "to secure the person of Sitting Bull, and deliver him to the nearest Commanding Officer of US Troops." It was the general's hope that Cody could convince his old friend to surrender—for the last time.

Cody contacted three friends, Dr. Frank Powell (aka White Beaver, a member of his show), Pony Bob Haslam (another cast member), and Lieutenant G. W. Chadwick—although the record varies and he may have enlisted the aid of other friends. On Thanksgiving Day, November 27, they arrived by train at Mandan, North Dakota, announcing via telegram to McLaughlin that they would be checking in at Standing Rock the following day. Meanwhile, Arizona John Burke and a contingent of Indians were heading for Pine Ridge as part of a two-pronged peace mission. Sometime during this period, Cody received a telegram with more news of import, this time regarding a personal matter: his ornate, three-story house in North Platte, Nebraska, was on fire. Friends and neighbors were trying to save it with a bucket brigade, as his wife, Louisa, and daughter Irma retrieved valuable possessions amid the inferno. "Save Rosa Bonheur's painting," he wrote back, referring to the famous portrait of him that Bonheur had painted when the Wild West was in Paris. "The rest can go to blazes." And it did; except for the painting, the house was destroyed, along with souvenirs and mementos from his travels around the world. But when Cody reached Fort Yates on the reservation, he was not able to continue any further; it was as if everything in his life had come to a halt. Apparently he was drunk, and according to Dr. Powell, Cody needed to rest for a few hours before continuing. His friends left, and when they returned he was completely incapacitated, having spent the entire afternoon drinking. Later, Powell and Pony Bob learned that McLaughlin's officers had plied him with liquor to prevent him from heading to Sitting Bull's cabin. Given his fondness for spirits, this would not have been difficult. And the fact that his beloved home on the Platte was aflame may have contributed to the urge to knock himself out. In any case, one thing is certain: even as his wife and daughter were trying to save his home his friendship with Sitting Bull came first. Behind it all, perhaps there was a distant echo of his midnight ride to save his father long ago; now the moment was back again, offering a chance to resolve itself, regardless of whether Cody was aware of the offering.

Early the next morning, he sobered up and announced that he was on his way to see his friend. Unable to prevent his departure, the officers provided him with a wagon and he loaded it up with sweets from the supply store, knowing that Sitting Bull liked candy. In addition to his three companions, he was now accompanied by five newspaper reporters. "I was sure," he wrote later, "that my old enemy and later friend would listen to my advice." But he confessed to also being concerned; he was going to "a hostile camp of Indians, risking all on the card of friendship and man-to-man respect (willing to test the ghost-dance shirt . . . perhaps, if pushed); but above all, desirous to save my red brother from a suicidal craze." Meanwhile, McLaughlin was still trying to prevent Cody's intervention; he had wired the Interior Department, asking for someone to overrule General Miles's order for Cody to bring Sitting Bull in. En route, Cody's party was headed off by Joseph Primeau, McLaughlin's interpreter. He told them that Sitting Bull was not at home, and that he was heading to Fort Yates on another trail, driving a wagon pulled by two horses, one shod and the other not. Changing course, Cody found a trail that matched and followed it. Unbeknownst to him, the day before Primeau had seen such a trail, and used the information to send Cody on a detour. That night, at his camp along Four Mile Creek, he received the news that President Benjamin Harrison had rescinded the order for him to bring in Sitting Bull. The following day, Cody and his party returned to Fort Yates and soon left for the railroad station at Mandan.

But sometime during the chaotic forty-eight hours of his mission, a moment of which we must take note was under way. It's mentioned deep in the annals, buried in an avalanche of words, and as such is easy to overlook. Sitting Bull had gotten word that Buffalo Bill was looking for him—shortly after he left. "Is it true?" he asked the man who told him, a *wasichu* who had in fact warned McLaughlin that Sitting Bull was planning to leave. Yes, it's true, the man said. What meaning did this have for the medicine man as things were careening toward a conclusion? We can imagine that perhaps it strengthened him along this bend in the path. Perhaps it gave him heart, or affirmed his friendship with Cody when most needed. Perhaps he was even wearing the hat that Cody had given him before he left the show—a sombrero, some said. Once, a friend had tried to put it on and Sitting Bull waved him off. "No," he said. "Pahaska gave that to me." The hat was his and his alone. Now, hearing that his old friend had been nearby, he may have wondered if he sought his return to the Wild West. Or maybe it was another kind of lifeline. You never knew about those *wasichu*. It could have been anything—someone wanted something, that was for sure. The man who told Sitting Bull about Cody asked him to surrender; everyone knew that the endgame was afoot. Sitting Bull declined, and said he had to go see his people about "The New Religion." He knew that doing so was a death sentence—or an arrest. Yet at that moment there may have been only one thing that mattered. Cody had been there and Sitting Bull knew it, and on he continued. Their friendship lived on another road.

Several days after the failed intervention, newspapers heightened the call for an end to ghost dancing. The following item ran in the *New York Herald*, to which Sitting Bull had given his first interview with a white man so long ago. There was no mention of the things that were conveyed at that time, no indication that what Sitting Bull had said reverberated at all.

> It is stated today that there was a quiet understanding between the officers of the Indian and military departments that it would be impossible to bring Sitting Bull to Standing Rock alive, and that if brought in, nobody would know precisely what to do with him. He would, though under arrest, still be a source of great annoyance, and his followers would continue their dances and threats against neighboring settlers. There was, therefore, cruel as it may seem, a complete understanding from the Commanding Officer to the Indian Police that the slightest attempt to rescue the old medicine man should be a signal to send Sitting Bull to the happy hunting ground.

There are certain atrocities involving Native Americans that have occurred around important holidays of the white man. Partly, this is because these holidays—Thanksgiving, Christmas, New

Year's—are in the winter, and when the ground is frozen, say, or during a snowstorm, it is difficult to fight back if you are hunkered down against the cold. But why the spirit of these festive occasions has led to bloodshed rather than brotherhood is a question for another time.

The cascade of moments preceding Sitting Bull's death involved a cadre of tribal policemen comprised of former followers as well as personal enemies and Indians from other tribes who did not revere the chief as the Hunkpapas did. They were backed by cavalry troops in case things went awry. The night before the arrest, First Sergeant Shave Head, a member of Sitting Bull's tribe, told his relatives that they mustn't be ashamed to see him reeling around as if he were drunk since he had every reason to act that way. "I am a dead man," he said, uttering remarks regarding his role in a play within a play—a fate that enveloped all of the horse tribes. "As good as dead. I am here in spirit, but my body is lying on the prairie. We have been ordered to arrest Sitting Bull."

On December 14, twenty-eight Indian policemen gathered at the home of Bull Head. "They were wearing their blue uniforms and badges," Stanley Vestal reported after years of correspondence and meetings with participants. "The more important among them had tied white handkerchiefs around their necks as identification. The moment was somber; some among the group had fought with Sitting Bull at Rosebud and the Little Bighorn. Others had starved with him in Canada." All were aware of the fact that they were on hallowed ground; Bull Head's home was nearly the exact site on Grand River where Sitting Bull had been born fifty-nine winters before. Lone Man said that they all felt sad. Bull Head outlined his plan and, now joined by eight more men, at four on the following morning, with an icy drizzle falling, the police gathered in front of his cabin. Bull Head offered a Christian prayer and they mounted their horses and headed out in a column of twos. Two miles downstream, they paused at Grey Eagle's cabin, where they were joined by more men, for a total of forty-four. They crossed the Grand River to the north side, with the horses' hooves rattling and slipping on the ice. Coyotes howled and owls hooted, and at least one of the men considered it a warning.

Sitting Bull was sleeping on his pallet with the elder of his two wives and one of his two small children. There were others in the room, including dancers from that night's event and Crow Foot, his seventeen-year-old son. Other members of his family were in a smaller cabin nearby, across the wagon road. Just before 6 a.m., dogs began barking and there came the clatter of hooves; someone pounded and kicked at the door, calling out for Sitting Bull.

"Brother, we came after you," Shave Head said.

"How," the chief said, "all right."

The standard and even at this point mythological accounts of what happened next state that Sitting Bull was dragged naked into his front yard. But his great-grandson LaPointe writes that according to Sitting Bull's stepsons, eyewitnesses to the event, the police waited for him while he got dressed, putting on his shirt and leggings.

Tatanka Iyotake then walked toward the door of the cabin. "I will stand with you," Crow Foot said, and picked up his weapon— as opposed to the early narratives, which state that Crow Foot was afraid and went to hide under his bed.

"At the door," LaPointe writes, "*Tatanka Iyotake* paused, then turned around and sang a farewell song to his family. 'I am a man and wherever I lie is my own.'" And then he walked out of his cabin. Crow Foot was behind him, carrying a weapon.

Sitting Bill was immediately flanked by Bull Head and Shave Head. Behind him was Sergeant Red Tomahawk, brandishing a pistol. By now, the ruckus had awakened the entire settlement, and people pressed in from all directions against the police cordon, shouting and calling out insults. Catch-the-Bear, an ally of Sitting

Bull's, barreled through the crowd and confronted Bull Head. "Now here," he said, "just as we had expected all the time. You think you are going to take him. You shall not do it." Then he turned to the crowd and yelled, "Come on now, let us protect our chief."

Bull Head asked Jumping Bull for help. "Brother," Bull Head said, "you ought to go with the police and not cause any trouble."

"Uncle," added Lone Man, "nobody is going to hurt you. The agent wants to see you and then you are to come back. . . . Please do not let the others advise you into any trouble."

Sitting Bull pulled back, and Bull Head and Shave Head tightened their grip, trying to haul the chief toward a waiting horse. "You are arrested," said Red Tomahawk, pushing from behind. "You can either walk or ride. If you fight, you shall be killed here." The crowd erupted in a frenzy, shouting at the police and calling out, "You shall not take our chief."

Suddenly Catch-the-Bear shouldered a Winchester, aimed, and fired. Bull Head went sprawling, his right side ripped open. As he fell, he grabbed his revolver and shot Sitting Bull in the chest. Red Tomahawk fired into the back of his head, killing Sitting Bull. Then Strikes-the Kettle fired, hitting Shave Head's stomach. The three men fell to the ground as more shots were exchanged and a vicious battle erupted, with Sitting Bull's men swarming over the police with knives, clubs, and guns fired at point-blank range. Within minutes, the fight was over. Five of Sitting Bull's followers had been killed and three more were wounded. Five of the police had taken fatal rounds. The dancers fled to a grove of trees behind the cabin. Red Tomahawk took charge, and ordered the wounded policemen dragged into the cabin. The others took up defensive positions in the barn and corral.

Red Tomahawk then ordered Hawkman No. 1—No. 2 had been killed—to mount a horse, ride fast, and bring soldiers. Indians were firing from the top of a knoll at Sitting Bull's cabin. From the timber beyond it, there was more firing. And shots were being directed at both places. Expecting trouble, Captain Fechét and his cavalry squadron arrived quickly. He raised a white flag, unable to tell friend from foe. The firing continued, and Fechét ordered Lieutenant E. C. Brooks to blast a shell from a Hotchkiss gun into the open space between the cabin and the timber. Lone Man, still inside, tore the white curtain from a window, tied it to a stick, and rushed out, waving it at soldiers. Sitting Bull's allies scattered, breaking for the hills and nearby valley, then fleeing upriver. The cavalry searched every cabin within two miles above Sitting Bull's, but found no one. As Captain Fechét surveyed the bloody scene around the chief's cabin, Sitting Bull's widows, in a house nearby, maintained a great wail. Relatives of one of the dead policemen arrived, and added to the chorus. One of them picked up a yoke in a stable where Sitting Bull's body had been dragged, smashing his face with a savage blow. "What the hell did you do that for?" demanded one of the soldiers. "The man is dead. Leave him alone."

To make sure the settlement had been cleaned out, the soldiers searched Sitting Bull's second cabin. There they found the chief's two wives and other women and children. Under some bedding on the floor, Lieutenant Matthew F. Steele found two young men, one of them Sitting Bull's deaf-mute stepson. On the cabin's wall, framed in gilt, was the portrait of Sitting Bull painted by Catherine Weldon. A policeman mourning the death of his brother in the shootout tore down the painting, smashed the frame with his rifle butt, and ripped a gash in the canvas with the barrel. Steele grabbed the painting, and later bought it from Sitting Bull's widows for two dollars.

Now the morning sun was rising, and the soldiers were feeding their horses and making breakfast. As Fechét began to sip his coffee, the police shouted an alarm. From the timber just eighty yards away an Indian on a black horse, brandishing a long staff and singing a song, raced at full speed toward the soldiers. This was Crow

Woman, one of the most zealous of the apocalyptic dancers. The police fired, and he retreated, emerging four hundred yards up the valley, driven back to the timber with another volley. But he tried again, this time galloping into the open, heading right through two cavalrymen who opened fire, escaping unscathed. He was wearing a ghost shirt, and to this day it is said that Crow Woman's ride is proof of the shirt's power.

The wounded policemen were hoisted into Fechét's ambulance, and the dead were loaded into an old farm wagon taken from the settlement and hitched to Indian ponies. Sergeant Red Tomahawk ordered that Sitting Bull be thrown into the wagon as well; after all, his assignment was to bring the chief in. But his fellow policemen balked; Sitting Bull had caused the death of their brothers, and to take him away in the same wagon would have been a dishonor. Red Tomahawk insisted and the men threw Sitting Bull's mangled corpse on the bottom and on top of him, four dead policemen. A little after noon on December 15, 1890, the caravan headed across the trail to Fort Yates. The troops were preparing for Christmas, the holiday that celebrated a figure whose sacrifice led to resurrection—the same thing that the Indians had been dancing for when they tried to call up their ghosts.

Upon learning that Sitting Bull was killed, his old friend Major Walsh expressed a terrible sadness. "I am glad to hear that Bull is relieved of his miseries," he said, "even if it took a bullet to do it." Walsh compared Sitting Bull to a king, with dominion over a "wild-spirited people." Such a man, he said, "cannot endure abject poverty without suffering great mental pain, and death is a relief." Trying to correct the record, he noted that "Bull was not bloodthirsty. He was not cruel. He was kind of heart. He was truthful. He loved his people and was glad to give his hand in friendship to any man who was honest with him." The tribute was all the more poignant because it came from a man who now had little standing in Canadian military ranks. After Sitting Bull and his tribe had returned to the United States, a scandal had erupted. Sitting Bull's chief protector Walsh was blamed for it and forced to resign, suggesting that careers could be made or broken according to one's treatment of "the man who killed Custer." (Ironically, years later it was revealed that Sitting Bull had saved Colonel Marcus Reno. On day two of the Little Bighorn battle, Reno's company was under siege, with no place to run. According to Stanley Vestal, Sitting Bull came to the front lines and saw the shooting. "Let them go!" he said. "They are trying to live!")

As December of 1890 played itself out and word of Sitting Bull's ambush spread through the camp, some of his followers and those of the Minneconjou Big Foot fled south, hoping to get to the reservation at Pine Ridge, where perhaps there was sanctuary with the Oglalas. On December 28, three days after Christmas and in the midst of a winter blizzard, they were intercepted by soldiers of the Seventh Cavalry—Custer's outfit—at Porcupine Creek just outside their destination. There was discussion and Big Foot, weakened by pneumonia, agreed to an escort to the agency. That evening, the group of 230 men and 230 women and children arrived at a creek named Wounded Knee, just inside the reservation. There they set up an immediate village, a thing to which they were accustomed, and there, on the following morning, they were told to disarm. Surrounded by armed soldiers and faced with Hotchkiss repeating weapons on a hill overlooking the campsite, they relinquished their guns, which were stacked up on the frozen ground. Already stunned by the death of Sitting Bull, the villagers grew increasingly wary and nervous. They could not flee, this they knew, lest they risk a massacre. They could not negotiate; this latest incident, after years of others, including the assassination of Crazy Horse and the vanishing of the buffalo, suggested that things were coming to a close. The soldiers too had become more agitated.

A search for concealed weapons was ordered, and two more rifles were found. Black Coyote, later said to be deaf, balked at turning over his weapon. A scuffle ensued and hell broke loose, with the Indians grabbing their guns and the soldiers blasting them at close range and from the bluffs above. When it was over 162 Lakota had been killed, including sixty-two women and children; others may have gotten away and died of their wounds later. Big Foot was killed in this encounter, his haunting image forever preserved in a photograph of his frozen and gnarled body, found on the site on a travois several days later, along with the other bodies. The Seventh Cavalry also suffered casualties; twenty-five men had been killed and thirty-five wounded in this horrific action, which has come to be seen as a coda to the Battle of the Little Bighorn. On New Year's Day 1891, army wagons came from Pine Ridge to retrieve the dead. Surviving children were found wrapped in shawls amid the carnage, and one soldier uncovered a baby under its mother and adopted her. The bodies were taken to a hilltop where one of the Hotchkiss guns had fired at them, and buried in a mass grave.

Sometime after Sitting Bull had been killed, Buffalo Bill ran into President Benjamin Harrison in Indianapolis. In what must have been a very sad thing to hear, the president told him that he regretted rescinding the order issued by General Miles. He explained that he had been unduly influenced by some philanthropists who made the case that a visit from Buffalo Bill would result in the killing of Sitting Bull, and a war would ensue. "So," Cody later wrote, "it was to spare the life of this man that I was stopped!" All for a political donation, it sounded like, if that was indeed the case—one more thing that would not have surprised Sitting Bull.

There are always questions about tragic events, many of which are concerned with whether they could have been averted. In this case, could Buffalo Bill have headed off the death of Sitting Bull? The question can't really be answered, and even Cody knew that he could have been killed in the chaos that was building prior to the arrest of Sitting Bull. Or perhaps, in the event of a fight, Sitting Bull might even have killed him. But this most horrific event should not be seen as a near-miss between the two unlikely friends. At the time of the ambush, there was an unexpected convergence of their lives in a way that brings a moment of grace, wrenching though it may be. It is said that the horse that Buffalo Bill had given to Sitting Bull upon his departure from the show was outside his cabin when the shooting began. He recognized the sound, having heard it many times in performance, and perhaps even in other battles. As Sitting Bull was being assassinated, his horse began to dance. He drew himself up and snorted, the story goes. He arched his neck and pranced in a circle. He bowed and then stood up and shook his long mane and pawed the ground, and reared up and leaped into the air. He cantered around and around in a circle, stopped and backed up, and then cantered some more. He did all of this while the battle was raging around him, and the bullets never touched him. And there the legend stops and the facts begin: Sometime amid the siege he was mounted and ridden off by a policeman seeking reinforcements. He carried the rider for several miles until they encountered troops, who headed to Sitting Bull's cabin upon hearing that they were needed. And on galloped the horse and rider, spreading the news. The days passed and the horse was returned to Sitting Bull's widows. Sometime later, Buffalo Bill returned to Standing Rock for an audience with them. Could he purchase the horse? he inquired. Yes, they said, and he did. According to various accounts, the horse was gray or white. If white, he was indeed a ghost horse.

The four-legged soon rejoined the Wild West. "Sitting Bull's horse has been shipped from Mandan to New York by express," reported the *Aberdeen Daily News* on June 17, 1891. "The horse was presented to Sitting Bull by Buffalo Bill. Bill is now in Germany and he just called for the animal. It will go on the first fast steamer from New York to Germany." In 1893, the horse made another appearance, during the Columbian Exposition in Chicago. He was draped with an American flag, and ridden in a parade by either Cody or someone else, the record is not clear, a silent tribute to his friend. Just inside the entrance to the midway, there were five stuffed buffalo in a grove of poplar trees. On the midway, Sitting Bull's cabin was on display. After he was killed, it had been dismantled and shipped from the plains. A Ghost Pole was next to the cabin, around which dancers had tried to conjure their world before it fell. Under the direction of one P. B. Wickham, the exhibit employed Oglala Lakota as well as Crow Indians who were veterans of the Little Bighorn (on opposing sides), performing dances and songs and posing for pictures. Cast members included Plenty Horses, a survivor of Wounded Knee, said to still have five bullets from the incident lodged inside him. Red Cloud's son Jack was a participant, along with Young-Man-Afraid-of-His-Horses, who had urged his fellows not to kill the army commissioners who had come to buy the Black Hills in the famous meeting after which Sitting Bull had granted his first interview with a white man. Inside the cabin, two women said to be Sitting Bull's widows sold baskets and moccasins. The Sitting Bull Cabin Exhibit netted the World's Columbian Exposition Company $2,575, a hefty sum for that time. A local reporter noted that Rain-in-the-Face "kindly relapsed into barbarism" for the show. Recall that the Lakota warrior is believed to have killed Custer—as opposed to Sitting Bull, who was blamed for it. Two other exhibits on the fairgrounds claimed to have the authentic Sitting Bull cabin. It was a frontier crime scene that had become a bonanza.

Every afternoon and evening at the Expo, the Wild West presented its show, apart from the midway, its own spectacle, now grander than ever, with centaurs from all corners of the earth.

"While the cowboy band played its opening medley," wrote Walter Havighurst, "scores of riders worked into formation outside the gate. The band played the national anthem, the crowd sat down, the ringmaster's whistle filled the air, and Buffalo Bill loped around the track on his cream-white stallion. He was forty-seven, his long hair thinning, his face lined with indulgence and dissipation, but he was still an imposing figure on a horse." Then came the announcement that the Congress of Rough Riders was about to enter; it was an addition to the show that came after Sitting Bull's departure, the final incarnation of the "equestrian extravaganza" that Cody and Salsbury had first imagined. With fanfare from the band, in galloped American cavalry troops with guidons, British Lancers, French Chasseurs in blue coats and scarlet britches, Russian Cossacks, Argentine gauchos in sombreros and serapes, Arab Bedouins, and cowboys from the West. Buffalo Bill "doffed his hat to the flags of all nations," wrote Havighurst, and "the riders circled the arena, men and horsemen of all colors, a World's Fair of horsemen." They continued to gallop, now in concentric circles, crisscrossing lines and weaving patterns, and then raced into the wings as the band sent up a flourish. The arena was now empty, except for one rider with a star on her hat. She stopped in the center of the ring as the announcer made his introduction: "The peerless woman marksman, the maid of the Western plains—Annie Oakley!"

That season she was thirty-three, but "she looked seventeen," Havighurst wrote, adding that "she still had her quick lithe movements and her girlish charm." The band quickened its tempo and she hopped off her pony and ran to her gun table. She picked up the weapons quickly, becoming a whirlwind of shooting, firing on foot, from a bicycle, from both shoulders, and behind her back, remounting her horse, shattering targets everywhere and then racing away. The rest of the cast dashed in, performing feats of horsemanship, reenacting frontier scenes as always. But now the show's finale was the Battle of the Little Bighorn, performed very elaborately, with heightened drama when it was presented at night, under artificial lighting. "After a moment of silence and emptiness, floodlights showed an Indian village at the foot of colored buttes and ridges," said Havighurst. "For twenty thousand spectators, it is daybreak on the Little Big Horn, with ponies picketed and fires gleaming." A scout sneaks in through the trees and returns with Custer. They count the Indians and horses but are spotted as they ride away. The Indians prepare for battle, and head off the returning cavalry in a circle of running fire. Amid their war cries, the soldiers fall one by one, and finally Custer himself is shot out of his saddle, falling to the ground to join his soldiers. All is silent and then Buffalo Bill enters on his white horse, heading for Custer and stopping there, pausing above Custer's body for a farewell. He removes his hat and thus concludes the Wild West.

Sometime later, after the Wild West went bankrupt, Cody began traveling with other Wild West shows. There is nothing in the record that indicates he was tired of the act, weary of the jokes that must have come—"Hey, Bill, how about a trick? Hey, Bill, will you take me hunting? Hey, Bill, you're not gonna buffalo me, are you?" In fact, by all accounts, he seemed to maintain his happy demeanor, that quintessentially cheerful and self-effacing American facade that masked the heart of a killer. Yet according to various accounts, he was drinking more than ever, a thing that began happening shortly after the death of Sitting Bull and continued throughout the prolonged and sensational divorce hearings that erupted during the early part of the twentieth century when, it seems, he had reached a breaking point. "God did not join two persons together for both to go through life miserable," he wrote to his sister Julia, who was managing his ranch in Wyoming. "When such a mistake was made—a law was created to undo the mistake." Quite simply, after a life on the road and numerous affairs—some quite serious and few hidden at all—the man who made and sold mythology could no longer live a lie. If his wife, Louisa, did not grant him a legal separation, he further explained, the result would be "war and publicity."

He hoped that his daughter Arta, then thirty-seven, might see things his way, but because of his long absences from the family, including the fact that he did not attend her wedding, along with his unfaithfulness toward her mother, she did not. "I'm going through with the divorce," he told Julia. "I think I'm entitled to be at peace in my old age. And I surely can't have it with Lulu." As the proceedings unfolded, the Cody family was roiled by more turmoil. Arta's husband died, and months later her father returned from abroad to attend her second wedding. Not long after that, Arta died; Louisa said it was from a broken heart due to Cody's desire to seek a divorce, and she sent Arta's new husband a telegram saying so. Cody returned from London, where he was then touring, and they traveled to Rochester to bury Arta next to her brother, Kit, who had died long ago when Cody was performing there during one of his first shows, and her sister who had passed away later.

Louisa would not accompany her husband to the gravesite, and from then on the divorce proceedings became more acrimonious, with Cody accusing his wife of poisoning his prized staghounds given to him by the czar of Russia and Louisa filing statements that Cody was a drunk and a cheat, naming two of his mistresses in her claim. According to reporting by Chris Enss in her book, various witnesses were called to testify, stating that over the years Cody had been involved with "four or five nice Indian girls and other women on different occasions." In spite of much testimony that indicated Cody was a reprobate, when Louisa took the stand and was asked if she still loved him, she said yes, and yes to whether she wanted a reconciliation, and she added that she would welcome him home. Unbeknownst to many, she had devoted much of her life to the making of Buffalo Bill, sewing the costumes that made him so desirable, making sure he was shown off in a way that suited him, right down to the buttons and fringe. In that regard, she was part of the myth.

When it was Cody's turn, he enumerated his many good acts as a husband, and said that he "was universally kind to Louisa." Further, he said that he had always been in a position to give his wife and family more money than most men ever possess. To support his claim, he produced a telegram that he had sent Louisa saying, "Ranch is yours. Take it and run it to suit yourself." This was the property at North Platte, which had been rebuilt after the fire. He had deeded it to his wife, he explained, "so as to have less nagging and a little peace," hoping that it would pave the way for their separation. But the plan failed, and in a dramatic statement outside the courthouse, she reiterated her love for her husband.

A month after the case was filed, the lawyers made their final summations. On March 23, 1905, in a kind of Samsonesque ruling, the judge dismissed the claims and counterclaims of both parties. He ordered that the names of Cody's mistresses be stricken from the record, unconvinced that there had actually been affairs. Nor did he believe that Louisa had once tried to poison her husband, as Cody testified, supporting her explanation that she had been trying to cure his hangover. Cody lost an appeal in another court and then told reporters that he was taking *Cody v. Cody* to the U.S. Supreme Court. Meanwhile, he headed to France for a prolonged tour with the Wild West. Several months later, he wrote to his sister Julia that he had found God in his old age and that he had quit drinking. "Everything is running smooth. And I hope to make a lot of money before coming home. . . . I must fix myself for my old age—and for those I love." While he was away, his daughter Irma wrote to him and asked that he withdraw his petition for divorce. She was his only living child and he responded that he would stay married to Louisa forever.

Yet there was one woman whom Buffalo Bill may have loved more deeply than any of the others. He and she did not have a physical affair but they had a connection that no one could break and that he proclaimed to everyone. This was Annie Oakley, whose rise to prominence he shaped and urged along. His affection for her—even as a kind of sister—was apparent. They had been drawn together by similar backgrounds, and they had a deep respect and admiration for one another. She and husband Frank often visited Cody and Louisa in Nebraska, and Annie and Bill would often ride and rope and shoot together throughout the years that they traveled as colleagues and friends. In 1889, Cody gave her a horse named Black Jack, and Annie was one of the few who could ride the once wild mustang. While touring, he would confide in her about some of the women in his life, and she apparently would advise him. Clearly, they were confidants, for she did not speak of these affairs to Louisa; it was through others, including private detectives, that Cody's wife learned of them. What else Buffalo Bill and Annie Oakley spoke of, we do not know. Annie would not have betrayed Frank, but her relationship with Cody incurred Louisa's jealousy, according to many accounts. They not only spent much time together, but their names were often linked in newspaper coverage of the Wild West, and the show's programs and posters. For Louisa, there was no getting away from Annie Oakley—except for much later, as noted in Chris Enss's *The Many Loves of Buffalo Bill*, when she omitted any mention of her husband's costar in her own memoirs, a strange blank in a chronicle of her life and times.

"She is the single greatest asset the Wild West show ever had," Cody told a press agent, and this was not hyperbole. Sitting Bull may have been the representative of an ancient kingdom, but he toured with Buffalo Bill for only four months; Annie Oakley was with Cody for a decade. "To the loveliest and truest little woman both in heart and aim, in all the world," Cody once wrote to her. Sometime later, she expressed a similar sentiment. "There were hundreds of people in the outfit," said the woman he had nicknamed Little Missie, "and the whole time we were one great family, loyal to one man, Buffalo Bill Cody. His words were better than most contracts."

With the film industry beginning to flourish, sooner or later most of the surviving frontier characters converged in Hollywood. Trapped in their personas, they had nothing else to do except get paid to be some version of themselves. Like the others, Buffalo Bill turned to the new mythmaking machinery for the last phase of his life. But he was not content with his accomplishments and wanted to be more than "Buffalo Bill." "I grow very tired of this sort of sham hero-worship sometimes," he told a friend in 1897. He wanted to present the real story of the West, which is to say, not the myth at all. Thomas Edison had already filmed his show in 1894, and in 1910 and 1911 he himself had filmed parts of it as well. He understood the power of film and it was time to set the record straight. He decided to produce a movie called *The Last Indian Battles from the War Path to the Peace Pipe*. Among other things, it featured General Miles, the cavalry acting out the massacre of the Indians at Wounded Knee, and participants, including Native Americans, playing themselves. Some of the cast members had not only survived Wounded Knee, but had served on one side or the other in the Battle of the Little Bighorn as well.

The film had the blessing of the Departments of War and Interior, with Interior Secretary Franklin K. Lane asking the Pine Ridge Agency superintendent to make sure that it "included pictures of the children in school working and on the farm, and otherwise industrially engaged. The whole presenting an historical event of the progress of the Indians for the last twenty years," according to the *Rapid City Daily Journal* on October 22, 1913. The military was hoping that the film would present the army in a positive light, portraying its role in paving the way for settlers and protecting them in their westward journeys.

Yet there was disagreement as to how to depict Wounded Knee. One military advisor asked Cody to hold back footage of the incident unless the War Department approved it. Cody agreed. General Miles did not want Wounded Knee included at all. He blamed subordinates for the massacre, stating in his autobiography that "I have never felt that the action was judicious or justifiable, and have always believed that it could have been avoided." But Cody did go ahead and film the event; after all, re-enactments were what he was known for—and this one was to be placed in a context that was not sensational like his shows, but an accounting that pulled no punches and portrayed exactly what happened. Yet this time women and children were not part of the story; General Miles had ordered that they not be included. He himself remained at the Pine Ridge Agency away from the action while the Wounded Knee segment was filmed.

It was a complicated enterprise. To make this part of the movie, Cody reconstructed the Lakota village along the creek where Big Foot's band had assembled. "Painted canvas teepees sheltered extended families," reported *American History* magazine, "few of which did not grieve for an absent loved one." There were wails and sobs, and hundreds of soldiers were cleaning their rifles and wheeling in Hotchkiss guns. "Some Sioux wondered if the coming morning's battle would really be pretend. Or were they to be slaughtered like their ancestors? Painted stick markers shuddered above the sacred grave as the increasing wind filled it with snow. Younger braves thought perhaps the time had come for vengeance. Some talked of loading their rifles with live rounds instead of blanks. Soon death songs shrilled above thudding drums." From the bluffs above, Cody was watching the action, along with Louisa, who had recently rejoined him after their estrangement. Some of the Indians who had traveled with Cody warned him of the threats; a council was quickly arranged in the mess tent and Cody assured the young men that they were indeed making a movie and no one was to be killed.

On the morning of October 13, the cameras rolled. "The air erupted with gun smoke, shrieks and howls. Rifles crackled and ponies whirled," reported *American History*. "With the camp aflame, people fled down into the ravine and the artillery lobbed shells into their midst. It was a tragic, bloody business."

In the following days, other aspects of the final days of the Lakota were filmed: the Sioux in starving conditions, Ghost Dances, Sitting Bull's arrest and death. Even the final siege of the Lakota in the Badlands was filmed, after an arduous fifty-five-mile trek for fifty Sioux families, and a company of troops and heavy wagons loaded with hay, grain, and provisions. Finally, day-to-day life on the reservation was filmed, featuring children in school and farmers harvesting crops. On October 30, Cody hosted a grand celebration to mark the end of production. Fifty-three of the Native American actors had been stranded in Denver when his show had gone bankrupt earlier, and he had not yet paid them. "You have been my friends and I am going to be yours," he said, and then he wrote a check for $1,313 in back salaries. Later he headed south in his new seven-passenger Ford touring car.

In February of 1914, Cody went to Washington, D.C., to screen his series of films for members of President Woodrow Wilson's cabinet, congressmen, and reporters. "Cody was still straight as the arrows that have whizzed around his noble head," one reporter said. The audience of one thousand was spellbound. "It has been my object and my desire," Cody said, "to preserve history by the aid of the camera, with the living participants who took an active part in the Indian wars of America." On March 8, he was back in Denver, introducing the films to a full house for a weekly run, twice daily, at the Tabor Grand Opera House. "Nothing like this has ever been done before," said the *Denver Post*. "It is War, itself, grim, unpitying and terrible, and it holds your heart still as you watch it and leaves you in the end, amazed at the courage and the folly of mankind."

On March 28, Cody's publicist Major Burke announced that once again Cody had a fortune in sight and "the world by the ears." But that did not happen. The film fared poorly, perhaps because it was too real or too intense, criticized by Indians for excluding women and children from the massacre scene, and not appreciated by whites, who were unimpressed by the anticlimactic ending in which Indians were assimilated and went to school, instead of going on the warpath.

The move was cut down into a shorter version called *The Adventures of Buffalo Bill*. The entire documentary was supposedly donated to archives at the War and Interior Departments, but there is no record that it was ever received. However, a two-minute segment of it was viewed nearly twenty years ago at the Buffalo Bill Historical Center in Cody by Andrea I. Paul, reporting for *Nebraska History Magazine* in the winter 1990 edition. While the clip does not include the incident at Wounded Knee, it does include footage of the Wounded Knee period. The rest of the film portrays scouting and cavalry maneuvers at the Battle of Warbonnet Creek, and a scene of Cody en route to Sitting Bull's cabin, intercepted by Indian police before he can intervene for his friend. Yet to this day, remnants of the film are rumored to exist elsewhere—a disintegrating and mysterious relic, a side of Cody that may be lost to the ages.

With the failure of his film and the vanishing of the Wild West show, Buffalo Bill went back on the road, as himself, in the Sells-Floto Circus. He appeared in every show and parade. Some said that he had a fear of dying in the arena. Suffering from arthritis, he had trouble getting in and out of the saddle, and waited for a cue before shows to climb aboard—aided by a close associate. "Without hope, one is dead," he wrote to his sister Julia. His last touring season ended in 1916, with two performances in Portsmouth, Virginia, billed as the last ones before the show went into winter quarters at Norfolk. By now, Cody was generally in a carriage, standing on the buckboard in full showman dress, as a team of horses took him through town. "WILD WEST ON PORTSMOUTH STREETS" said the headline in the women's section of the local paper following the show. The streets were thronged. The band played "Memphis Blues" and then "Home Sweet Home" was offered on the piano. It was a memorable event, as always, and soon Cody was indeed going home.

Back in Colorado to visit his sister May, his health broke down, and then he briefly recovered. "You can't kill an old scout," he would say as the pattern repeated itself. But soon, doctors told him there wasn't much more time. He prepared for his final scene, calling in his friends for a last round of poker just before he died, on January 10, 1917. Although Cody had wanted to be buried in a beloved and remote spot in Wyoming, the *Denver Post* paid his wife $10,000 to bury him in Colorado, so that's where he was eventually laid to rest, on Lookout Mountain in the town of Golden, overlooking the plains. Months earlier, so many people had gathered for Cody's funeral that the country had its first traffic jam—or so newspapers reported. His body was carried by caisson past a sea of spectators, escorted by fellow members of an Elks lodge, all wearing top hats. One of his favorite horses, McKinley, followed the caisson. When the casket was lifted and carried into the lodge, according to a witness, McKinley tried to break free from his handler. As the lodge doors closed, the horse whinnied, bolted, and ran to the caisson—like Sitting Bull's horse, and Comanche before him, looking for his rider. Then he sniffed and whinnied again. The handler grabbed his reins and led McKinley away. But he turned his head and stared at the doors, longing for Buffalo Bill. It was all a fitting end to the equestrian age.

At his burial service sometime later, Native Americans filed past the grave, placing the recently minted buffalo head nickel atop the stone. Aptly, the Indian portrayed on that famous nickel was Iron Tail, an Oglala figure of note, friend of Buffalo Bill's, and member of the Wild West. On the other side is the buffalo, and he has a name too. It's Black Diamond, who lived in a small cage at the Central Park menagerie, the offspring of a pair of buffalo that were once in the P. T. Barnum circus. "Its head droops as if it had lost all hope in the world," one observer said, "and even the sculptor was not able to raise it."

One person conspicuously absent as Cody's body lay in state in Denver was Annie Oakley. She had endured her own share of travails, both during and after her years of touring. In her first season with the Wild West, Frank Butler's poodle, George, the dog who had played Cupid in their courtship and then became part of their act, got caught in the rain, developed pneumonia, and died while the show was in Cleveland. A company carpenter built a small wooden coffin and Annie and Frank covered him with the satin and velvet table cover where they placed their weapons during their act. Indian girls chanted and made wreaths, and an old friend offered his lawn as a resting place. Two cowboys dug a grave and there George was buried.

Although this happened early in Annie's career with Buffalo Bill, it was the end of the shooting team of Butler and Oakley. Other dogs would take George's place and Annie was devoted to them all, especially a dog named Dave. During the First World War, Annie and Frank raised money for the Red Cross by giving shooting exhibitions at army bases around the country. Dave was part of their show, sniffing out money hidden in a red handkerchief that would be donated to the charity. They signed their Christmas cards "Annie, Frank, and Dave," and Annie's countless fans clamored to meet him. Time passed and Annie continued to appear in shooting exhibitions, now wearing eyeglasses, but still just as fast on the draw. One day she was traveling in Florida with friends.

Their car overturned and Annie was pinned underneath—one more accident since a horrific Wild West train crash in 1901 during which she and other performers, including animals, had incurred serious injuries. Now with a fractured hip and shattered ankle, she was hospitalized for six weeks. Frank took a room across the street from the hospital, visiting daily with Dave, who posted himself at her side. Later, Frank wrote a story called "The Life of Dave, As Told by Himself," describing Annie's hospital stay from the dog's point of view. "She looked very feeble and could only put out one hand to stroke my head," Dave said. "She was always so gentle and careful in combing and brushing me." Upon recovery, she needed a cane to walk and had a steel brace on her right leg. She wrote a public letter of thanks to the thousands of admirers who had sent get-well telegrams and notes.

Shortly after her accident, while out for a walk with Frank, Dave was hit and killed by a car. He was eulogized in the paper as "The Red Cross Dog," and it was said that Annie and Frank never recovered from his loss. Annie continued to tour, giving shooting exhibitions in spite of her limp and sometimes from a chair. In an interview with the *Philadelphia Ledger*, she had some advice for "the modern girl." "Learn to ride a horse," she said, "not merely to hold one." She also wanted girls to learn how to shoot and said that they should concern themselves with "other people's troubles," lest they spend too much time thinking about their own. Over the years, she taught thousands of women and girls to shoot, and probably some boys too. But it was as a role model for girls that she had become known; in her quiet and unassuming way, she was passing along knowledge of self-defense to part of the population that may have never had it.

Over the next few years, Annie weakened, and at some point began preparing for her death. She gave away possessions including mementos from the Wild West, such as a pipe and a newspaper clipping showing Sitting Bull with that very item. Her fondness for him was known to all; not only did she speak of him to friends, but once she had dressed as Sitting Bull for a costume ball, wearing a war bonnet of pheasant feathers on Valentine's Day. On November 3, 1926, Annie Oakley died in her sleep. Described in newspaper reports as "the friend of monarchs and Sitting Bull," she was sixty-six. Her doctor said the cause of her death was pernicious anemia, but some said she was simply worn out. Others attributed her death to lead poisoning caused by a lifetime of handling weapons and ammunition. If accurate, this surmise suggests that any number of other frontier characters could have been afflicted by the same condition, flowing with toxins. Not quite three weeks later, Frank passed away at the age of seventy-six. He had stopped eating upon her death and although he had not been well for some time, close friends said he died of a broken heart. They were buried together in Greenville, Ohio, Annie's hometown.

It was said that Annie had a dislike for anything that was not of the present, an understandable characteristic for a sharpshooter who was clearly in tune with the here and now. In fact, when she learned of Buffalo Bill's death, she was at a shooting exhibition. Her reaction indicated how much Cody had in common with his old friend and touring partner Sitting Bull. "It may seem strange," she observed, "that after the wonderful success attained that he should have died a poor man. But it isn't a matter of any wonder to those that knew and worked with him. The same qualities that insured success also insured his ultimate poverty. . . . He was totally unable to resist any claim for assistance that came to him, or refuse any mortal in distress." A short time later, as Buffalo Bill's body lay in state, Annie penned a note. "Good bye old friend," she wrote. "The sun setting over the mountain will pay its tribute to the resting place of the last of the great builders of the West, all of which you loved, and part of which you were."

And now, there is one more item for our tale. After Wounded Knee, Kicking Bear, the Minneconjou Indian who met Wovoka and returned to his people to speak of resurrection, joined the Wild West. There were others who had danced the Ghost Dance as well, and they too entered the American dreamtime in the parade without end led by Buffalo Bill. To this day, the show is still touring.

EPILOGUE

Let us speak once again of Wovoka, the man whose vision triggered the unfortunate cascade of events leading to the death of Sitting Bull. His fame grew after the Ghost Dance prophecies failed to materialize, with many seeking his counsel, healing, rain-making abilities, and blessings. With a partner, he established a business selling his autograph and pictures, and then one winter day in 1924 he had a visitor from Hollywood. This was the cowboy Tim McCoy, who had been working as a technical director on *The Thundering Herd*, which was filming in Bishop, California, with various Native American stuntmen and extras. Realizing that he was a day's car ride from Wovoka in Yerington, Nevada, he set out to explore the place where Short Bull and Kicking Bear had journeyed over twenty-five years earlier, in search of the messiah. He too wanted to find this man, after hearing so much about him from the Indians with whom he was now working. On the outskirts of town, he found the shack to which he had been directed, and he knocked on the door. A Paiute in his twenties opened the door and McCoy asked if this was the home of Wovoka. Furtively looking around, the young man nodded and then closed the door.

McCoy headed back to his car, and then the door opened. Out came Wovoka. He was no longer the vibrant conveyor of salvation, now an old man, in a dark beaver skin hat, a rumpled suit and vest, with a flourish, perhaps, of a white shirt and boots.

"His face showed much sadness," McCoy told his son in their book, "though neither then nor later to determine for whom that sadness had been experienced; for the hundreds who had been blasted to smithereens at Wounded Knee or for himself and a dream that had become a nightmare." McCoy explained that he wanted to talk about the Ghost Dance, and Wovoka said he did not want to discuss it. Then he headed back to his cabin. "That's too bad," McCoy responded, adding that he had greetings from some of his old friends. "What friends?" Wovoka said. "Two men from Wind River," McCoy replied. "Yellow Calf and Sage. Two Men from Pine Ridge: Short Bull and Kicking Bear." Wovoka said that he remembered them. "What do they say?" he asked. "They say that they respect you," McCoy answered. Wovoka relaxed a little and said that they were all good men when they knew him. "They still are," McCoy said. "And I know some others who would like to see you. They are Arapahos and were all ghost dancers. They believed in you. I think they still do." Wovoka replied that he would like to see them too. But they lived so far away. "I've never been to their country," he said. "It's a long way off." That was for sure, McCoy thought to himself. By all accounts, Wovoka had not been anywhere. He remained in Nevada during the ghost dance years, perhaps never stepping out of Mason Valley. After Wounded Knee he vanished.

McCoy told Wovoka that the Arapahoes did indeed live far away. But he explained that they came from their country to see him. Wovoka asked where they were, and McCoy said that they were just across the state line, in California. "They are too far away," Wovoka said again. "But think of how far they have come just to see you," McCoy replied. "They have been told so often by the white man that you are a fraud and yet they continue to believe. It would be the greatest thing in their lives if they could lay their eyes upon you just once before they die."

Wovoka relented and asked McCoy to send a car for him on the next day. Then he turned around and headed back to his shack. "Bring some of your friends," McCoy called after him. "There'll be a dance."

On the following day there was no film shoot. McCoy did not tell the Arapahoes that Wovoka was coming, lest he not show up. The car had been sent, and the Indians were dancing at an outdoor fire, eating, having a good time. "At about four-thirty that afternoon," McCoy recalled, "the long black limousine carrying Wovoka and his grandson arrived. It was followed by a convoy of five jalopies filled with Paiutes."

McCoy asked for the men to gather in a circle, and then he told them that the Messiah had arrived, the man who started the ghost dance. At first there was no reaction. But then the Arapahoes became excited, whispering among themselves, and Wovoka got out of the car. The Arapahoes bowed their heads, afraid to look at him. The members of his entourage also avoided his eyes. "My children! Hear me!" Wovoka said. "I wish to speak with you. But first, dance and eat some more!" And so they did, and then they made music, and then Wovoka began to speak. He explained the vision that he had on that fateful New Year's Day in 1889 when he died along with the sun and he met with God, who told him to tell his children to tell no lies and live in peace with everyone. And that was all he did, he explained, and nothing more. "But some of them," he continued, "particularly the Sioux, got carried away and took back this idea about ghost shirts, because they wanted to fight the white man. God was not pleased with this and the Sioux were killed and the Medicine turned bad. So God decided that the spirits of the dead Indians and the elk, antelope and buffalo, would not return. At least not now."

But there was still time to get things right, he added, and announced that he was going to teach them a dance. "It's good Medicine," he said. They were told to take it back to Wind River and teach it to their fellow tribesmen. "And I'll be damned if it wasn't the Ghost Dance," McCoy said. "Here it was 1924 and Wovoka, his grandson, twenty-some Paiutes, nine old Arapahoes and I were dancing in a circle, shuffling along, painted with sacred paint, singing the songs. The same old songs, the same old dance."

After an hour of dancing, Wovoka said it was time to go. He stood in front of the limousine, making his final blessings. "The old buffalo hunters and warriors put their hands into their pipe bags," McCoy remembered, "drew out five- and ten-dollar bills, and then marched single file toward the Messiah, presenting their offerings." Wovoka accepted them and then got into the limo. He settled in, looking out the window at McCoy and then rolled it down. Out came his hand, which dropped a cake of red paint into the cowboy's coat pocket. It was the same paint that Wovoka had given to Kicking Bear and the other pilgrims upon their original visit, and it was to be applied to the face for the dance that called up the ghosts. And then from the back seat of the fancy car came a whisper. "I will never die," Wovoka said. "Is that so?" McCoy replied, gazing at the man who dreamed an apocalypse. Wovoka nodded. "Never?" McCoy asked one more time. "No, never," he said. Eight years later, he walked on. His wooden grave marker in the Paiute cemetery in Yerington said "Jack Wilson. Died Sept. 20, 1932, Age 64." One day, a new headstone was added. "Founder of the Ghost Dance," it says. "His teachings of hope, good will, and promise of life after death will live as long as man inhabits this earth."

CODA:

Ghost Dance II

"On January 27, 1913," wrote Steven Rinella in *American Buffalo*, "twenty-five presses at the Philadelphia Mint began stamping out three thousand buffalo nickels a minute. Production continued until 1938, and Black Diamond's profile became the most widely distributed image of a buffalo in the world. In the midst of that production, in 1915, Black Diamond himself was put up on an auction block in New York City. There were no bidders. His keeper then offered Black Diamond for private sale." He was purchased for $300, less than the starting bid of $500, and taken to a slaughterhouse on Fourteenth Street. "The carcass yielded 1020 pounds of meat," Rinella noted, and his head was mounted on the wall of the packer's office. Its whereabouts are now unknown.

A few years before the death of Black Diamond, fifteen buffalo from a seed herd at the Bronx Zoo were loaded onto a railcar and shipped to Cache, Oklahoma. They had been living at the zoo under the auspices of the American Bison Society, a group that was started by New York aristocrats including Andrew Carnegie, which also included the artist Frederic Remington. President Theodore Roosevelt was the president of the society. Once a buffalo hunter himself (in fact, his hunting cabin had been shipped from the Badlands to the Columbian Exposition and sat near Sitting Bull's on the midway), it was his belief that the buffalo must be returned to the Great Plains, lest its disappearance diminish the American spirit. "In Oklahoma," Rinella wrote, "the train was approached by a group of curious Comanche Indians. The Indians remembered buffalo, though the children had never seen one."

On May 7, 2016, President Barack Obama signed the National Bison Legacy Act. The animal that gave its name to Sitting Bull and Buffalo Bill had now come full circle; it was officially the national mammal. A few months later, on November 1, there was a ceremony to mark this moment at Wind Cave National Park in Wyoming. The ceremony celebrated the buffalo's restoration across the West as well as the herd that originated in this region. According to Lakota tradition, the cave is the place from which the ancients emerged, followed by the buffalo. Its high, barometric winds roil and blow through one of the world's great natural labyrinths—the breath of the earth, as the legend goes, right here under the grasses of the prairie. Two days after the ceremony in the park, there was another one nearby. This was on the Wind River Reservation of the eastern Shoshone, honoring the release of ten buffalo from a federal refuge in Iowa, with help from the National Wildlife Restoration—an effort that was forty years in the making. There had been no buffalo on this reservation since 1885, two years after Sitting Bull had gone on the last buffalo hunt elsewhere on the Great Plains. Accompanied by native drums and prayer and song, the small herd headed right out onto the plain as soon as the corral gate was opened.

Sitting Bull and Sacajawea now lie near a remote rural highway, and neither site is well maintained. (Some say, however, that Sacajawea is actually buried on the Wind River Reservation, home of her ancestors. There are many memorials to her across the West, statues portraying her with her child on her back, which was how she accompanied Lewis and Clark. Each statue seems to invoke the petrified woman and child after which Standing Rock was named. In

North Dakota, the Sitting Bull and Sacajawea burial sites each have statues marking their graves.) Occasionally tourists making a pilgrimage, especially those from faraway lands, stop to pay their respects, and notice the beer cans and shotgun shells that litter the graves and find themselves cleaning. Appalled at the manner in which we treat our icons, especially Sitting Bull, for he is a hero to many, they make note of it in their journals and wonder how it has come to this.

If you go to the grave of Sitting Bull, and if you have seen his few photographs, you will note that his statue does not really look like him. That's because the person who posed for it was Nancy Kicking Bear, his granddaughter. There's a family resemblance but not enough of one to make anyone who has seen his images feel his power in this representation. But this brings us to another puzzle of the Great Plains. Not everyone believes that Sitting Bull was buried at this location, although other accounts place him nearby.

After his body was returned to Fort Yates, there was a funeral for the metal breasts, the Native American police who had been killed in the fight at his cabin. They were buried in the Standing Rock cemetery with full military honors, a three-volley gun salute, and the playing of taps. A little while later, Sitting Bull was buried in the Fort Yates military cemetery. "The grave had been dug by four Army prisoners from the guardhouse," writes Judith St. George in *To See with the Heart*. "With only McLaughlin and three Army officers present, Sitting Bull's body, wrapped in canvas and placed in a crude wooden box, was hauled from the Dead House to the grave in a two-wheeled cart pulled by a mule. Silently the box was lowered into the grave, with no honors at all."

In 1915, Red Tomahawk, the man who killed Sitting Bull, was interviewed at Fort Yates by Colonel A. B. Welch, army veteran and adopted son of the Yanktonai Sioux Nation.

"Does his spirit ever come back here?" Welch asked.

"Yes, sometimes," was the reply. "He rides in on an elk spirit."

"I want to go to his grave," Welch said. "Come with me."

"No," Red Tomahawk replied. "I do not go. I am afraid. There are mysterious flowers on his grave every year. We do not know where they come from. They are *wankan*. They should bury him in a church yard."

Somewhere between the time Sitting Bull's body had arrived at Fort Yates and was buried there, a lock of his hair was taken and so were his leggings. It was just as he had once told a reporter in something of an aside—he had feared not receiving proper rites when it was time. Years later, some of his descendants carried out a stealth operation and removed the bones from his grave at Fort Yates, taking them to the new site on a highway in South Dakota. There the bones were reinterred. In 1952, a ceremony marked the grave's unveiling. But like so many things around Sitting Bull, a sad litany of disputes arose. Some said his bones had been spirited away long ago, and were never buried at Fort Yates at all. Perhaps the bones in that grave were someone else's, a soldier's maybe, or an Indian scout's. Whose bones were really in the new grave? Should he have been buried there anyway? And if so, why isn't the site turned into a museum that attracts more tourists and sells things?

Meanwhile, the dream of the ghost dancers is being dreamed again on the Great Plains. At Standing Rock, the vibrations of those who have gathered to pray and sing and drum have resounded around the world. Tribes from the four directions have arrived on foot, horseback, by canoe, and by car. In Wyoming, to the west of Standing Rock, when the buffalo were released, although it was a small herd, there arose a sound and it is said that the gusts at Wind Cave from where the ancestors of the animals emerged swirled in response, the breath of the earth accompanying the dance of the four-legged.

About ten years ago, when the Sacajawea visitors center

opened up in Salmon, Idaho, a descendant of hers asked an elder if Sacajawea ruined it for everyone by helping Lewis and Clark on their expedition into the West. "No," came the reply. "It would have happened anyway."

And so we play our parts, all creatures great and small, and Sitting Bull knew this well—a meadowlark and other animals foretold the turns on his path, and he listened and was not surprised. Now his great-grandson Ernie LaPointe would like to make a course correction. A few years ago, the U.S. government returned Sitting Bull's leggings and hair to LaPointe's family. They were received with ceremony, but of course the work is not done. Since then, LaPointe has been hoping to move Sitting Bull's bones one more time—to the Little Bighorn battlefield. There he would join the others, Native American and *wasichu* alike, and the spirits of the horses who carried them—all who rest in the greasy grass, all whose legacy is there.

> *A dawn*
> *Appears,*
> *Behold it.*
>
> —Lakota Dawn Song

> *The tribe*
> *Named me,*
> *So*
> *In courage*
> *I shall live*
> *It is reported*
> *Sitting Bull*
> *Said this.*
>
> —Song of Sitting Bull

ACKNOWLEDGMENTS

I would like to thank my editor, Bob Bender, for acquiring this book and his patience and assistance along its path; his assistant Johanna Li, for being there during the process; copyeditors Kathy Higuchi and Fred Chase and the entire crew at Simon & Schuster for all their work on my behalf. Also, I must thank my agent BJ Robbins for helping me take *Blood Brothers*—one more years-in-the-making endeavor—to fruition.

I would like to say that I am ever so grateful to my biggest fan, my mother, Eleanor Stillman, who wanted so much to help with this endeavor, and did, going through my library and writing down on index cards the names of every book that I read and consulted for this one—the bibliography. Now, as my book goes to press and she nears the end of her life, she doesn't remember doing that. Although she has read chapters of *Blood Brothers* in progress, my most fervent hope is that she can see the book itself when published.

And now, let me say that it's always difficult to face what Tennessee Williams has called "the pale judgment"—the blank page and its terrors. Who shall bear witness to the writer's travails? Who shall provide comfort and aid when the page is full (for a moment)? To that end, I would like to thank Rex Weiner, George Solomon, and Sonnie Buttiglieri, all there at different times in my life, and let it be said, for no one can know the time or the hour.

Others who have helped me during my journey through this

book, and in all sorts of other ways—a gesture, aid, solace, time, an ear, a venue, a hand—whether in this dimension or from afar: Jo Anderson, Pamela Berkeley, Mickey Birnbaum, Alaina Bixon, the late Charles Bowden, Jamie Brisick, Jeffrey Burbank, Gimique Camp, John Carver, Leslie Caveny, the late Rebecca and Sam Cohen, Lee Cohn, John Coinman, Lynda Crawford, John Densmore, Samantha Dunn, Jill Alexander Essbaum, Jeff Eyres, Eric Feig, Tony Gilkyson, Tod Goldberg, the late Zelda Gorodetzer, Kevin Hancock, Amy Handelsman, Melissa Henderson, Chief Arvol Looking Horse, Betty Lee Kelly, Lenora Kelly, Michael Kelly, Andrea Lankford, Tom Lutz, Kate MacMurray, Joshua Malkin, Anthony McCann, Mary Martha Miles, Victor Mongeau, Mary Otis, Carol Park, Jon Pierson, Michele Raphael, Luis Reyes, the late Helen Rosenberg, Patricia Roth, Bobbi Royle, Jessica Sampson, Barry Siegel, Pam Slipyan, Pamela Diane Gilbert-Snyder, the late Susan and Peter Stern, Ariana Stillman, Denise Stillman, Jon Stillman, the late Ron and Linda Stillman, Kathleen Sublette, Mark Sublette, Tom Teicholz, Mark Treitel, Stanley Triggs, Maggie Towers, Jean Waszak, John Waszak, Andrew Winer, Cisco, Buster, and Zoe the rescued cats, and others whom I have most likely forgotten to mention. You are all in the house and will be, always.

NOTES ON THE WRITING OF THIS BOOK

To write this book, I traveled across the Great Plains to visit many of the locations mentioned in it, and as I do with all of my work, I talked with a wide range of people and consulted a number of texts. Those I spoke with included scholars, librarians, museum curators, members of the Lakota and other tribes, current Wild West reenactors, and various other relevant figures. The texts that ground my writing include first-person Native American and cavalry accounts, government records, nineteenth-century newspaper reports, oral histories, auction house records, letters, interviews, maps, songs, poems, books, films, television documentaries, and plays. Many of these sources are cited in my narrative, so are not included in the following chapter-by-chapter notes and list of references. A number of books served as a kind of foundation for my book, and they are cited where quoted, but I'll mention them here as well, as they are essential reading on the matters at hand.

They are: *Buffalo Bill's America* by Louis Warren; *The Lives and Legends of Buffalo Bill* by Don Russell; *Wild West Shows and the Images of American Indians* by L. G. Moses; *Buffalo Bill and the Wild West* by Henry Blackman Sell and Victor Weybright; *Buffalo Bill: His Family, Friends, Fame, and Failures* by Nellie Snyder Yost; *True Tales of the Plains* by William F. Cody; *Woman Walking Ahead: In Search of Catherine Weldon* by Eileen Pollack; *The Ghost-Dance Religion and Wounded Knee* by James Mooney; *Sitting Bull: His Life and Legacy* by Ernie LaPointe; Robert Utley's books about Sitting Bull, including *Sitting Bull: The Life and Times of an American Patriot, The Lance and the Shield: The Life and Times of Sitting Bull,* and *The Last Days of the Sioux Nation; Sitting Bull: Champion of the Sioux* by Stanley Vestal; *Sitting Bull, Prisoner of War* by Dennis C. Pope; *Sitting Bull* by Bill Yenne; *Annie Oakley of the Wild West* by Walter Havighurst; *Annie Oakley* by Shirl Kasper; *The Life and Legacy of Annie Oakley* by Glenda Riley; *The Destruction of the Bison* by Andrew C. Isenberg; and *Black Elk Speaks* by John G. Neihardt.

It should be noted that there is some controversy surrounding *Black Elk Speaks.* First published in 1932, and then in subsequent editions, it is the account of the Lakota holy man Black Elk as recorded by John G. Neihardt, longtime Nebraska resident and state poet laureate whose affinity for Native Americans led him to record Black Elk's visions. After the book was published, it gained an ever-growing following and was, and still is, regarded by many (including this author) as a great work of theological import. Yet over time, some critics said that Neihardt embellished the stories, and that perhaps the account is a blending of his and Black Elk's visions. Let's defer to the Native American writer Vine Deloria, Jr. on this matter. As he says in the latest edition of the book (2000), "Neihardt's *Black Elk Speaks* and *When the Tree Flowered,* and *The Sacred Pipe* by Joseph Epes Brown, the basic works of the Black Elk theological tradition, now bid fair to become the canon or at least the central core of a North American Indian theological canon which will someday challenge the Eastern and Western traditions as a way of looking at the world. . . . The very nature of great religious teachings is that they encompass everyone who understands them and personalities become indistinguishable from the transcendent truth that is expressed. So let it be with *Black Elk Speaks.*"

Other books and texts that have informed my work but are not listed here are mentioned inside the narrative and/or are included in my extensive bibliography. What follows is a look at each chapter and the main sources used in addition to the above-mentioned essential reading. I should also note that certain passages from this book previously appeared in my book *Mustang: The Saga of the Wild Horse in the American West*, as noted in the chapter breakdown below. Some material also originally appeared in my "Letter from the West" columns on www.truthdig.com and in the *Los Angeles Review of Books*.

For the introduction, I drew from "Celebration of Forgiveness at Black Elk Peak," by David Rooks, *Indian Country Media Network*, September 30, 2016, and "Oglala Veteran Pushed for Black Elk Peak," by Jim Kent for *Lakota Country Times*, reprinted on www.indianz.com, August 26, 2016.

For Chapter 1, "In Which Public Enemy Number One Comes Home," I drew from the following books: *The Wild West: A History of the Wild West Shows* by Don Russell; *Adventures of the Ojibbeway and Ioway Indians: In England, France, and Belgium*, Volume 1 and Volume 2 by George Catlin; *Sitting Bull in Canada* by Tony Hollihan; *My Friend, the Indian* by James McLaughlin; and *Prairie Man: The Struggle Between Sitting Bull and Indian Agent James McLaughlin* by Norman E. Matteoni. I also referred to "Enemies in '76, Friends in '85—Sitting Bull and Buffalo Bill," an article by Louis Pfaller in *Prologue: The Journal of the National Archives*, Fall 1969.

The books *Sitting Bull* by Bill Yenne and *Sitting Bull: Prisoner of War* by Dennis C. Pope were of much aid and insight, and the fact that one of Sitting Bull's wives, Four Robes, gave birth to a daughter en route to Fort Randall was determined by Pope in his examination of population records of that period.

For Chapter 2, "In Which the Wild West Is Born—and Dies and Is Resurrected from the Bottom of the Mississippi River," I drew from *Buffalo Bill's Life Story, An Autobiography*; *Buffalo Bill and His Horses* by Agnes Wright Spring; *Last of the Great Scouts (Buffalo Bill)* by Zane Grey and Helen Cody Wetmore; *Mustang: The Saga of the Wild Horse in the American West* by Deanne Stillman; *The Buffalo Hunters: The Story of the Hide Men* by Mari Sandoz; the archives at the Buffalo Bill Historical Center in Cody, Wyoming; the Buffalo Bill Museum and Grave in Golden, Colorado.

For Chapter 3, "In Which the Seventh Cavalry Is Defeated at the Battle of the Little Bighorn, and Buffalo Bill Stars as Himself in 'The Red Right Hand, or the First Scalp for Custer,'" I referred to *Custer, Cody, and Grand Duke Alexis: Historical Archaeology of the Royal Buffalo Hunt* by Douglas Scott; *Custer's Gold* by Donald Jackson; *The Last Stand: Custer, Sitting Bull, and the Battle of the Little Bighorn* by Nathaniel Philbrick; *Mustang: The Saga of the Wild Horse in the American West* by Deanne Stillman; *His Very Silence Speaks* by Elizabeth Atwood Lawrence; *To Kill An Eagle: Indian Views on the Last Days of Crazy Horse* by Edward and Mabel Hadlecek; *Crazy Horse and Custer* by Stephen Ambrose; *Son of the Morning Star* by Evan S. Connell; *Boots and Saddles, or Life in Dakota with General Custer* by Elizabeth B. Custer; *Buffalo Bill on Stage* by Sandra K. Sagala; and *American History*, August 2011, the article from *US History in Context* described "Soothsayer Sitting Bull's ability to embrace the Great Mystery and commune with meadowlarks made him one of America's greatest spiritual leaders." The Walter Stanley Campbell (pen name Stanley Vestal) papers at the University of Oklahoma were also of service; they contain numerous interviews with contemporaries of Sitting Bull, including One Bull, and transcriptions of Sitting Bull's songs.

For Chapter 4, "In Which Sitting Bull Is Hired and Heads East for the Wild West," I referred to various newspaper accounts regarding the occasion of his hiring by Buffalo Bill's advance man, John Burke, including those in the *San Francisco Daily Evening Bulletin*, June 11, 1885, entitled, "Sioux Warriors: Sitting Bull and Other Braves Coming to Join a 'Wild West' Show,'" *Milwaukee Sentinel*, June 11, 1885; "The Sitting Bull Party," *Bismarck Daily Tribune*, June 12, 1885; and "Greek Meets Greek: A Thrilling and Romantic Encounter Between Redskins and Pale Face Chieftains," *Buffalo Courier*, June 13, 1885.

For Chapter 5, "In Which Sitting Bull and Buffalo Bill Join Up in the City of Buffalo, and *Tatanka Iyotake* Reunites with Annie Oakley," I consulted the above-mentioned *Buffalo Courier* article; the archives at the National Annie Oakley Archives at Garst Museum in Greenville, Ohio; the Annie Oakley and Buffalo Bill chapters of *The Wild West* PBS documentary series for *The American Experience* (available on DVD); and *Annie Get Your Gun* (original film, 1950).

For Chapter 6, "In Which an Indian and a *Wasichu* Certify Their Alliance Across the Medicine Line," I drew from *William Notman: The Stamp of a Studio* by Stanley G. Triggs; *William Notman's Studio: The Canadian Picture* by Stanley G. Triggs; *Buffalo Bill and Sitting Bull: Inventing the Wild West* by Bobby Bridger; the play *Indians* by Arthur Kopit and the Robert Altman film based on it, *Buffalo Bill and the Indians, or Sitting Bull's History Lesson* (with Paul Newman as Buffalo Bill); the catalogue for Buffalo Bill and the Wild West, an exhibition presented at the Brooklyn Museum November 21, 1981–January 17, 1982, and its essay, "The Indians," by Vine Deloria, Jr.; "Sitting Bull Talks," *New York Herald* interview, Jeremy Stilson, October 17, 1877; and *Teton Sioux Music and Culture* by Frances Densmore.

For Chapter 7, "In Which There Comes a Ghost Dance, or, A Horse from Buffalo Bill Responds to the Assassination of Sitting Bull, and Other Instances of the Last Days of the Wild West,"

I referred to *Tim McCoy Remembers the West* by Tim McCoy and Ronald McCoy; the Mary Collins Collection at the South Dakota State Archives; the Indian Rights Association records (online), 1830–1986, at the Historical Society of Pennsylvania, Philadelphia; Indian Rights Association Pamphlets (online), 1884–1985, Center of Southwest Studies, Fort Lewis College, Durango, Colorado; *American Indian Policy in Crisis: Christian Reformers and the Indian, 1865–1900*, by Francis Paul Prucha; http://nativeamerican netroots.net/diary/958 regarding Indian rights of the 1880s; poem "Omeros" by Derek Walcott (regarding Catherine Weldon); *My People, the Sioux*, by Luther Standing Bear; Sitting Bull College online library—www.sittingbull.edu for archive of photographs and images of Sitting Bull and other information; *The Arrest and Killing of Sitting Bull* by John M. Carroll; *Eyewitness at Wounded Knee*, by Richard E. Jensen, R. Eli Paul, and John E. Carter; *Bury My Heart at Wounded Knee* by Dee Brown; *A Century of Dishonor* by Helen Hunt Jackson; and *Buffalo Bill's Own Story of His Life and Deeds*, by William Lightfoot Visscher, who recorded his friend's "heroic career" in his own words, as stated on the book's cover. "Tell me a story, Buffalo Bill!" said the young boys who gathered around him in his last days. He would and then they'd say, "Tell me another."

Finally, regarding the Ghost Dance, my phone conversation with Chief Arvol Looking Horse while I was working on this book opened up a new way of thinking about this—and my entire story. I had long thought about the legend of the horse from Buffalo Bill that was outside Sitting Bull's cabin at the time of his killing. This was the four-legged that began dancing at the sound of gunfire as it had been trained to do while touring as Sitting Bull's mount in the Wild West. This too was the Ghost Dance, I realized when I first learned of its occurrence, and as I said in the introduction to this book, it was an element of the story from which I could not turn away. When Chief Looking Horse suggested that it was even something more, that it was the horse metaphorically taking bullets for Sitting Bull as he was being assassinated, I had to take a moment or two, and I am still taking them, for of all the images that have come my way while writing this book—Sitting Bull's son handing Sitting Bull's rifle to the authorities at his father's request; Sitting Bull and Buffalo Bill meeting for the first time in Buffalo, of all places; Sitting Bull and Buffalo Bill posing for a photograph in full dress—this is the heartbeat behind the story, the trinity of the West, the two icons nearly crossing paths just before Sitting Bull died, and joined in the end by a horse that "died" along with our great Native American patriot.

BIBLIOGRAPHY

Bates, Edward V. *In Search of Spirit: A Sioux Family Memoir*. Spokane, WA: Marquette Books, 2009.

Bear, Luther Standing. *My People, the Sioux*. Lincoln: University of Nebraska Press, 1975.

Blackstone, Sarah J. *The Business of Being Buffalo Bill. Selected Letters of William F. Cody, 1879–1917*. New York: Praeger Publishers, 1988.

Blevins, Win. *Buffalo*. Tucson: Rio Nuevo Publishers, 2005.

Brandes, Ray. *Frontier Military Posts of Arizona*. Globe, AZ: Dale Stuart King, 1960.

Bridger, Bobby. *Buffalo Bill and Sitting Bull: Inventing the Wild West*. Austin: University of Texas Press, 2002.

Brown, Dee. *Bury My Heart at Wounded Knee*. New York: St. Martin's Press, 1970.

Buel, James William. *Heroes of the Plains*. St. Louis and Philadelphia: Historical Publishing Company, 1883.

Burke, John. *Buffalo Bill*. London, Great Britain: Cassell & Company Ltd., 1974.

Calvert, Patricia. *Standoff at Standing Rock: The Story of Sitting Bull and James McLaughlin*. Bismarck, ND: Twenty-first Century Books, 2001.

Carroll, John M. *The Arrest and Killing of Sitting Bull: A Documentary*. Mattituck, NY: Amereon House, Ltd., 1986.

Carter, Robert A. *Buffalo Bill Cody: The Man Behind the Legend*. Hoboken, NJ: John Wiley & Sons, 2000.

Cody, William F. Cody. *True Tales of the Plains*. New York: Cupples & Leon Company, 1908.

Connell, Evan S. *Son of the Morning Star: Custer and the Little Bighorn*. New York: North Point Press, 1997.

Coward, John M. *The Newspaper Indian: Native American Identity in the Press 1820–90*. Chicago: University of Illinois Press, 1999.

Crummett, Michael. *Sitting Bull*. Tucson: Western National Parks Association, 2003.

Custer, George Armstrong. *Sitting Bull: Adapted from Wild Life on the Plains*. Bedford, MA: Applewood Books, 1886.

Densmore, Frances. *Teton Sioux Music and Culture*. Lincoln: University of Nebraska Press, First Bison Book printing, 1992.

DeWall, Robb. *The Saga of Sitting Bull's Bones*. Sioux Falls, SD: Modern Press, Inc., 1982.

Diedrich, Mark. *Sitting Bull, the Collected Speeches*. Rochester, MN: Coyote Books, 1998.

Drury, Bob, and Tom Clavin. *The Heart of Everything That Is: The Untold Story of Red Cloud, an American Legend*. New York: Simon & Schuster, 2013.

Easton, Robert, and MacKenzie Brown. *Lord of Beasts: The Saga of Buffalo Jones*. Tucson: The University of Arizona Press, 1961.

Enss, Chris. *The Many Loves of Buffalo Bill. The True Story of Life on the Wild West Show*. Guilford, CT: A Twodot Book, a division of Globe Pequot Press, 2010.

Friswold, Carroll. *Frontier Fighters and Their Autograph Signatures*. Tuscon, AZ: Westernlore Press, 1968.

Fugle, Eugene. *The Nature and Function of the Lakota Night Cults*. Kendall Park, NJ: *Museum News*, vol. 27, no. 3–4, 1966.

Garst, Shannon. *Sitting Bull: Champion of His People*. New York: Julian Messner (Simon & Schuster), 1956.

Grey, Zane, and Helen Cody Wetmore. *Last of the Great Scouts (Buffalo Bill)*. New York: Grosset & Dunlap Publishers, 1918.

Hamilton, Charles. *Cry of the Thunderbird*. Norman: University of Oklahoma Press, 1972.

Hardorff, Richard G. *Indian Views of the Custer Fight*. Norman: University of Oklahoma Press, 2005.

Havighurst, Walter. *Annie Oakley of the Wild West*. Lincoln: University of Nebraska Press, 1992.

Hinman, Eleanor H. *Oglala Sources on the Life of Crazy Horse*. Lincoln: Nebraska History, 1976.

Hittman, Michael. *Wovoka and the Ghost Dance*. Lincoln: University of Nebraska Press, 1997; First Bison Books printing, 1997.

Hollihan, Tony. *Sitting Bull in Canada*. Edmonton, AB.: Folklore Publishing, 2001.

Hoover, Herbert T. *The Sioux: A Critical Bibliography*. Bloomington: Indiana University Press, 1979.

Hyde, George E. *A Sioux Chronicle*. Norman: University of Oklahoma Press, 1993.

Isenberg, Andrew C. *The Destruction of the Bison*. Cambridge, UK: Cambridge University Press, 2000.

Jackson, Donald. *Custer's Gold: The United States Cavalry Expedition of 1874*. Lincoln: University of Nebraska Press, 1966.

Jackson, Helen Hunt. *A Century of Dishonor*. New York: Harper & Brothers, 1885; reprint, University of Oklahoma Press.

Jensen, Richard E., R. Eli Paul, and John E. Carter. *Eyewitness at Wounded Knee*. Lincoln: University of Nebraska Press, 1991.

Johnson, Dorothy M. *Warrior for a Lost Nation: A Biography of Sitting Bull*. Philadelphia: The Westminster Press, 1969.

Johnson, Willis Fletcher. *The Red Record of the Sioux: Life of Sitting Bull and History of the Indian War of 1890–91*. London: Forgotten Books, 2012.

Josephy, Alvin M., and John S. Bowman. *The World Almanac of the American West*. New York: Ballantine Books, division of Random House, 1987.

Kasper, Shirl. *Annie Oakley*. Norman: University of Oklahoma Press, 1992.

Kasson, Joy S. *Buffalo Bill's Wild West: Celebrity, Memory, and Popular*

History. New York: Hill and Wang, division of Farrar, Straus and Giroux, 2000.

Kelly, Fanny. *Narrative of My Captivity Among the Sioux Indians*. Hartford, CT: Mutual Publishing Company, 1871; reprint from University of Michigan Library.

LaPointe, Ernie. *Sitting Bull: His Life and Legacy*. Layton, UT: Gibbs Smith, 2009.

Lawrence, Elizabeth Atwood. *His Very Silence Speaks—Comanche, the Horse Who Survived Custer's Last Stand*. Detroit: Wayne State University Press, 1989.

Lazarus, Edward. *Black Hills/White Justice: The Sioux Nation Versus the United States 1775 to the Present*. New York: Harper Collins, 1991.

Leonard, Elizabeth Jane, and Julia Cody Goodman. *Buffalo Bill, King of the Old West*. New York: Library Publishers, 1955.

Macy, Sue. *Bull's Eye: A Photobiography of Annie Oakley*. Washington, DC: National Geographic Society, 2001.

Marquis, Thomas B. *Wooden Leg: A Warrior Who Fought Custer*. Lincoln: University of Nebraska Press, 1931.

Matteoni, Norman M. *Prairie Man: The Struggle Between Sitting Bull and Indian Agent James McLaughlin*. Guilford: A Twodot Book, 2015.

McCoy, Tim, with Ronald McCoy. *Tim McCoy Remembers the West*. Lincoln: University of Nebraska Press, 1988.

McGaa, Ed (Eagle Man) J.D. *Crazy Horse and Red Cloud*. Rapid City, SD: Four Directions Publishing, 2005.

McGregor, James H. *The Wounded Knee Massacre*. Rapid City, SD: Fenske Printing Inc., 1993.

McLaughlin, James. *My Friend the Indian*. Boston: Houghton Mifflin Co., 1910.

McMurtry, Larry. *The Colonel and Little Missie*. New York: Simon & Schuster, 2005.

———. *Custer*. New York: Simon & Schuster, 2012.

McNenly, Linda Scarangella. *Native Performers in Wild West Shows, from*

Buffalo Bill to Euro Disney. Norman: University of Oklahoma Press, 2012.

Miles, General Nelson A. *Personal Recollections and Observations of General Nelson A. Miles.* Chicago: The Werner Company, 1896.

Mooney, James. *The Ghost-Dance Religions and Wounded Knee.* New York: Dover Publications, 1973.

Moses, L. G. *Wild West Shows and the Images of American Indians 1883–1993.* Albuquerque: University of New Mexico, 1996.

Neihardt, John G. *Black Elk Speaks.* Lincoln: University of Nebraska Press, 1932.

O'Moran, M. *Red Eagle, Buffalo Bill's Adopted Son.* Philadelphia and New York: J.B. Lippincott Company, 1948.

Pfaller, Louis. "Enemies in '76, Friends in '85—Sitting Bull and Buffalo Bill." Prologue, *The Journal of the National Archives,* Fall 1969.

Philbrick, Nathaniel. *The Last Stand.* New York: Penguin Group, 2010.

Pollack, Eileen. *Woman Walking Ahead: In Search of Catherine Weldon and Sitting Bull.* Albuquerque: University of New Mexico Press, 2002.

Pope, Dennis C. *Sitting Bull, Prisoner of War.* Pierre: South Dakota State Historical Society Press, 2010.

Powell, Lawrence Clark. *Southwest Classics.* Pasadena, CA: Ward Ritchie Press. 1975.

Powers, Thomas. *The Killing of Crazy Horse.* New York: Alfred A. Knopf, 2010.

Priest, Loring Benson. *Uncle Sam's Stepchildren: The Reformation of United States Indian Policy, 1865–1887.* Lincoln: University of Nebraska Press, 1942.

Reddin, Paul. *Wild West Shows.* Chicago: University of Illinois Press, 1999.

Riley, Glenda. *The Life and Legacy of Annie Oakley.* Norman: University of Oklahoma Press, 1994.

Rinella, Steven. *American Buffalo: In Search of a Lost Icon.* New York: Spiegel & Grau, 2009.

Rosa, Joseph G., and Robin May. *Buffalo Bill and His Wild West*. Wichita: University Press of Kansas, 1989.

Russell, Don. *The Lives and Legends of Buffalo Bill*. Norman: University of Oklahoma Press, 1960.

———. *The Wild West, or, A History of Wild West Shows*. Fort Worth, TX: Amon Carter Center for Western Art, 1970.

Sagala, Sandra K. *Buffalo Bill, Actor: A Chronicle of Cody's Theatrical Career*. Bowie, MD: Heritage Books, Inc., 2002.

———. *Buffalo Bill on Stage*. Albuquerque: University of New Mexico Press, 2008.

Sandoz, Mari. *The Buffalo Hunters*. New York: Hastings House, 1954.

Sayers, Isabelle S. *Annie Oakley and Buffalo Bill's Wild West*. New York: Dover Publications, 1981.

Scott, Douglas D., Peter Bleed, and Stephen Damm. *Custer, Cody, and Grand Duke Alexis: Historical Archaeology of the Royal Buffalo Hunt*. Norman: University of Oklahoma Press, 2013.

Sell, Henry Blackman, and Victor Weybright. *Buffalo Bill and the Wild West*. Cody, WY: Big Horn Books, 1979.

Spring, Agnes Wright. *Buffalo Bill and His Horses*. Fort Collins, CO: B&M Print Co., 1953.

Stillman, Deanne. *Mustang: The Saga of the Wild Horse in the American West*. Boston and New York: Mariner Books/Houghton Mifflin Harcourt, 2009.

Sublette, Ned. *The Year Before the Flood, A Story of New Orleans*. Chicago: Lawrence Hill Books, an imprint of Chicago Review Press, 2009.

Triggs, Stanley G. *Le Studio de William Notman/William Notman's Studio, Musée McCord d'Histoire Canadienne*. Montreal, Canada: 1992.

Triggs, Stanley G. *William Notman: The Stamp of a Studio*. Toronto: Art Gallery of Ontario/The Coach House Press, 1985.

Turner, Frederick W. *North American Indian Reader*. New York: Penguin Books, Ltd., 1973.

Utley, Robert M. *The Lance and the Shield: The Life and Times of Sitting*

Bull. New York, NY: Ballantine Books, a division of Random House, 1993.

Utley, Robert M. *The Last Days of the Sioux Nation*. New Haven, CT: Yale University Press, 1963.

———. *Sitting Bull: The Life and Times of an American Patriot*. New York: A Holt Paperback, Henry Holt & Company, 2008.

———. *The Story of the American West and Its People*. New York: DK Publishing, 2003.

Vangen, Roland Dean. *Indian Weapons*. Palmer Lake, CO: Filter Press, 1972.

Vestal, Stanley. *New Sources of Indian History*. Norman: University of Oklahoma Press, 1934.

———. *Sitting Bull: Champion of the Sioux*. Norman: University of Oklahoma Press, 1957.

Visscher, William Lightfoot. *Buffalo Bill's Own Story of His Life and Deeds*, 1917; introduction; public domain reprint.

Walsh, Richard J., and Milton S. Salsbury. *The Making of Buffalo Bill: A Study in Heroics*. Kissimmee, FL: The International Cody Family Association; reprint of first edition, The Bobbs Merrill Company, 1928.

Warren, Louis S. *Buffalo Bill's America: William Cody and the Wild West Show*. New York: Vintage Books, 2006.

Wissler, Clark. *Indians of the United States: Four Centuries of Their History and Culture*. Garden City, NY: Doubleday & Company, Inc., 1946.

Witt, Shirley Hill, and Stan Steiner. *The Way*. New York: Alfred A. Knopf, 1972.

Yenne, Bill. *Sitting Bull*. Yardley, PA: Westholme Publishing, 2009.

Yost, Nellie Snyder. *Buffalo Bill: His Family, Friends, Fame, Failures, and Fortunes*. Chicago: The Swallow Press Inc., 1979.

CATALOGUES

Buffalo Bill and the Wild West—Brooklyn Museum; Museum of Art, Carnegie Institute; Buffalo Bill Historical Center, including "The Indians," essay by Vine Deloria, Jr., distributed by the University of Pittsburgh Press, 1981.

"The Last Years of Sitting Bull" exhibit, North Dakota Heritage Center, State Historical Society of North Dakota, Bismarck, ND, June 1–September 30, 1984.

Legends of the West Auction—Heritage Auctions, Dallas, Texas, June 10, 2012.

Legends of the West II Auction—Heritage Auctions, Dallas, Texas, December 11–12, 2012.

ARTICLES FROM SITTING BULL'S TOUR WITH THE WILD WEST

Telegraphic Notes, "Daily Evening Bulletin," San Francisco, June 11, 1885.

"Sioux Warriors: Sitting Bull and Other Braves Coming to Join a 'Wild West'" Show," *Milwaukee Sentinel*, June 11, 1885.

"The Sitting Bull Party," *Bismarck Daily Tribune*, June 12, 1885.

"Greek Meets Greek: A Thrilling and Romantic Encounter Between Redskin and Pale Face Chieftains," *Buffalo Courier*, June 13, 1885.

"Chief Sitting Bull," *Evening Star*, Washington, DC, June 24, 1885.

"Sitting Bull in War Paint," *The Sun*, New York, June 24, 1885.

"The Wild West Visits the War Department in War Paint," *Wheeling Register*, June 28, 1885.

"Buffalo Bill's 'Wild West.'" *Boston Post*, July 20, 1885.

"The Wild West at Beacon Park." *Boston Post*, July 28, 1885.

"Buffalo Bill's Barbecue," *Boston Post*, July 31, 1885.

"Buffalo Bill et le Wild West Show," *La Patrie*, August 11, 1885.

"The Day That Custer Fell." *Springfield Globe-Republic*, August 11, 1885.

Arkansas City Republican, August 15, 1885, as quoted on Little Big Horn Associates Message Board: http://thelbha.proboards.com/thread/1707/1st-sgt-john-ryan.

"Les Adieux de Buffalo Bill," *La Patrie*, August 17, 1885.

"The Bill and Bull Show," *Toronto Globe*, August 24, 1885, excerpted here: http://sandyscollectedthoughts.com/buffalo-bill-and-sitting-bull -play-cowboys-and-indians-in-toronto-wild-west-sho/

"With Sitting Bull/How the Chief Traveled as a Star," *Salt Lake City Herald*, August 30, 1885.

"Buffalo Bill's Wild West." *Grand Rapids Evening Leader*, September 12, 1885.

"Sitting Bull/A Half Hour in the Tent of the Sioux Chief—He Talks about the Campaign Against His People." *Grand Rapids Evening Leader*, September 12, 1885.

"Buffalo Bill's Wild West." *Weekly Graphic*, Kirksville, MO, October 2, 1885.

"Buffalo Bill." *St. Louis Sunday Sayings*, October 18, 1885.

OTHER ARTICLES

"General Custer's Expedition into the Sacred Land of the Sioux," *New York Herald*, June 19, 1874.

"The Black Hills, A Timely Caution," *The New York Herald*, August 29, 1874.

"Sitting Bull Tells the Story of the Fight," *New York Times*, April 3, 1881.

Bates, Charles Francis. "Redmen and Whites Honor Custer's Memory; Fiftieth Anniversary of Famous Battle to Be Celebrated this Week on Little Big Horn," *New York Times*, June 10, 1926.

Coggeshall, Bruce. http://www.readex.com/blog/sensational-hair-raising -blood-curdling-penny-awful-american-life-ned-buntline, June 1, 2012.

Collard, Edgar Andrew. "Buffalo Bill's Big Show Thrilled Montrealers," *Montreal Gazette*, January 18, 1986.

Deahl, William E., Jr. "Buffalo Bill's Wild West Show in New Orleans." *Louisiana History: The Journal of the Louisiana Historical Association*, vol. 16, no. 3, summer 1975, pp. 289–98.

Goodyear, Frank H., III. "Wanted: Sitting Bull and His Photographic Portrait." *South Dakota History*, vol. 40, no. 2, 2010.

Hittman, Michael. "Wovoka, Paiute Prophet and the Ghost Dance." *History*, March/April 2011.

Houting, Beth A., "Indian Rights Associations." www.Philadelphia Encyclopedia.org.

Kerstetter, Todd. "Spin Doctors at Santee: Missionaries and the Dakota-Language Reporting of the Ghost Dance and Wounded Knee." *The Western Historical Quarterly*, vol. 28, no. 1, spring 1997, pp. 45–67.

Lalire, Gregory. "More Than the World's Greatest Showman: Buffalo Bill Was a Brave Scout Who Impressed Generals." *Wild West*, February 2009.

Lemons, William E. "History by Unreliable Narrators: Sitting Bull's Circus Horse." *Montana: The Magazine of Western History*, vol. 45, no. 4, autumn–winter, 1995.

Markley, Bill. "Guarding Custer's Guidon." *True West*, May 13, 2013.

Rinehart, Melissa. "To Hell with the Wigs! Native American Representation and Resistance at the World's Columbian Exposition." *The American Indian Quarterly*, Fall 2012.

Salsbury, Nate. "The Origin of the Wild West Show." *Colorado*, vol. 52, no. 4, fall 1975.

Stillson, Jerome. "Sitting Bull Talks." *New York Herald*, November 16, 1877.

West, Elliott. "Soothsayer Sitting Bull's Ability to Embrace the Great Mystery and Commune with Meadowlarks Make Him One of America's Greatest Spiritual leaders." *American History*, August, 2011.

LIBRARIES AND ARCHIVES

Annie Oakley Center at Garst Museum, Greenville, Ohio—questions regarding Annie Oakley and her friendship with Sitting Bull, http://www.annieoakleycenterfoundation.com/centeratgarst.html.

Buffalo Bill Historical Center, Cody, Wyoming. Records and news accounts of Buffalo Bill, Sitting Bull, and the Wild West.

Buffalo Bill Museum and Grave, Golden, Colorado. Records and news accounts of Buffalo Bill, his travels, and the Wild West.

Center of Southwest Studies, Fort Lewis College—Indian Rights Association Pamphlets, Years: 1884–1985. Durango, Colorado.

Historical Society of Pennsylvania—Indian Rights Association, Records, 1830–1986 (Collection 1523), hsp.org.

Huntington Library, San Marino, California. Extensive holdings in American history, especially the West, including rare books and early cavalry manuals; accounts of the Indian wars in newspapers, magazines, academic journals, and periodicals published by historical associations; explorer, settler, and war veteran diaries and memoirs; nineteenth-century documents and records.

Kalamazoo Public Library—newspaper accounts of the Wild West in Michigan.

Library of Congress—American Memory digital archives for a range of material, including photographs of Sitting Bull, Buffalo Bill, and Annie Oakley and cast members of the Wild West, images and postcards from the Wild West, nineteenth-century treaties, documents, and memorabilia.

New-York Historical Society—newspaper accounts of the Wild West in Buffalo, New York.

New York Public Library—"Reminiscences of Nate Salsbury," Billy Rose Theatre Division.

New York State Library—newspaper accounts of the Wild West in Buffalo, New York.

St. Louis Public Library—newspaper accounts of the Wild West in St. Louis, Missouri.

The State Historical Society of Missouri—newspaper accounts of the Wild West in St. Louis, Missouri.

State Historical Society of North Dakota—holdings pertaining to life at the Standing Rock Agency, Sitting Bull, and the Indian wars.

State Archives of the South Dakota Historical Society, South Dakota

Manuscripts Collection, Autobiography of Mary C. Collins in Her Handwriting.

University of Michigan Libraries—newspaper accounts of the Wild West in Michigan.

Walter Stanley Campbell Collection, "Correspondence with Chief Standing Bear," author of *My People, the Sioux*, University of Oklahoma, Western History Collections, includes information from One Bull regarding Sitting Bull and the Little Big Horn.

Welch Dakota Papers, *Oral History of the Dakota Tribes, 1800s–1945, as told to Colonel A.B. Welch*, Welch Dakota Papers, Red Tomahawk interview, 1915–http://www.welchdakotapapers.com/

DOCUMENTARIES

PBS, *The West*, directed by Stephen Ives, episodes about William F. Cody and Sitting Bull.

PBS, *American Experience*, Annie Oakley episode.

ILLUSTRATION CREDITS

1. Wikimedia Commons
2. Published in *Heroes of the Plains* by J. W. Buel, Historical Publishing Company, 1881
3. Library of Congress
4. Library of Congress
5. Library of Congress
6. Cowan's Auctions
7. Library of Congress
8. No credit
9. Library of Congress
10. South Dakota Historical Society, South Dakota Digital Archives
11. University of Michigan Libraries
12. Library of Congress
13. Library of Congress
14. Library of Congress
15. Library of Congress
16. Wikimedia Commons

INDEX

Aberdeen Daily, 224
abolitionism, *see* slavery
Adirondack Murray (W. H. Murray), 146–47, 179
Adventures of Buffalo Bill, The (documentary), 234
Alexander II, Czar, 62
Alexis Alexandrovich, Grand Duke, 62–63, 66–72
Allen, Alvaren, 94
American Bison Society, 245
American Buffalo (Rinella), 46, 245
American History, 232, 233
Annie Get Your Gun (play), 126
Annie Oakley (Kasper), 92, 128
Annie Oakley of the Wild West (Havighurst), 98
Arlington and Fields Combination, 20
Arthur, Chester A., 16
Arvol Looking Horse, Chief, xix
"Attack on the Settler's Cabin" (Wild West performance), 163–64
Autobiography (Cody), 60

Barry, D. F., 177, 201
Basil Brave Heart, xvi

Batchelor, C. W., 13, 14
Bear's Heart, 114
Bedloe's Island, 54
Bell, Alexander Graham, 51
Benteen, Frederick, 78, 79
Bentley, Emma, 15
Berlin, Irving, 126
Big Foot, 222, 223, 232
Billings, Horace, 36
Bills, C. J., 31
Black Coyote, 223
Black Diamond (buffalo), 236, 245
Black Elk, xv, xvi, xvii, 81–82, 105–7
Black Elk Peak, xv, xvi
Black Elk Speaks (Neihardt), xvi
Black Hills, 73–74, 87, 176
Black Jack (horse), 230
Black Kettle, 46
Black Moon, 64
Black Shield, 192
Bleed, Peter, 68
bloketu (Time of the Warm Moons), 97
Bloody Knife, 79
Blue Water, Massacre at, xv
Bogardus, Captain, 137
Bone Tomahawk, 6, 13

Boston, 142
Wild West in, 164–68
Sitting Bull dines with reporters, 166
adoption of Nate Salsbury, 167–68
Breckenridge Place, 34, 40
Brigham (horse), 44, 47–48
Brooklyn, Hatching of idea for Wild West in restaurant, 52–53
Brooklyn Bridge, Native American band at opening, 197–98
Brooks, E. C., 220
Brotherton, David H., 4, 6, 8–9, 12
Brown, Dee, 19
Brown, John, 36
buffalo, buffalo hunting:
appearance at Lakota ceremony, 161
appearance of white buffalo, 108
Black Elk's dream and, xv
buffalo endurance and, 110
called "PTE" in Lakota, 118, 119
by Cody, 43–45
depletion of herds, 46–47, 155
in Hickok's Wild West show, 93–94
impact of railroads on, 43–45, 118–19
meaning of *wasichu* and, 104
"The Millionaires' Hunt" 62
Native Americans and, 44, 46
Notman photo and newborn calf, 180–81
restored to West, 245–46
Royal Buffalo Hunt, 62–63, 66–72
Sitting Bull's respect for, 118
as star of Wild West, 159–60
U.S. government and, 34

Buffalo Bill, the King of the Border Men (Buntline), 50
Buffalo Bill and His Horses (Spring), 43
Buffalo Bill and the Wild West (Sell and Weybright), 36, 92–93
Buffalo Bill Cody (Carter), 36
Buffalo Bill Historical Center, 87, 234
Buffalo Bill's America (Warren), 38, 62, 164
Buffalo Courier, 116, 120, 124, 138
Buffalo Soldiers (Twenty-fifth Infantry), 17–18
Bull Head, 211, 217, 218, 219
Bunnell's Museum, 125
Buntline, Ned, 48–50, 52
Bureau of Catholic Indian Missions, 23
Bureau of Indian Affairs, U.S., 11, 23–24, 94
Burke, John M., 116, 138–39
as Cody's publicist, 166, 234
hires Sitting Bull for Wild West, 24, 91–102
takes Sitting Bull on tour of St. Louis, 181–82
on Wild West's copyright, 162
Bury My Heart at Wounded Knee (Brown), 19
Butler, Frank, 21, 133–35, 230, 236–38

Camp Alexis, 67
Canada, Sitting Bull flees to, xiii, 3–4, 84, 87
Cannupa Wakan (sacred pipe), 116
Captain Jack, 192
Carnegie, Andrew, 245
Carr, Eugene Asa, 24, 181–82
Carter, Robert A., 36

Catch-the-Bear, 218–219
Catlin, Clara, 2
Catlin, George, 1–2, 199–200
Chadwick, G. W., 213
Charlie Almost Human (horse), 69
Charlie Joe (horse), 31–32
Cheyenne River Agency, 17
Cheyenne tribe, xiii, 44, 46, 64, 75,
    77, 78, 80, 81, 84, 86, 90, 115,
    187, 188, 189, 190, 191
Chief Joseph and the Nez Perce, 100
Circling Bear, 192
Clark, Wesley, Jr., xiv–xv
Cleveland, Grover, 24, 173–74
Clifford, Captain, 12
Cody, Arta (daughter), 228
Cody, Isaac (father), 34–35, 37–39
Cody, Kit Carson (son), 60, 228
Cody, Louisa Frederici (wife),
    28–29, 43, 60, 87, 214,
    227–29, 232
Cody, May (sister), 235
Cody, Sam (brother), 35
Cody, William Frederick "Buffalo
    Bill":
  acquires name "Buffalo Bill," 44
  Annie Oakley and, 26, 57, 137,
      229–30, 258
  appears in *The Scouts of the
      Prairie*, 50, 91
  appears in Sells-Floto Circus,
      234–35
  attempt to save Sitting Bull,
      212–15
  birth and early life, 33–40
  as buffalo hunter, 43–46, 61–62
  Canadian reception of, 146
  death and burial of, 235–36
  death of son, 60
  description and personality of,
      26–28, 143, 159

  drinking habits, 214, 227, 229
  duel with Yellow Hand, 84–86,
      87
  friendship with Custer, 61
  gives horse to Sitting Bull,
      xi–xii, xvii, 182–83, 224–25
  gypsy's prophecy to mother, 156
  home catches fire, 213–14
  kills first Indian, 41
  Lakota call "Long Hair," xvi
  love of horses, 30–32, 34, 35,
      36, 38
  makes movie, 231–33
  meets President Harrison, 223
  meets Sitting Bull in Buffalo,
      138–40
  as mythical figure of Great
      Plains, xiv, 52
  photographed by Notman,
      177–81
  publicized by Buntline, 48–50, 52
  receives bear claw necklace from
      Sitting Bull, 183
  *The Red Right Hand or Buffalo
      Bill's First Scalp for Custer*,
      88, 91
  rides for Pony Express, 41–42
  Royal Buffalo Hunt and, 62–63,
      66–72
  Salsbury and, 51–53
  scouts for army, 43, 48, 60–61, 84
  seeks to hire Sitting Bull, 21–24,
      91
  Sitting Bull's desire to meet
      president and, 15
  wife and, 28–29, 43, 60, 87,
      227–29, 232
  women and, 27, 145–46, 227–29,
      230
  writings, 39, 60
  see also Wild West

Cody's Combination, 59
Collins, Mary, 196–97, 208–9
Comanche (horse), 80, 83–84
Company K, 86
Compton, Cy, 31
Comstock, William, 45
Congress of Rough Riders, 226
Conquering Bear, 99
Cortés, 117–18
Council Fire, 192, 193, 198
cowboy church, 145
Crazy Horse, xv, 66, 75, 87, 115
    Battle of Little Bighorn and, 3,
        77, 78, 79, 80
    surrender and death of, 100, 187,
        222
Crazy Horse Memorial, xiii
Crook, George, 75, 77
Crow Eagle, 101, 170
Crow Foot (SB's son), 7, 8, 9, 218
Crow's Ghost, 101
Crow Woman, 221–22
Curtis, Edward S., 177
Custer, Cody, and Grand Duke Alexis
    (Scott, Bleed, and Damm),
    67–68
Custer, George Armstrong, xvi, 59,
    61, 63
    Battle of Little Bighorn and,
        74–83, 149
    gold expedition led by, 73–74
    Royal Buffalo Hunt and, 67–72
    Sitting Bull on, 174–75
    treatment of animals and, 68,
        70, 73
Custer, Libbie, 75
Custer's Gold (Jackson), 73

Daily Picayune, 56
Dakota Territory, 63, 65
Dakota War of 1862, 114

Damm, Stephen, 68
Dave (dog), 236–37
Davies, Henry, 62
Dawes, Henry, 198
Dawes Act, 198–99, 200, 203, 205,
    206
Denver Post, 233, 235
de Smet, Pierre Jean ("Black
    Robe"), 64, 170
"Don't Fence Me In" (song), vii
Drum, Richard C., 173

Eden Musee, 96, 155
Edison, Thomas, 231
English Metropolitan, 162
Enss, Chris, 27, 28, 228, 230

Fallen Timbers, Battle of (1794), 127
Faribault, Louis, 204
Fechét, Captain, 220
Filgate (steamer), 147
Fire Cloud, 194–95
Fishing Elk, 101
Flynn and Sarsfield, 20
"Foes in '76, Friends in '85," xii, xvi,
    117, 180
Fool Thunder, 101
Forrest, Edwin, 49
Forts:
    Abraham Lincoln, 64
    Buford, 4, 6, 10, 119
    Hays, 43
    Kearny, 40, 41
    McPherson, 62
    Randall, 16, 17–18, 83
    Stevenson, 12, 65
    Yates, 11, 24
    see also Treaty of Fort Laramie
        (1868)
Four Horns (SB's uncle), 6, 13, 64,
    104, 105, 107, 108, 115

Four Prairie Knights Casino and Resort, xiv
Four Robes (SB's wife), 17

Gall, 53, 64, 65, 79, 94, 174
Garfield, James, 16
General Sherman (steamboat), 11–12, 15, 16, 17
George (poodle), 134–35, 236
Ghost Dance, vii, 186, 190, 208, 210, 211, 216, 233, 242, 243–44
ghost shirts, 161, 185, 186, 190–91, 215, 221, 243
Gibbon, John, 75
gold, 73–74, 173
Good Feather (SB's sister), 13
Goodman, Julia Cody, 34, 227, 228, 229, 234
Graham, John, 135
Grand Opera House, 20
Grand Rapids Leader, 169–71
Grant, Ulysses S., 51, 63
Grattan, John Lawrence, 99
Grattan Massacre, 99
Great Black Moose, 101
Great Mystery (*Wakan Tanka*), 76, 89
Great Plains:
    buffalo hunting on, 46–47, 62
    Cody as mythical figure of, xii, 52
    war against Indians of, 63
    Wounded Knee ends Lakota era on, 187
Great Sioux Reservation, 199
Grey Eagle, 205–6

Halsey, William, 97, 100, 101, 120
Hamlet (Shakespeare), 49, 51
Harney, William S., xv

Harney Peak, *see* Black Elk Peak
Harrison, Benjamin, 215, 223
Haslam, Bob ("Pony Bob"), 55, 213, 214
Hat Creek, 85–87
Havighurst, Walter, 98, 147, 226
Hawkman No. 1, 219
Her Holy Door Woman (SB's mother), 104
Hickok, Wild Bill, 43, 92–93, 95
High as the Clouds, 6, 13
Higheagle, Robert, 113
Higley, Brewster, 57
History of Darke County, Ohio (Wilson), 129
"Home of the Brave" (exhibit), 161
"Home on the Range" (song), 57
horses:
    at Battle of Little Bighorn, 78–83
    Black Elk's dream and, xv, xvii
    ceremony to honor Sitting Bull, 109
    Crazy Horse carves petroglyph of, 78
    Custer's treatment of, 68, 70
    return of wild, 161
    Sitting Bull's, and legend of dancing horse, xi–xii, xvii, 182–83, 224–25
    Sitting Bull's rescue of, 112–13
    as star attractions of Wild West, 161–65, 226
    see also specific horses
Hotchkiss guns, 232
Hunkpapa tribe, 3, 6, 7–12, 14–18, 23
    see also Sitting Bull
Huntley, Robert, 112
Hurricane Katrina, 55
Hutton, Betty, 126

Ilges, Major Guido, 8
Indian Rights Association (IRA),
    174–75
Infirmary (county poor farm),
    130–31
Interior Department, U.S., 23, 34,
    95, 172, 200, 215, 231, 234
interpreters, *see* translators and
    translation
Iron Hawk, 78
Iron Tail, 236
Iron Thunder, 101

Jack (Red Cloud's son), 225
Jackson, Allie, 20
Jackson, Andrew, 55
Jackson, Donald, 73
John Grass, 173
Johnston, Albert Sidney, 40
Jumping Bull (SB's adopted
    brother), 76, 112
Jumping Bull (SB's father, formerly
    Returns Again), 104, 108–10,
    111–12

Kansas Pacific Railroad, 43, 47
Kasper, Shirl, 92, 128
Katzenberger, Charles, 131–32, 133,
    134
Katzenberger, G. Anthony, 131–32,
    133
Keogh, Myles, 79–80, 81, 149
Kicking Bear, 189–90, 212, 239,
    242
Killdeer Mountain, Battle of (1864),
    114
Know Nothing Party, 49

Lakota Sioux, 3
    at Battle of Little Bighorn, 80–81
    Battle of the Rosebud and, 77

competition with Canadian
    tribes, 155
forgiveness sought from, xiv–xv
gold found in territory, 74
humility as virtue in society, 97
inaccurate translations and, 99
matriarchal culture, 177
name for buffalo, 118
reburial of Long Wolf in U.S.,
    161
see also Hunkpapa tribe
Lamar, Lucius, 172
Lame White Man, 80
Lane, Franklin K., 231
LaPointe, Ernie, 102–3, 104, 109,
    115, 218, 249
*Last Indian Battles from the War Path
    to the Peace Pipe, The* (movie),
    231
Last Stand, The (Philbrick), 76
Last Stand Hill, 79
Légaré, Jean-Louis, 5, 8, 10
Leonard Crow Dog, Chief, xv
Lewis and Clark, 142, 184, 246, 249
"The Life of Dave, As Told by
    Himself," (Butler), 237
Life on the Border (play), 59
literature wagons, 143
Little Bear, 78
Little Bighorn, Battle of (1876),
    xv–xvi, 3, 8, 21, 59, 74–83,
    174–75, 227
Little Gray (horse), 36
"Little Raindrops" (poem), 135
Lives and Legends of Buffalo Bill, The
    (Russell), 55
Lone Man, 217, 219, 220
Long Wolf, 160–61
"Lucretia Borgia" (Cody's gun), 45,
    69
Luther Standing Bear, 198

McCarthy, Frank, 41
McCoy, Tim, 189–90, 241–44
MacDonnell, Alexander, 10
McKinley (horse), 235
McLaughlin, Major James:
    approves "Sitting Bull
        Combination" tour, 23, 94
    Cody and, 21–22
    as nemesis of Sitting Bull, 18–19,
        93–94
    permits Sitting Bull to join Wild
        West, 24, 97–98, 100
    prepares to arrest Sitting Bull,
        210–12
    Standing Rock ceremony and,
        194
    takes Sitting Bull to St. Paul, 20
    Weldon and, 201–2, 204–6
McMartin, Lieutenant, 145
McNulty, James, 54
Macready, William Charles, 49
Many Loves of Buffalo Bill, The
    (Enss), 27, 230
Meacham, Alfred, 192–93
meadowlarks, 112, 197, 204, 210, 249
Medicine Line, 3, 8, 51, 148, 149,
    155
Medicine Tail Coulee, 79
Merchants Hotel, 14
Merman, Ethel, 126–27
Merritt, Wesley, 84
Miles, Carlo, 30–31
Miles, Nelson A., 187, 213, 223,
    231, 232
"The Millionaires' Hunt," 62
Mississippi Jaeger (Cody's rifle), 41
Modoc tribe, x, 192
Montezuma, 117–18
Montreal, 146–47
    Sitting Bull and Buffalo Bill in
        (photo session), xii–xiii, 147

Morlacchi, Mademoiselle, 91
Morning Star (steamship), 29
Moses, Hulda (AO's sister), 130
Moses, Jacob (AO's father), 127–29,
    129
Moses, John (AO's brother), 129, 132
Moses, Mary Jane (AO's sister), 129
Moses, Susan (AO's mother), 127–9
Muldoon's Picnic (play), 20
Murray, W. H. "Adirondack
    Murray," 146–47, 179
*Mustang: The Saga of the Wild
    Horse in the American West*
    (Stillman), xi
My Friend the Indian (McLaughlin),
    194
My People the Sioux (Luther
    Standing Bear), 198
"My Western Home" (poem), 57

Nancy Kicking Bear (SB's
    granddaughter), 247
*Narrative of My Captivity Among
    the Sioux Indians, with a Brief
    Account of General Scully's
    Indian Expedition in 1864,
    Bearing Upon Events Occurring
    in My Captivity* (Kelly), 115
National Bison Legacy Act, 246
National Indian Defense
    Association (NIDA), 192,
    196, 197, 198, 199, 203, 206
National Wildlife Restoration, 246
Native Americans:
    contemporary protests at
        Standing Rock, xvi, 248
    gain citizenship in 1924, 173
    in movies, 231
    rights movement, 192–93
    see also specific individuals
Nebraska History Magazine, 234

Ned Buntline's Own, 48
Neihardt, John G., 105
Nelson, John, 141
New Orleans, Wild West flooded
 during tour, 55–57, 136–37,
 144
 Annie Oakley appears out of the
 waters, 57
New Orleans, Battle of, 55
New York, Sitting Bull at Eden
 Musee, 96, 155
New York Herald, 67, 84, 113, 148,
 216
New York Tribune, 73, 74
New York Weekly, 50, 87
No Neck, 64
North, Major Frank, 52
Northern Pacific Railway, 12, 13, 19
Northwest Indian War, 127
Northwest Mounted Police, 8, 147
Notman, William, 147, 177, 178–81
Notman Museum, 179

Oakley, Annie:
 birth of, 128
 Butler and, 21, 133–35, 230,
 236–38
 Cody and, 26, 57, 229–30, 238
 death of, 238
 hunting prowess, 128–29,
 132–34
 at the Infirmary, 130–31
 performing pets and, 236–37
 Sitting Bull and, 20–21, 124,
 136, 172, 238
 as Wild West star, 137, 147,
 159–60, 226
Obama, Barack, 246
Olympic Theater, 20
Omohundro, J. B. ("Texas Jack"),
 50, 91

One Bull (SB's nephew), 16, 88
Osawatomie Brown (play), 36
Outdoor Life, 134, 145–46

Parker Brothers gun, 133
Patrie, La, 146
Paul, Andrea I., 234
Philadelphia, Sitting Bull on tour
 in, 174–75
Philbrick, Nathaniel, 76–77
Pine Ridge Reservation, 189, 231
pipe, sacred (*Cannupa Wakan*), 116
Plenty Coups, 161
Plenty Horses, 225
Pollack, Eileen, 199, 200, 202
Pony Express, 41–42
Pope, Dennis C., 5
Porcupine, 189
Powell, Frank (White Beaver), 213,
 214
Primeau, Joseph, 97, 100, 211, 215
Prince (horse), 38

railroads, 43–45, 118–19
 see also specific railroads
Rain-in-the-Face, 80, 225
Red Cloud, 53, 192, 201, 205
Red Cloud Agency, 84, 86
Reddin, Paul, 157
Red Horn, 64
*Red Right Hand or Buffalo Bill's First
 Scalp for Custer, The*, 88, 91
Red Thunder, 6
Red Tomahawk, 218, 219, 221, 238,
 247
Remington, Frederic, 26, 245
Reno, Major Marcus, 78, 79, 165, 222
Returns Again, *see* Jumping Bull
Reynolds, Charley, 43
Richmond, Frank, 163
Rinella, Steven, 46, 245, 246

Rob Roy (Scott), 43
Rogers, Katherine, 125
Roosevelt, Theodore, 245
Rosebud, Battle of the (1876), 77
Royal Buffalo Hunt, 62–63, 66–72
Running Antelope, 16
Russell, Don, 55
Ryan, John, 165–66

Sacajawea, 184, 246–47, 248–49
Sacred Horse Dance, 113
Sage, 190, 242
Salsbury, Nate, 51–53, 56, 167–68, 174–75
Salsbury's Troubadours, 51, 52, 56
Sand Creek fight (1864), 46
Sandoz, Mari, 43, 44, 46, 47
Sardinia (steamer), 147
Sarnia (steamer), 147
Scarlet Thunder, 13
Scott, Douglas D., 67–68
Scott, Walter, 43
Scout's Best Ranch, 29
Scouts of the Prairie, The (Buntline), 50, 91, 95
Sell, Henry Blackman, 36, 92–93
Sells Brothers Circus, 57, 135, 136–37
Sells-Floto Circus, 234–35
Seventh Cavalry, xiii, 3, 61, 74–83, 222–23
    see also Little Bighorn, Battle of (1876)
Seventh Kansas Cavalry, 61
Seventeenth U.S. Infantry, 145
Shakespeare riots of 1849, 49
Sham (horse), 30–31
Shave Head, 217, 218, 219
Shaw, Joseph, 132
Sheridan, Philip, 61, 62, 63, 66–72, 74, 87

Sheridan House, 13
Sherman, William Tecumseh, 24, 74, 95, 128, 173
Short Bull, 189–90, 242
Sioux Nation, 63, 247
    see also Hunkpapa tribe
Sitting Bull:
    Annie Oakley and, 20–21, 57, 124, 136, 172, 238
    arrest and killing of, 217–21
    arrives in Buffalo, 120–24
    Battle of Killdeer Mountain and, 114
    birth of, 102
    Buffalo Bill attempts to hire, 21–22
    burial site, 245–48
    Catherine Weldon and, 195–97, 198, 199, 200–211, 220
    considered for Wild West, 53
    denounces government at railroad ceremony, 19
    desire to meet president, 15, 97
    flight to, and return from Canada, 51, 84
    gives bear claw necklace to Cody, 183
    grants interviews, 148, 150–54, 168–72
    known as Jumping Badger, 104–8
    learns of Cody's attempted final visit, 215–16
    legend of dancing horse and, xi–xii, xvii, 182–83, 224–25
    life at Standing Rock, 191, 193–94
    marriages, 111
    Mary Collins and, 196–97, 208–9
    meets Cody in Buffalo, 138–41

Sitting Bull (*cont.*)
   meets with Indian Rights
     Association, 174–75
   negotiations for Dawes Act and,
     199–200
   not present at Little Bighorn,
     88–89
   poses for Notman, 177–81
   reception at Merchants Hotel, 13
   saves white woman captured by
     Sioux, 115
   "Sitting Bull Combination"
     entourage and, 23
   spurns army commission seeking
     his return to U.S., 149–50
   Sun Dance ceremony and,
     76–77, 181
   temperament of, 175, 176
   as thunder dreamer, 113
   tours St. Paul with McLaughlin,
     20
   transfer to Fort Randall, 16–17
   transfer to Fort Yates, 11–15
   Treaty of Fort Laramie and,
     63–65, 74
   Trobriand puts price on head,
     65
   visits Washington, D.C., 172–74
   warns against looting battlefield,
     82
   wildlife and, 105, 112, 118
   as Wild West performer, 24–25,
     91–102, 146–47, 155–56,
     181–82
Sitting Bull (Yenne), 111
Sitting Bull: Champion of the Sioux
   (Vestal), 108
Sitting Bull: His Life and Legacy
   (LaPointe), 102
Sitting Bull: Prisoner of War (Pope), 5
Sitting Bull Cabin Exhibit, 225

"Sitting Bull Combination," 94
slavery, 33, 35–39
Slow White Bull, 101
smallpox, 2, 98, 114, 153
Smith & Wesson gun, 63, 69
Smithsonian National Museum of
   Natural History, Repatriation
   Office, 103
Spotted Eagle, 6
Spotted Tail, 70
Spring, Agnes Wright, 43
Standing Bear, 78
Standing Rock Agency and
   Reservation, 10
   contemporary protests at, xvi,
     248
   dedication ceremony at, 194–95
   Hunkpapas and, 11, 17
   Indians ordered to return to, 156
   Sitting Bull and family at,
     93,174, 176, 191, 195, 196,
     199–200
Statue of Liberty, 54
Steele, Matthew F., 220
St. George, Judith, 247
St. Louis, Sitting Bull's final
   appearance with Wild West,
     181–83
   Cody gives Sitting Bull a horse,
     182–83
St. Paul, Minn., Sitting Bull on tour
   meets Annie Oakley, 20–21
St. Paul Pioneer Press, 8, 10, 12, 20
Stillson, Jerome, 148, 150–54
"The Story of American Hunting
   and Firearms," 133–34
Strikes-the-Kettle, 211, 219
Stronghold, 212
Sublette, Ned, 55
Sully, Alfred, 64, 114
Sun Dance ceremony, 76–77, 119

Tabor Grand Opera House, 233
Tatanka Iyotake, see Sitting Bull
Tecumseh, 127–28
telephone, 51
Teller, Henry M., 95
Tennis (buffalo hunter), 43, 44
Terry, Alfred Howe, 12, 74, 81–82, 149
"There's No Business Like Show Business" (song), 126
thunder dreamer, 113
Thunder Hawk, 192
Thundering Herd, The (movie), 241
Tim McCoy Remembers the West (McCoy), 189
Toronto Globe, 144, 176
To See with the Heart (St. George), 247
translators and translation, 82, 97, 99–100, 136
  for Sitting Bull, 8, 15, 19, 120, 124, 145, 150, 165, 166, 169, 170, 171, 182, 201, 212
Treaty of Fort Laramie (1868), 63–66, 74
Triggs, Stanley, 179
Trobriand, Regis de, 65
True Tales of the Plains (Cody), 39
Twain, Mark, 26, 48
Twenty-fifth Infantry (Buffalo Soldiers), 17–18
Two Lance, 70, 71

Valley of the Little Bighorn, 75–76
Vermilye, B. D., 13, 14
Vernon, Diana (fictional character), 43
"Verses on the Prospect of Planting Arts and Learning in America," 142
Vestal, Stanley, 18, 108, 110, 196, 202, 205, 217, 222

Victoria, Queen, 31, 49, 162, 177
Victoria Bridge, 177

Wakan Tanka (Great Mystery), 76
Walsh, Major James Morrow, 10, 147, 148, 150, 176, 221–22
Warbonnet Creek, Battle of, 234
War Department, U.S., 11, 173, 231–32, 234
Warren, Louis, 38, 62, 163
Washington DC, Wild West cast members visit, 172–74
wasichu (white man):
  meaning of, 4
  misunderstanding of Native Americans, 110
  original meaning of, 104
Wayne, "Mad" Anthony, 127
Welch, A. B., 247, 248
Weldon, Catherine (Woman Walking Ahead), 195–97, 198, 199, 200–211, 220
Wertz Brothers, 20
"Westward the Course of Empire Makes Its Way" (mural), 142
Wetmore, Helen Cody, 38, 43
Weybright, Victor, 36, 92–93
White Buffalo Calf Woman dream, xv, 106–7
White Dog, 6, 13
Wickham, P. B., 225
wildlife:
  Custer's killing of, 68
  depiction of Lewis and Clark's encounters with, 184
  importance of bear to warriors, 183
  no hunting limits on, 46, 133–34
  Sitting Bull and, 105, 112, 118
  see also specific wildlife

Wild West, 224–27
　advertising for and popularity of,
　　157–59
　bankruptcy of, 30, 227
　Black Elk and, xvi
　Cody's first attempts to hire
　　Sitting Bull for, 21–22
　copyright, 152
　as equestrian extravaganza,
　　161–65, 226
　launch of, 22, 54–57
　multicity tours, 142–46
　Oakley joins, 137
　Pawnees as participants in, 55, 95
　performance in Buffalo, 125
　rebranding of, 184
　reenactment of Battle of Little
　　Bighorn, 227
　"Shake 'Em Up, Bill"
　　(stagecoach ride
　　reenactment),72
　still in existence, 239
Wild West Shows (Reddin), 157
Wilson, Frazer, 129
Wilson, Woodrow, 233
Winchester (gun), 7, 8, 143, 179,
　180, 219
Winchester, Sarah, 180
Wind Cave National Park, 246

Wind River Reservation, 246
Woman Walking Ahead (Pollack),
　199
Wooden Leg, 81
World's Columbian Exposition
　Company, 225
World's Industrial and Cotton
　Centennial Exposition, 55,
　56, 94
Wounded Knee, xiii, 83, 187,
　222–23, 225, 231, 232, 234
Wounded Knee Survivors
　Association, 161
Wovoka, 185–86, 188–91, 241–44

Yankton Daily Press, 201
Yankton Press and Dakotian, 74
Year Before the Flood, The (Sublette),
　55
Yellow Calf, 190, 242
Yellow Hand (Yellow Hair), 84–86,
　87
Yellowstone Line, 13
Yellow Wolf, 46
Yenne, Bill, 13, 15, 111, 112
Young-Man-Afraid-of-His-Horses,
　225

Zahn, William, 101